PENGUIN CANADA

A LIFE IN THE BUSH

ROY MACGREGOR has been a journalist for more than thirty years, and for many years has written his immensely popular "This Country" column on page two of *The Globe and Mail*, Canada's national newspaper. He is the author of numerous bestselling and award-winning books, including *Escape, Canoe Lake, The Home Team, The Weekender*, and the popular children's mystery series *The Screech Owls*. MacGregor was named an Officer in the Order of Canada in 2005 and currently resides in Kanata, Ontario.

Also by Roy MacGregor

The Dog and I: Confessions of a Best Friend

The Weekender: A Cottage Journal

Escape: In Search of the Natural Soul of Canada

A Loonie for Luck

Canoe Lake

The Last Season

The Home Team: Fathers, Sons and Hockey

Road Games: A Year in the Life of the NHL

Chief: The Fearless Vision of Billy Diamond

Home Game: Hockey & Life in Canada
(with Ken Dryden)

The Screech Owls Series
(for young readers)

A Life in the Bush
Lessons from My Father

ROY
MacGREGOR

PENGUIN
CANADA

PENGUIN CANADA

Published by the Penguin Group

Penguin Group (Canada), 90 Eglinton Avenue East, Suite 700, Toronto, Ontario, Canada M4P 2Y3
    (a division of Pearson Canada Inc.)

Penguin Group (USA) Inc., 375 Hudson Street, New York, New York 10014, U.S.A.
Penguin Books Ltd, 80 Strand, London WC2R 0RL, England
Penguin Ireland, 25 St Stephen's Green, Dublin 2, Ireland (a division of Penguin Books Ltd)
Penguin Group (Australia), 250 Camberwell Road, Camberwell, Victoria 3124, Australia
    (a division of Pearson Australia Group Pty Ltd)
Penguin Books India Pvt Ltd, 11 Community Centre, Panchsheel Park, New Delhi – 110 017, India
Penguin Group (NZ), 67 Apollo Drive, Rosedale, North Shore 0745, Auckland, New Zealand
    (a division of Pearson New Zealand Ltd)
Penguin Books (South Africa) (Pty) Ltd, 24 Sturdee Avenue, Rosebank, Johannesburg 2196,
    South Africa

Penguin Books Ltd, Registered Offices: 80 Strand, London WC2R 0RL, England

First published in a Viking Canada hardcover by Penguin Group (Canada),
    a division of Pearson Canada Inc., 1999
Published in Penguin Canada paperback by Penguin Group (Canada),
    a division of Pearson Canada Inc., 2000
Published in this edition, 2007

(WEB) 10 9 8 7 6 5 4 3 2 1

Copyright © Roy MacGregor, 1999

Text design and typesetting by Laura Brady.

Manufactured in Canada.

LIBRARY AND ARCHIVES CANADA CATALOGUING IN PUBLICATION

MacGregor, Roy, 1948–
    A life in the bush : lessons from my father / Roy MacGregor.

ISBN 978-0-14-027551-3 (bound).—ISBN 978-0-14-305331-6 (pbk.)

1. MacGregor, Duncan Fisher, 1907–1995. 2. MacGregor, Roy, 1948–.
3. Outdoor life—Ontario—Algonquin Provincial Park. 4. Algonquin Provincial Park (Ont.)—
Biography. 5. Loggers—Ontario—Algonquin Provincial Park—Biography. I. Title.

FC3065.A65M32 2000   971.3'147   C00-931624-8

Visit the Penguin Group (Canada) website at **www.penguin.ca**

Special and corporate bulk purchase rates available; please see
www.penguin.ca/corporatesales or call 1-800-810-3104, ext. 477 or 474

For Helen MacGregor, the caregiver, 1915–1999.

For Jim and Tom, who were there, and for the grandchildren—Alison, Craig, Karen, Kerry, Christine, Jocelyn and Gordon—who knew him only briefly, but who will also never forget.

ACKNOWLEDGMENTS

Thanks to Cynthia Good at Penguin, and especially to Meg Masters, who had the original idea. Thanks, too, to Sean Conway, who insisted Dunc's story be told. The author is also grateful to Mark Webber and Janet McRae Webber for making available precious tapes of Janet McRae's reminiscences, and to historian Ian Radforth for sharing his tapes on the early McRae logging operations. Thanks to Iain Higgins for hints on the literature of nature. Jim and Tom MacGregor were invaluable in reading, correcting and adding to earlier drafts. A special thanks to Helen MacGregor, who would never have believed her "pictures" would end up inside a book.

"What went ye out into the wilderness to see?"
—The Gospel according to Matthew, 11:7

Jim and Ann MacGregor in a boat with their father, Duncan.

A Life in the Bush

PROLOGUE

Dunc MacGregor at the Rock Lake mill—seventy years old and no intent of quitting, ever.

I HAVE NO IDEA HOW or where to begin this story. Those who write mysteries—and let's face it, he was impossible to figure out at times—might suggest starting at the end and working backwards, so let us begin there for lack of any other clear point of departure. And start with numbers rather than words, since he so treasured statistics and what they could tell you about a given situation, whether it was Ty Cobb's determination to make second base, or the chances of drawing to your hand, or, for that matter, the number of board feet in a missed stand of white pine back of his beloved Mosquito Creek. So let us, then, tally the count of his final day above earth:

Twelve white-tailed deer, six of them—including two bucks with soft budding antlers—in a single grouping at the turnoff to Rock Lake and, for those very few who know how to get there, Mosquito Creek. Nine moose. Four red fox. One black bear. And one timber wolf.

Not a bad turnout, he might have said. Not bad at all, in the circumstances.

The circumstances, unfortunately, were his own death, less than three months short of his eighty-eighth birthday and four weeks short of opening day for smallmouth bass. Not that the Old Man would have marked it that way; bass, he believed, lacked personality, and they interested him as little as people who react predictably to whatever passes them by. A rubber worm on a hook or a new trend—if they bit too easily, fish or fool, they weren't considered worth the effort. The best fish was the lake trout, deep and moody; the best people were those who required long study as well. Plutarch, for example. Or Andy Capp. People who had something to say that was worth remembering. Like the week earlier, when he had sat up in what he never expected would be his deathbed and recited, from memory as well as experience, all sixty-eight lines of Hugh Antoine D'Arcy's "The Face on the Barroom Floor":

> 'Twas a balmy summer evening, and a goodly crowd was there,
> Which well-nigh filled Joe's barroom, on the corner of the square;
> And as songs and witty stories came through the open door,
> A vagabond crept slowly in and posed upon the floor. . . .

He could quote them all when he felt so moved. The Bible. Dizzy Dean. Mark Twain. Mickey Spillaine. Robert Service. Capp. Plutarch. A curious, sprawling mind that captured almost everything that ever passed through it—common sense often excluded —and contained no filter, no pretension, no care whatsoever for the class and intellectual breaches that might separate, say, Plutarch's

Parallel Lives from *Ellery Queen*. So what? Picasso was enthralled with the Katzenjammer Kids; Shaw said that a good bookshelf holds both classics and trash. If it was there, the Old Man read it. If he was here, he would read this—and offer his usual critique on those matters that failed to make much sense to him.

"*Tch-tch-tch-tch-tch-tch-tch.*"

"Don't look back," he would say, quoting the great philosopher Satchel Paige, a semi-literate ballplayer whom he would rank with anyone who wrote in Greek or Latin. "Something may be gaining on you."

In his case, it was time. Eighty-eight years, seventy-six of them as a hard, no-filter, roll-your-own—or in a crunch, Player's Plain—cigarette smoker, seventy or so as a man who loved a drink and may have been saved from it by two mitigating factors. First was the isolation and inaccessibility of the Algonquin Park bush, where he could sometimes go months without seeing so much as a bottle of beer. The second factor came by grace of a bitterly cold December day and a massive wood-chip truck skidding down an icy mill-yard hill. It was his last day of work. He was seventy-three years old and had come to believe he had successfully fought off "forced retirement." The Old Man had the hood of his jacket up over his hardhat, and the big, silently, helplessly sliding truck struck him from behind, throwing him down on his stomach and pinning him under locked wheels that drove him down the hill and along the flat and up the next incline until it came to a soft, precarious stop. For more than fifty yards, the huge locked wheels ground his hip and pelvis into the ice and ruts of the frozen, pitted road. He never lost consciousness. He never even cried out. The men who pried and dragged him out from under the wheels had no more idea what to do with him hurt than they had when he was well, for they lifted him into the open box of a half-ton truck and hauled him, crushed bones and all, nearly thirty miles over rough roads to the Ottawa Valley village of Barry's Bay, where there was a small hospital. It was twenty-two degrees below zero. He never said a word.

Those who had worked with him saw the sliding truck as a bit of a blessing, for it solved the problem of what to do with the ancient worker who refused to quit. The doctors who worked on him in Barry's Bay, and then Peterborough, where they transferred him, and finally Toronto, where they operated, said he'd never walk again; but medical expertise knows little of the miracles that can be performed by a library and a beer parlour that sit four blocks away, all downhill. Nearly a year after the ice accident he was living in the small town of Huntsville, on the western edge of Algonquin Park, where he and his wife, Helen, had owned a large clapboard house for thirty years, but where he had never really lived. There he had to get used not only to walking with a cane, but also to television reception and newspapers that weren't a week old and a wife who had, over those thirty years, known him only through random weekends and the summer months, when the family would move back up into the park and the life of bare feet, wild raspberry pies, fresh trout, wolves calling by night and the mill whistle by day.

Fortunately, she was a person of large heart. If she could forgive him, even coldly, for the car he had lost through gambling, for the winter wages he threw away on phony mining stock, for the day the Mounties pulled up in front of all the neighbours with a summons for failing to pay his income taxes, for the beer he hid in the creek at the edge of the road, even for the garter snake he once "forgot" was in the pocket of the pants he handed her as she fired up the gasoline-burning washing machine, she could forgive him surviving the truck accident and having to move into town. They would spend the next fourteen years together, two different entities joined by treaty as much as marriage, a situation largely made acceptable by the fact that the cane, the bad leg and the four blocks downhill to the town library and the beer parlour kitty-corner to it forced a strict three-drink limit. He could hobble down in late morning with books to exchange, a hour of searching for something, anything, that he had not already read, and then two hours at a Formica-covered table in the old Empire Hotel, delighting himself with the passing, stumbling parade.

"Tch-tch-tch-tch-tch-tch-tch."

And books, in an odd way, gave them both escape. C.S. Lewis might have said we read in order not be alone, but Lewis wasn't speaking for all. Even in the heart of a family Christmas morning, the Old Man would begin his books immediately, instantly alone and happy, every page of every gift quickly bookmarked with tobacco droppings and ash. She, too, was happiest when he was reading, left alone to do as she wished as well. There was no point in giving him clothes; he had the clothes he was wearing and, if necessary, a change. There was no point in giving him new lures to try, for even if fishing was his second great passion in life, he never used anything but one of two or three scratched and worn William's Wablers, which he kept, along with a few copper leaders, a couple of extra treble hooks and a single, cracked floater, in a small and rusty tackle box. For all those decades he passed deep in the Ontario bush, a trolling rod for the daylight hours and fresh books for the coal-oil lamp of evening was all the company he ever needed. And once forced retirement sent him to town, reading filled the mornings and afternoons as well—the morning pages separated from the afternoon by three drinks at the Empire and a quick stop at the pharmacy for the latest lottery tickets.

The only books he never seemed to read had to do, oddly enough, with the very bush in which he had lived and worked almost all of his life. Perhaps this was because he never found any—the literature of the Canadian wilderness being so largely the estate of those who came from elsewhere; who pretended to be something they were not; who visited rather than stayed, in good weather more than bad; who had the luxury of education and time to write; and who delivered back exaggerated stories they thought their distant readers and theatre audiences would like, rather than stories in which those who actually lived in the wild would recognize themselves and, for that matter, the creatures around them. Not for him Ernest Thompson Seton and his cute, "human" animals of the brightly lighted woods. Not for him Susanna Moodie and her high sense of social status, her contempt for commoners and her ultimate detestation for the bush he so loved. Not for him the phony Indian names and costumes of the transplanted Englishmen Seton and Archie Belaney. He would have shaken his head at the poet Pauline Johnson heading off to England as Princess Tekahionwake and claiming that the "scalp" hanging from her belt was, to her, the equivalent of the Victoria Cross to the British soldier. He would have howled with laughter at the works of Sir Charles G.D. Roberts, that silly, puffed-up fool who is still held up as the father of Canadian nature writers. Roberts, who dared write a poem about his type, "The Solitary Woodsman," and claim that the wily woodsman could find, in "the partridge drumming, / The belated hornet humming, / All the faint, prophetic sounds / that foretell the winter's coming." Partridge are notoriously stupid birds, but most know enough to drum in the spring when they mate. And hornets are rare where partridge are found. No, the Old Man would have stood with his beloved Teddy Roosevelt, who railed against such frauds as Seton and refused to have anything to do with "yellow journalists of the woods." If the Old Man wanted to escape to the Canadian woods, he had only to open the door, not a book.

"Tch-tch-tch-tch-tch-tch-tch."

He was different. "Drive on your own track," Plutarch advised, and he certainly did on his, amusing, delighting, and at times exasperating. He belonged, as Service rather accurately recorded in another northern wilderness, to that "race of men that don't fit in." In those final years, he was, by and large, well-behaved. There was that one incident when he was well into his eighties and was banned from the local Legion for "causing a disturbance," but that was an exception, and he—and we, for that matter—believed he was perfectly justified in trying to put the cane to a Nevada lottery-ticket seller who was out to rip off what he mistook for a doddering old fool.

He was, of course, perfectly behaved at his own funeral. There had been nothing that day like the day two decades earlier when they buried Roy, his brother-in-law and deep-bush soulmate who was less able to handle strong drink and responsibility and who had ended up, in his mid-fifties, the victim of a lifetime of bad habit. Handsome, gifted in sports, brilliant in the bush and cursedly charming, Roy had died broke and estranged, and yet he had been laid to rest, in this same small-town cemetery on a similar sun-blistered day, in a beautiful red-cherry casket. My two brothers and I and three cousins had served as pallbearers, and we had stood by this lovely casket facing the priest and a handful of mourners as the Old Man stepped back from them and ducked behind a nearby hedge to take a long, leisurely leak while the priest raised his fist and spilled out the sign of the cross in sand. None of us even blinked, even though others, facing in the opposite direction, fidgeted and half turned at the sound of liquid spraying through juniper branches. As far as the pallbearers were concerned, the Old Man could do as he damned well pleased. He, after all, was paying for the funeral.

He paid for his own as well. The day before his three sons had sat in the local bank while the manager openly puzzled about how a man who had lived to nearly ninety, who had worked for the same lumber company for more than half a century, who had raised a family and owned his own house could possibly have to his name only one bank account.

"There must be something more," she kept saying, as if she, not we, were to inherit.

But of course there wasn't more; nor had we expected it. There was precisely enough to pay for his funeral. No more. No less. His entire worldly possessions, trolling rod and lure aside, had fit into one desk drawer: four watches, three of them not running; some old black-and-white photographs; a wallet that had never held a credit card; some dated lottery tickets; a few letters; and a silver jackknife with a chip out of the blade. His entire wardrobe hung on five hangers in the closet of the bedroom that had once been mine.

"There must be something more."

It is hard to say how bank managers measure life, but accumulation—whether of money or of possessions—told nothing of the life of Duncan Fisher MacGregor, August 28, 1907–May 29, 1995. When the Old Man himself looked back on where he had been (nowhere) and what he had done (quit school, went to work in the bush), he tended to see himself as a minor player in a long, glorious tale that included Babe Ruth and Lou Gehrig barnstorming through the Ottawa Valley, Al Capone supposedly hiding low in a secret hideout in the valley woods in the late 1930s, the fact and fantasy of—what? a hundred thousand? two hundred thousand?—books and short stories and magazine articles and Andy Capp collections, even a family lineage that included his own great-grandfather, Jack Carson, striking off for the Nile with 385 other loggers, voyageurs, Mohawk, Iroquois and Métis to rescue Maj.-Gen. Charles Gordon before the fall of Khartoum.

Stories real and imagined, they were what mattered to him, as well as the shivers that such names could call forth, the magic of the printed word and the sense that, every now and then, his tiny hidden pocket of Algonquin Park could reach out and touch that other, more mysterious world, and survive the experience.

He loved incongruity. Al Capone afraid to use the outhouse after dark. David Thompson, the world's greatest mapmaker, taking on the Algonquin Park area when he was old and half-blind and, very likely, half out of his mind as he winced out at the endless tangle of alders and aspen and poplar until he had convinced himself that he could see nothing but fine farmland in the future. Tom Thomson, the great Algonquin Park painter and distant family connection who, many of us believe, was murdered at Canoe Lake, then honoured by his naive city friends with, of all things in Ontario, a totem pole that sat on the shore as natural as an orangutan hanging from the branches of a sugar maple.

"Tch-tch-tch-tch-tch-tch-tch."

There was incongruity in his own life, as well. He loved humanity and all its foibles and conceits, yet lived a virtual hermit's life in the bush. He was the best-read person any one of us has ever known, yet had no access to daily papers, no magazine subscriptions, no library within an hour's drive. He knew more about the world at large than anyone else we knew, yet had no education to speak of and was into his eighties before he saw his first mountain or seashore. He smoked constantly for nearly three-quarters of a century, ate very irregularly (and then only fried or burnt food, heavy with salt), drank too much and never once was aware of exercising—yet threatened, it seemed at times, to live forever. He would have found nothing of interest in his own life to speak of. He lived and worked in the bush. He was a lumberman, meaning he had done everything from fell the trees in the woods to saw the logs in the mill and pile and ship the lumber from the yard. He had, up until his forced retirement at seventy-three, never taken a holiday and never planned for any life after work. Who could blame the bank manager? There had to be something more.

After that sliding truck put him out of a job, he kept it simple in Huntsville: a daily walk; a daily book, perhaps two; and a daily libation, probably three. He eventually came to realize that he was the only one left, that smoke and booze and bad decisions and even the truck accident had somehow left him impossibly healthy and sharp long after virtually everyone else had passed on. His best company became the daily sports scores, which got him up each morning "just to see what happened last night."

He missed them that last morning. And a lucky thing, too. The papers were filled with predictions—wrong, it would turn out— about the Ontario election, which was then less than two weeks away. He would miss it, but what the hell, he had run out of votes anyway. Typically Canadian, he had already thrown out the Tories, whom he had helped put in, then thrown out the Liberals, whom he had helped put in, then thrown out the New Democrats, whom he had helped put in. There being no one left he hadn't lost faith in, he had come to the conclusion that his voting days were done. The big sports story of the day was Jacques Villeneuve's becoming the first Canadian to win the Indianapolis 500, but since the Old Man believed, as I now believe, that the only connection cars have to sport is to get you to the game and home again, he would have been decidedly unimpressed. What would have bothered him even more, was that his beloved Blue Jays blew a late rally against the Cleveland Indians, the score 5–4 for the Tribe with Toronto runners on every base in the bottom of the ninth, Ed Sprague foolishly hitting into a double play to end the rally and the game.

"*Tch-tch-tch-tch-tch-tch-tch.*"

He lost himself that final morning to pneumonia. Quick and

silent. Dignified, almost, his final words a joke and his eyes open and fearless until very near the end. Thomas Wolfe thought that the most telling feature of a boy's dead father was the old man's hands, "still-living hands of power and strength [that] hung incredibly, horribly, from that spectral form of death to which they were attached." Not in this case. This old man's blue, blue eyes sparkled to the final hours, as if death itself was some private joke that he, and only he, was privy to, and that those of us staying behind would have to wait and hope that we, too, would one day get.

The last score he needed to know was the tally as we drove back through the park after burying him. Two moose is considered a good count running through Algonquin Park these days. A deer is unusual. A bear rare. A wolf never. And yet there were six witnesses, four of them his grandchildren, to the count that bright late spring day: twelve deer, nine moose, four fox, one bear and one wolf.

But there was more that was unusual. The little bear raced along the side of the road for some distance, running with the slowing car. The wolf came out to the side of the road opposite Whitefish Lake, where the Old Man had lived so many years, and sat on its haunches and stared hard while we slowed and stopped. I had come across timber wolves before, both while driving and while walking in the bush, and every one I had ever seen had averted its eyes and bolted instantly—until this one.

If you took all the animals and added in the ravens and whisky-jacks and squirrels that we passed that bright day, the fauna would outnumber the people who had gathered in the small Huntsville chapel to say farewell. His grandchildren, naturally, supposed that the animals of the park had come out to say their goodbyes, as well. I had no idea what to suppose.

If the grandchildren were right, then what was the purpose of the wolf, with his stern, yellow-eyed stare and his utter contempt for a slowing, then stopping, car? A rabid wolf had once attacked his cousin and best friend, Sandy, while he was cruising timber in another part of this Precambrian Shield, and although Sandy had eventually died of heart failure, it had been the wolf attack that began the descent. And wolves, in the mill yard not far from this very point, had once ripped his little dog Blackie to death while the Old Man stared on helplessly, the illegal rifle he kept in the park too far out of reach and the wolves too soon skittering away and howling into the night and the trees that swallowed them up and away.

The wolf unsettled me, sitting there, staring, the pavement ahead rippling with heat and the park air hot through the window. He stared and we stared, and slowly he turned and elegantly sauntered back into the bush, his darkness bleeding into the black of dense spruce shade.

I did not understand the animals' presence then, and do not today. But I do know that it was not the only time I could not explain to myself or to anyone else the strange pull the Old Man had on everyone, and perhaps everything, who came to know him.

Months later, after our mother had arranged for a small, simple stone to sit above the grave we had stood around that day, I returned to the cemetery after a late November snowstorm. There was about a half-foot of snow on the ground, wet, packy snow falling in on itself as the late fall sun shone down on it.

I had told no one I was going. I made my way from the road, where I had parked, to where I remembered the grave had been dug. There were no footprints in the snow. The only sound was of melting snow and, every now and then, heavy snow dropping from the branches.

He was buried in the southwest corner of the cemetery, and I made my way over, realizing that because of the snow, I could read none of the small flat stones. I might not be able to find him.

But then I came on a set of fresh prints. They came from

another direction, towards town, and they wound their way through the stones until they came to a place where whoever it was had leaned over and brushed away the snow covering with the sleeve of his or her coat.

It was the Old Man's marker, the lettering clear and sparkling wet in the bright sunlight.

And a single rose had been placed on the stone.

CHAPTER ONE

Donald—always known as "Dan"—McGregor, 1856–1912. Headed for prosperity when he struck off for the bush back of Mattawa, only to die at fifty-six, leaving Annie with little but a house filled with children and her own remarkable wits.

IN THE FORTY-SEVEN years I knew him, my father gave me only two gifts. The first was a shotgun, which quickly fell into disuse, as both of us eventually came to the conclusion that we would rather laugh at the foolishness of grouse than take advantage of it. The second was a canoe paddle hand-crafted out of Algonquin Park cherry by his old Whitney friend Alex Cenzura. Two gifts I still have and treasure, though one is used and one not. I suppose there is a third I should mention as well, though I failed to recognize it for a gift when he gave it to me. Once, when the Old Man was well into his eighties, I asked him how old he felt he was when he first popped awake in the morning, the late-night scores waiting for him. As one who spends months of each year waking up in strange and distant hotel rooms, unsure of his space, I wondered if others ever lost track of where they were in time. He thought about it for a while. "Forty-nine," he finally said. "I feel forty-nine until I actually think about it." I was forty-nine the day I began writing these pages. If it never gets worse than this, I will paddle forever.

My gifts to him are less memorable. Books, of course—dozens and dozens of them, all carefully inscribed, "To Dad, Christmas 19(whatever), Love, Roy," just the same as my brothers, Jim and Tom, and sister, Ann, wrote in the books they gave to him—each one to be quickly read and then, much to our early disappointment, passed on to the first bushworker or lumber piler or lost camper who happened to stumble into the little corner of the Rock Lake mill where, night after night, he would stay up smoking and reading in the pale, weak light of coal-oil lamps or, later, electric generators. Books, to him, were more like conversations to be shared than secrets to hoard.

The year he turned eighty-four, I decided I should give something back to him. Father's Day was coming on and the baseball season was in full swing. He was unusual for a Canadian in that, unlike me and most everyone else I knew, he found baseball a far more compelling sport than hockey. He had played senior hockey himself until he was into his early twenties, and had followed the National Hockey League all his life, but he preferred the Grand Old Game, as he loved to call baseball, for its endless analysis and easy anecdote. If he wasn't quoting Satchel Paige or Babe Ruth or Casey Stengel, it would be Dizzy Dean, particularly Dizzy's "It ain't braggin' if you done it" when applied to fishing. He could recite the fifty-two lines and 576 words of "Casey at the Bat" without missing a beat. The only poetry he ever found in hockey was the harsh rhyming couplet of Gordie Howe's elbows, which he admired in its own way as much as Ernest L. Thayer or Robert Service at the top of his game.

I called him from Ottawa, the Old Man shouting into the telephone as if it were more cupped hand than receiver. Most of his life had been spent without the invention—the telephone had not come to Whitney and Algonquin Park until the 1950s—and it was still regarded more as an emergency measure than a necessity.

"Eh?"

"Cooperstown," I repeated. "We should go to Cooperstown to see the Baseball Hall of Fame."

"It's in the United States," he said as if this were a fact of which I was unaware, the discussion now rendered moot.

"It's not far," I argued. "We can drive down."

"When?"

"This weekend. I'll come over and pick you up."

"You mean it?"

"Of course I mean it."

"I'll be ready."

When I got to Huntsville the following day, it looked like he had been ready from the moment he had hung up the telephone. His little travelling bag—fake leather, cracked, with one handle broken—was sitting in a chair out in the porch, waiting. He was upstairs, sitting, as always, at the edge of his bed, reading from a pile of books, tobacco shreds marking every page, the rickety old card table pockmarked with match blisters and deeper grooved cigarette burns. To comfort our mother, we had placed ashtrays within easy reach and installed smoke detectors throughout the house. He burned holes in his shirts and words out of his books, but somehow the disaster everyone kept predicting never quite seemed to catch.

"No smoking in the car, if you don't mind," I said. "I'll gladly stop anytime you want."

He answered with a grunt and his own rule for the ride: if I wasn't going to let him smoke, he wasn't going to wear his seat belt. The compromise struck—me far more uneasy about the lack of a seat belt than he was about the lack of nicotine—we set off to drive back through the park, with periodic stops for him to have a smoke. We stayed overnight in Ottawa and set off again early the following morning for the United States of America.

It was only our second trip together to the U.S. and only the third time he'd been there in his life. Back in the very early 1960s, a shipment of hardwood from the McRae Lumber Company had ended up under dispute in Dallas, Texas, the American buyer claiming that the maple was of inferior quality and thus refusing to pay the full cost of the contract. The complaint resulted in a representative of the National Lumbermen's Association and the scaler who had shipped the wood, Duncan MacGregor of Algonquin Park, being dispatched to Dallas to settle the disagreement, which was ultimately ruled in McRae's favour. It had been his first-ever plane ride, which had terrified him. It had been his first prolonged experience with Americans, which had delighted him. It was also his first, and only significant, foreign trip.

His other trip had been very minor, and very much on a whim. He had come to Ottawa to visit with my family for a few days, and, having run out of sights to show him, I had asked him if he'd like to drive down and over the border for something to do. Sort of travel to another country for the afternoon. He thought it a splendid idea, and off to Massena, New York, we headed on a dark fall day. It was the closest border town of any substance, and I figured we'd have a drink—he'd probably have a few—I'd pick up some American treats for the kids and we'd be home by suppertime.

We drove around by the old Massena hockey rink, an older, barn-style arena with great charm to it, and he naturally suggested we drop in at the nearest bar, the Penalty Box, for a quick drink. I had a beer. He had a double rum and Coke, and the bartender, with no other customers to worry about so early in the day, began chatting with us. I had travelled enough to know that if you're going to be meeting only on a superficial basis anyway, there are no better travelling companions than Americans, with their easy talk and contempt for privacy. The Old Man had spent decades in Algonquin Park walking up to total strangers and starting a conversation—invariably warmly welcomed by tourists who were searching for firewood, fishing hints or directions to the dump where the bears could be found—and he fell into the conversation as easily as the bartender.

It seemed to me a perfect opportunity to bow out for a hour or so. There was a shopping mall back down the road where I could get the treats I needed to buy, and the Old Man would be happy here having a second, or even third, drink to pass the time.

The two of them were talking hockey when I left, still talking hockey when I came back in. The rum and Cokes had piled up. The bartender, it turned out, had played the game at a high level for an American, even coming across the border to Canada at one point to play junior hockey, and had once fancied a professional career. It hadn't worked out, like most professional fancies, but he still followed the sport avidly, especially for an American, and was hanging on every word this elderly Canadian was dispensing over the bar.

I joined in for a while before finding an opportunity to break the spell, or ice, and hint that it was time to get going. The Old Man headed for the washroom, the bartender and I for the door. "Your father wouldn't be a scout, would he?" the man asked as I buttoned my jacket tight.

A scout? God but how he had loved that. An American bartender—"bright young man, knows his hockey"—had mistaken for a working scout a retired, eighty-year-old lumberman who plucked everything he knew about the National Hockey League out of the sports pages.

"He *said* that?"

"He did."

"Tch-tch-tch-tch-tch-tch-tch."

But said with a different tone than usual, one of delight rather than reproach.

We struck out for Cooperstown on a fine, sunny day, early June with a fine mist over the creeks and the eastern Ontario woods still dappled with the fading blossoms of hawthorn and service-berry. We drove down Highway 16 and crossed the St. Lawrence River at Prescott, his excitement growing as we headed onto the high, arching green bridge and could look down at long, black-and-rust-coloured ships headed upstream into the Great Lakes and downstream towards Montreal, Quebec City and the North Atlantic beyond. He wondered where they were destined, what they were carrying. It seemed, in conversation, that I was the parent and he the child, with one profound difference. No matter how I tried to answer, I hadn't a clue; and he knew it.

He had on a new button-down cap, light blue and, for him, clean. An Andy Capp cap, he called it, and had it set on a slightly rakish tilt. He also wore an old brown-tweed sports jacket that I had long ago given up on and he had claimed for his own. The arms were a bit long, but with them folded over his chest, still defying the seat-belt signs, he looked well-turned out and, I think, far younger than his actual age. There was so much weather in his face, from more than half a century of working in the wind and snow and sun of the bush, that he kept the pink glow of youth rather than taking on the pallor of age. He had no need of glasses for distance, his blue eyes still clear and always, invariably, dancing with whatever delight happened to be passing through them. A sloping Bob Hope nose only underlined the sense of mischief. Sitting in the car where he had no need to walk—and thereby to

limp badly from the smashed pelvis and broken hip that had been
his retirement presents—he must have looked little more than a
middle-aged man travelling with another middle-aged man.

We passed by Ogdensburg and headed towards the Adirondacks
—not the easiest route to Cooperstown, but the more scenic one.
I drove looking in the rear-view mirror for state troopers. He sat,
beltless, staring straight ahead as we moved onto Highway 3 and
headed up into the hills after a half-hour of dairy farms and small
towns with, it seemed, the Stars and Stripes flying from every
porch. The hills caught him by surprise.

"So much goddamned bush," he marvelled.

"There's a lot," I agreed. I wound down the driver's side window, the car filling with the sweet smell of spring pine.

"I had it all wrong all these years," he said. "I always thought
Americans would never have seen anything like Algonquin Park—
but hell, they've got just as much here, haven't they?"

"They're different trees," I said. He looked at me as if I had just
told a child there are different television channels.

"You know what I used to dream?" he said suddenly.

"What?"

"I used to dream that I would find a walnut tree."

"What?"

"A walnut tree."

I have had my own recurring dreams. One takes place at Lake
of Two Rivers, not far up the road from the park mill at which he
worked. Our mother had once lived at Lake of Two Rivers on a
long rocky point that held the huge log home that her father, the
park ranger, had built with his own hands. We spent every summer
there from the moment school got out until it went back in the
fall, as well as most weekends and all holidays. It was, and remains,
the place that matters most. In this dream, the lake has dried up
and I am scrambling about the mud bottom finding lost lures and

dropped outboards and even, finally, just exactly how large the trout are off the far shoal. Sometimes I am worried there will be a body there instead of the trout, a rotting, ghostly body tied down with fishing wire like Tom Thomson was in another park lake farther down the road. But this dream is not nearly so worrisome as the one where there has been a mistake at school and I must repeat grade twelve for a *third* time, having barely scraped through, wide awake, on my second attempt, and I know in my sleeping heart that I cannot do it. In a third recurring dream, I am floating above the house in Huntsville, careful not to drop below the hydro lines, careful not to rise too high, and able to stare through the roofs of all those friends and neighbours who are, mercifully, returned to precisely the state they were in in 1961 or 1962, whenever it was that my shameful sentimentality locked into the small-town experience. In none of my dreams do I ever worry about what type of tree I am seeing.

For most people, such a dream would be impossible. They walk through parks and nature trails and sit in their backyards, and though they may admire the trees surrounding them and shading them, they are mostly all "trees," with few bothering to make much more distinction than that between evergreen and deciduous. A good woods walker can tell balsam from spruce and recognize three different types of birch, but it takes a timber cruiser to know where bird's-eye maple can be found, or how to look for the square scales on the bark of the black cherry. I have seen the Old Man sit in the passenger seat of a car being driven through the Algonquin Park woods and tell how many board feet of silver maple would be found along the slope of the nearest hill.

One fall in the early 1960s, the government decided to test all those ill- and self-educated men who were handling the shipping of lumber to export markets. The Dallas dispute was far from uncommon, and not all arguments were ending in Canada's favour.

There had been too many complaints of confused shipments—bur oak for white oak, scotch pine for white pine—and it was decided that there needed to be consistent standards established. The Old Man was petrified of the examinations, and reluctantly came out of the bush to write them. He was sure he would fail and had all but convinced himself that his days as the McRae Lumber Company shipper were numbered. But he breezed through them, scoring 99 per cent on the hardwood portion of the tests. Perhaps walnut, never having seen it, was the one question he missed. Perhaps walnut attracted him because it is the one hardwood that has never been found in a pure, natural stand, but insists on scattering. It puts down roots, of course, but the roots give off a toxic substance that prevents anything else, even walnut seedlings, from growing too close to it. A loner, like him.

We drove on a while in silence, the engine heating slightly as we rose higher and higher into the Adirondacks. I had purchased a map back at Ogdensburg, where we stopped for cheap gas, and had it opened, clumsily, on my lap to make sure we didn't lose our way. We were near Childwold when a sharp turn to the left put us in sight of a dark mound of soaring treeline.

"Is that a mountain?" he wanted to know.

"According to the map," I answered, reading and driving at the same time. "Yes . . . Mount Ma . . . Matumbia—2,700 feet."

"A *real* mountain?"

"An *old* mountain."

"First one I ever saw."

I turned and stared at him. He was still leaning out of the window, looking back for as long as he could take it in. Almost eighty-four years old and here he was seeing his first mountain, one so minor it barely made the official New York State road map.

I suppose I shouldn't have been so surprised. There were watersheds but no mountains in Algonquin Park. We called the big rock-face hill overlooking Huntsville "the mountain," but only because it made the high-school gym class runs seem more challenging. Its more appropriate name was the Lookout, which came from the expansive view it afforded of the little town, but the only climbing that ever took place there was in the back seats of absurdly modified cars on Saturday nights.

He had never travelled. Like Thornton W. Burgess' Grandfather Frog, "He heard all about the Great World and what a wonderful place it was, but he couldn't and wouldn't believe that there could be any nicer place than the Smiling Pool, and so he made up his mind that he would live there always." And yet his sister Isobel had once told me that he had been so world-aware as a child that she and the other youngsters in Eganville, where they lived, had invented a game in which the object was to stump young Duncan. They would name a country, and he would answer with that country's capital city. They would name a mountain range, and he would list the countries it covered. They would name a sea, and he would tell the countries it touched; a large lake or river, and he would tell where it could be found. From hours of studying atlases and spinning the small globe one of the teachers had on her desk, he knew, perfectly, where every significant thing on earth was located, and yet he had never seen a single capital city outside Ottawa and had never seen a real mountain until this moment, when I thought I would be soon showing him something truly amazing, like Ty Cobb's cleats.

"A *real* mountain?"

He was born Duncan Fisher MacGregor on August 28, 1907, though there was some minor dispute over the year. His older sister Janet always maintained that it had been 1906, which would have made him a year older than we thought he was. But that was not the only confusing thing about his beginning. The "Fisher" was not, as I once believed, an honorary title, like "colonel," that paid homage to his great passion, but was, rather, an older family name that his father also carried.

If he was born on that day in 1907 that his driver's licence listed, he entered a world where the big news out of Ottawa was that a horse had drowned in the Rideau Canal and its young drover was very nearly lost with it. In Berlin, the American steel magnate Andrew Carnegie was urging a European union to ensure that Germany, now chasing the United States in steel production, be kept in line. Rasputin was taking control of the court of Czar Nicholas II, and the stock market was undergoing its first genuine panic.

All of this was far, far removed from little Eganville, on the banks of the Bonnechere River in the Upper Ottawa Valley. Here, runaway horses were more threatening to the general public than the rise of Germany. The village was quietly growing, a happy mix of Irish, Germans, French and Scots. Donald "Dan" McGregor— the lost *a* in the surname would not be returned for several years—worked in lumbering, as did most of the men of the area. The magnificent, hundred-foot-tall white pine that had gone to ship masts and house construction around the world was still being felled, though some of the more observant loggers were starting to wonder how long it would be before the once seemingly limitless stands were exhausted. Dan McGregor's lively, good-humoured wife, Annie, was a Keenan, whose parents, John Keenan and Mary Hogg, had come from a small farming community just outside Ottawa. They had settled in Eganville, and Annie was born there on May 12, 1870. Dan and Annie were married in 1893. Relatives attending included Campbells and Fishers and Carsons, but beyond a handful of surnames little is known of Dan's and Annie's ancestors, where they came from and how they got here.

The typically Canadian family tree, with the roots running into impenetrable rock just below the surface and clinging to whatever holds can be found.

They were, according to what little oral history has survived, mostly stonemasons who arrived, as McGregors, in the first half of the nineteenth century and settled on farms around White Lake, a tiny village just north and west of Ottawa. They arrived around the same time as the other Scots who had been rounded up by the infamous Laird MacNab, who was setting up his notorious serf system along the nearby Madawaska River, but the name, happily, is not found on any of the MacNab lists of the time. MacNab was typical of the stories the Old Man adored of the Upper Ottawa Valley, a disgraced and bankrupt Highland chieftain arriving in full battle regalia, personal piper included, setting out to establish his own fiefdom along the lower Madawaska between 1823 and 1840, and very nearly succeeding. "Larger than life" would not even begin to describe the six-and-a-half-foot tyrant, who loved to brood for days alone with his beloved Bachelor, a fancy clay drinking cup said to hold a gallon of whisky, and who offended the settlers he tricked into coming here to the point of numerous often violent uprisings. They took offence, apparently, to having to sign a contract binding themselves and all future generations to the laird. They didn't like it that he forbade them to leave the township boundaries; that he owned all valuable resources, such as timber; and that he was magistrate and priest, controlling everything from marriage to prison terms. But as he proudly claimed, "The land is mine and all the people on it!" The colonial authorities finally tired of the complaints and accused him of "wanton oppression and outrages on humanity." He was tried as a "public nuisance" before being booted out of the country, ending up in France, where he died penniless in 1860. But he left behind a township still called MacNab and a curious plot in the White Lake cemetery, where the Old Man and Tom and I once roamed one hot August day until we found what had been, for more than a century, the unmarked grave of Granny Fisher, MacNab's house-keeper, and her illegitimate son, Allan Dhu, a nasty, criminal type who was remembered as "the bastard" in Dunc's youth but had now been upgraded to "son of Chief MacNab" by the local historical society and given a brand-new, polished marker.

"Tch-tch-tch-tch-tch-tch-tch."

The Mc is another matter of confusion. It may be that some of them were Irish-Scots, MacGregors who had been driven out of the Scottish Highlands generations earlier when a bounty had been placed on their heads and any link with the great Scot patriot Rob Roy MacGregor was considered a crime. Or it may be that they merely slightly abridged the spelling when it was for some time declared illegal to go by the MacGregor name. Whenever, and however, they came to North America, they arrived with little but blessed luck. They either survived or missed entirely Grosse Isle, the death stop downstream from Quebec City where the ships seeking to land during the time of the Irish crop failures dropped their destitute loads. Men, women and children who had lasted the hideous two months at sea often dropped dead on the beach, convinced they had been saved, more than five thousand of them consigned to mass graves in 1847 alone.

For those who survived the typhoid, the pattern was often similar. They were dispatched to new settlements—in the McGregors' case, the Upper Ottawa Valley—cleared their land, which was too often useless, built their homes and raised the children that had survived. With the cleared land unable to keep pace with the growing children, families began to spread deeper into the Upper Canada bush, where the squared-timber trade was far more enticing and profitable than trying to farm land that frequently turned from bush to rock clearing to thin and depleted soil. The bush made more sense to them than the land. The coming of steam had reduced the value of the white pine for the perfect masts they made, but the Industrial Revolution and the rush of immigrants were causing a European and North American building boom unlike anything seen before or since, and the straight, solid timber of the Canadian Shield was suddenly in demand everywhere.

They cut the trees in winter and then shipped the logs in spring, sending them down rivers like the Madawaska, Bonnechere, Quyon, Petawawa and Schyan into the wider Ottawa River and down the Ottawa to Bytown, now known as Ottawa, Queen Victoria's odd choice as a capital city for the colony, and then even farther down the Ottawa to the St. Lawrence to, eventually, Quebec City. Each winter they cut deeper, and soon along the Bonnechere there were timber chutes skirting five waterfalls, the fifth at the point where the lumber baron John Egan also constructed a gristmill to serve the farms that were being cleared along the riverbanks. Eganville was soon a tiny centre, with a number of small sawmills along the water, including one run by a Mr. McGregor in the early 1850s, and a few supporting farms spreading back from the Bonnechere. Egan and other timber barons backed the opening up of the Opeongo Road, and a colonization trail was soon twisting eastward towards the wilderness that would eventually form Algonquin Park.

Settlers quickly followed. Scots, Irish, French, German, Polish—a mix that would eventually make the Ottawa Valley "accent" as instantly identifiable to other Canadians as the Newfoundland way of talking. *Th* often comes close to *d*; "cookies" become "kookies"; a "car" can sound like "care"; "bank" becomes something like "boink"; chickens lay "ehhggs," "bush" is often "boosh" and still water is "cam" rather than "calm." In its rawest form, it can be a remarkable conversation carried by Irish lilt, connected by the peculiarly Canadian conjunction "eh," and filled with the dry humour of the Scot, the passion of the French and the directness of the German. Valley Talk.

"What's *that* mean?" the Old Man asks as we skirt by a cottage community on Otsego Lake, now less than an hour from Cooperstown.

"What's *what* mean?"

"That sign," he says, jerking a thumb towards a small convenience store back of some gas pumps. He reads it out: "Eee-zed Shop."

"No, no," I say. "That's Eee-*zee* Shop. American pronunciation. Zee instead of zed. Eee-*zee* Shop. Get it?"

"Tch-tch-tch-tch-tch-tch-tch."

It is strange that a man who would devote his life to reading could have so much difficulty pronouncing. As Christmas approached one year, around the time of the various *Godfather* movies, he dropped a hint that he particularly liked books about the "*maa-fay-ya*" and it took us days to figure out he meant the mafia. He had trouble with prime ministers' names and athletes' names and technical words, yet could spell them out or write them down with no difficulty whatsoever. Some of this affliction he passed on, and I have often thought I went into print in part because I could not talk.

Donald—always known as Dan—McGregor was a solid man with a thick moustache, a flair for business and, like the children who would follow him, contempt for the conventional. A staunch Presbyterian, he built a large brick home on the Catholic side of the Bonnechere River, which ran in an eastern flow through the village of Eganville. Protestants lived on the north side, Catholics on the south—with rare exception, and Dan McGregor was one.

Annie had been trained as a schoolteacher, but her work was put on hold as the brick home soon filled up with children: William, Janet, Donald, Kenneth, Marjorie (actually baptized "Anna Margaret"), Duncan and Isobel. Donald died of a sudden fever in the summer of 1908, three weeks short of his twelfth birthday. Duncan had just celebrated his first birthday, and would have no memory of his brother.

Annie was absolutely in charge of the big house. Her husband was often gone, travelling by rail or cutter or snowshoe deep into the bush, where he looked after timber rights for the growing McLaughlin Lumber Company of nearby Arnprior. He visited the winter shanties and checked on the spring log drives. Dan McGregor was also entrepreneurial in his own right, buying timber off farmers as they cleared their land, selling pulpwood to the paper mills down on the lower Ottawa River and slowly building up investment in local property. He thought Eganville would one day grow to be a centre of some import, and it seemed as if he had already become a significant citizen. His faith in coming prosperity made him an easy touch for those who needed a respectable signature to back a loan or a mortgage, which he was always content to do. Dan McGregor's faith in the young country was such that, shortly after Saskatchewan became a province of the Dominion in 1905, he bought a section of grassland around Biggar, east of Saskatoon. He believed, as others did, that there would soon be a hardier brand of wheat that could be grown in the more northern prairies, and that it would transform the harsh homesteads into profitable farmland. The better Canada did, the better he would do.

Such unbridled confidence was not uncommon: in a speech to the Canadian Club in New York City some twenty years earlier, Edmund Collin had claimed, "Alone, the valley of the Saskatchewan, according to scientific computation, is capable of sustaining

800,000,000 souls." It is not hard to imagine that around Eganville and the Upper Valley, Dan McGregor was widely seen to be going places, following the same Horatio Alger curve that had taken the likes of John Egan and fellow timber barons like J.R. Booth and Daniel McLaughlin and the Gillies brothers from subsistence farms to substantial holdings. E.B. Eddy, the story went, arrived in Ottawa with only forty dollars to his name and began with nothing more than a wild scheme to go door to door selling matches he made from pine butt. Now Eddy matches are struck around the world. J.R. Booth apparently left his father's farm with only nine dollars and turned a contract to supply timber for the new Parliament Buildings in Ottawa into an empire that eventually included four thousand shantymen in the Upper Ottawa Valley and a five-hundred-mile railway that he blasted and dug through the heart of Algonquin Park—the largest railway ever built by one man. It was a time when anything was possible, and Dan McGregor was only beginning to see the possibilities.

The McGregor children were all expected to succeed as well. Annie offered extra schooling at home. She had a piano brought in by rail from Ottawa and taught the three girls to play. She shipped in books so the bookcases would be filled with Dickens and Defoe, Brontë and Shakespeare, the Romantic poets and Kipling. The works of Robert Louis Stevenson and Sir Walter Scott and James Fenimore Cooper were read aloud to them before they could begin their own reading. There were history texts and atlases and, of course, the Bible. Sunday for staunch Presbyterians was a day for worship—church in the morning and church again in the evening—with the afternoon reserved for quiet contemplation and reading. They were not allowed to play cards. They could not even go outside except to head down the hill and over the bridge to the Presbyterian church on the northern hill. Duncan, the youngest boy, despised Sunday.

He was, however, allowed to read between church services. He lost himself in the bookshelf. He was like the young T.E. Lawrence—later to become Lawrence of Arabia, one of young Duncan's favourite war heroes—in that he had discovered, at a very young age, "the joy of getting into a strange country in a book." He did not discover, as Lawrence also claimed, that climbing naked in a tree stimulated one's thoughts. Words alone were good enough for Duncan.

Great adventure seemed a matter that came to others from other worlds, not to him in Eganville. He knew personally of only one great adventure, and that had been his great-grandfather Jack Carson's trip up the Nile to rescue the British governor of Egyptian Sudan, Gen. Charles George Gordon. The Nile Expedition of 1884–85 stands as one of the most unusual quirks of history, yet is all but forgotten today. Nearly four hundred Indians and French-Canadian trappers and Irish-Scot loggers headed off to canoe up the Nile and save Gordon's hide before the Mahdi captured Khartoum. The expedition was the brainchild of a British general, Garnet Wolseley, who had commanded the Red River expedition during the first Riel uprising in 1870 and had never forgotten the skill and doggedness of the voyageurs who had led him and his men to the river. Wolseley believed such men, with canoes, might traverse the difficult Nile in time. They set out drunk, were kept on board the ship in London so they wouldn't get drunk again, got drunk and into fistfights in Gibraltar, almost passed out at the sight of nearly naked Egyptian girls coming down to greet the ship as it reached the Nile and lost whatever innocence they had left in the fleshpots of Cairo. In between, they tried to reach the doomed Gordon, eight of them losing their own lives as they paddled and portaged and tipped and traded their way up the difficult Nile. They were too late, but came home heroes anyway, the city of Ottawa even throwing a parade for the ones who made it back,

Wellington Street packed with grizzled bushmen walking about with raised spears and shields, some with cockatoos on their shoulders, a few with frightened monkeys scrambling up and around and pulling, painfully, on their beards. Such an adventure, and Duncan felt a small part of it because of Jack Carson, who later settled in the small Upper Ottawa Valley community of Round Lake Centre and ran an unprosperous hotel.

The McGregor family entered the second decade of the twentieth century in magnificent shape. Six of Annie's seven children were alive and healthy, a rarity in those days. Bill, the oldest, was about to be accepted into Queen's University. Brilliant and comical at the same time—he could quote Rudyard Kipling at length and, just as effortlessly, mimic the town drunks—he was thought to be headed for a career as a politician or a lawyer. Further education was presumed for all of them, and none of the children—not even Duncan yet—had any other ideas as to what they might be doing with their lives.

Very quickly, however, fortunes changed. On Sunday afternoon, July 9, 1911, three small boys with cigarettes—Duncan was innocent in that he was then only four and was kept indoors on Sundays—started a small fire in a shed on the Catholic side of the river. The flames spread quickly along the frame houses and business sheds. They leapt the river at the dam and began eating up the woodframe homes on the north hill. Soon most of Eganville was on fire. Families that had taken this exquisite summer day to travel by wagon out to Mink Lake, a few miles to the northeast of town, could see the smoke and, according to newspaper reports of the time, realized that their churches were lost when the charred pages of hymn books began landing along the little beach where the families were picnicking. The Catholic priest, thick-bearded Father Patrick Sylvester Dowdell, carried the Blessed Sacrament down into the business area and, according to Catholic witnesses, actually turned the flames back at one point. According to Protestant witnesses, it was simply a wind shift that unfortunately did not last. A workforce of worried men went into McElligott's Hotel along the river and carried out all the hard liquor and loaded it into a canoe, which they then paddled over to Patterson's house and hid in the root cellar. But they obviously didn't get all the liquor. Fire brigades arrived from Renfrew and Pembroke, but they came too late to do much about the fire. The gristmill caught and burned on into the night, the shocked families of Eganville gathering near the smouldering buildings to watch the sparks dance while the visiting firemen dragged a piano out of one of the houses, broke out the whisky they had "saved" and got roaring drunk.

More than half the town was gone, including three churches, the public school, two newspaper offices and seventy-five residences. The brick McGregor home, fortunately, had been spared. Dan McGregor, stunned by what three little boys had done to his prospects, helped set up a relief committee of local businessmen and clergymen and donated the first hundred dollars to begin a subscription list. A month later, however, only $3,500 had been raised, and much of it had come from other towns and municipalities. The people of Eganville were virtually bankrupt. The fire had caused damage of nearly $500,000, but only $100,000 had been covered by insurance. The money Dan McGregor had invested was gone. The loans he had so easily guaranteed were still outstanding, and he was expected to make good on them. His home had survived, but his community was in ruins.

Who knows what Dan McGregor felt as he headed out into the bush that fall. His town was trying to rebuild, he was himself trying to straighten out his finances, but he had to go to work. McLaughlin had acquired new timber rights far up the Ottawa River in the wild Mattawa area, and his job was to check the shanties along the rights and make sure that everything was in shape for the winter cut. He travelled north by rail and then canoe, and the weather turned bitterly cold as he reached long Lake Timiskaming. With a north wind howling and an early snow in the air, he moved even farther up the Ottawa watershed, heading into the Quebec side and Lac des Quinze and Lac Simard.

The Quebec lakes were iced over, and he and his travelling assistant had to cache the canoes and walk. It was twenty-four miles to the nearest camp, and they walked all day and into the night, reaching the warm shanty and waking up the men who had already gone to sleep. They ate and warmed themselves and went immediately to bed. In the morning, when Dan McGregor didn't get up, the men checked and found him semi-conscious, unable to talk or move.

They carried him out of the bush on a sled, and when they reached Lake Timiskaming a boat was used to break through the thin ice that had formed and they were able to take him to Mattawa. Here he suffered a second stroke. They took him by train from Mattawa to Ottawa, and then straight on to Montreal, where doctors had previously performed successful operations on brain hemorrhages. But they were hesitant to attempt anything on a man who had been so severely stricken and so late reaching medical care. He lingered, half-conscious, through the winter, finally suffering a third, fatal, stroke on April 21, 1912. Dan McGregor was two weeks short of his fifty-sixth birthday.

Annie McGregor was suddenly a widow with a half-dozen children. They had the large brick house, a couple of horses, a milk cow and several chickens. They were fine for the present, but what of the future? Two of the children, Duncan and Isobel, weren't even of school age. There would be no more money coming in from the lumber company. No pension. No insurance.

I have often wished I knew more of Annie. But she died on March 22, 1949, and the strongest image I have of her comes from, of all places, the inside cover of several of her treasured books, which Duncan managed not to give away or throw out. Inside, she has signed her name in elegant style and dated the year the book was purchased. In ballpoint pen, some seventy-five years later, her youngest son, had scribbled, "A wonderful mother." By Presbyterian measure, this is close to sainthood.

Annie became an entrepreneur herself. At the urging of her bright, history-driven oldest child, Willie, she inserted the *a* back into the family name and opened up A. MacGregor & Co. in the newly constructed downtown of the little village. She sold ice cream that came in by refrigerated car from the Ottawa Dairy. She sold soft drinks, chocolates, fresh fruit, groceries, tobacco and crockery. She received parcels shipped in for farm families. She even came up with her own version of Canadian Tire money, handing customers a fifty-cent coupon—"good in trade"—for every ten dollars' worth of purchased goods. She took over what few investments of her husband's had survived and, apparently, handled the small amount of money well. She sold the farmland in Saskatchewan, even though Marquis wheat was now a reality and the Biggar region would be opening up to wheat production. She wanted what little money she had to remain within sight, where she could keep a sharp Calvinist eye on it.

Annie told her older children—Willie, seventeen when his father died, and Janet, then fifteen—that they would have to help with the family situation. But she insisted that so long as she could afford it, they would still get their own educations. Willie she sent to Queen's University in Kingston. Janet she dispatched to the Ladies' College in Ottawa, where, Janet much later lamented, "They taught us a little French, some music and how to do needlepoint—nothing that you would ever use." Janet's ambition was to become a nurse, but Annie had already decided that her oldest daughter would be kept at home to help out. This was common practice in the area and at the time, and Janet, a quick, high-spirited girl who dreamed of one day seeing the world, found herself back in Eganville at seventeen, with few prospects other than the stove and laundry. The only way out of this accepted predicament for her and others—for that matter, my own mother a generation later—was to marry. "What else could you do?" she once said.

In Janet's case, the suitor turned out to be John Stanley Lothian McRae, from next door. The McRaes were among the most prosperous families in town, despite the setbacks of the Great Fire, and they owned the small hydro-electric mill, two gristmills, including one in nearby Douglas, a sawmill, timber rights and a general store. John—who would later become known throughout the valley as J.S.L.—was, however, seven years her elder. The day he got up the nerve to walk into the MacGregor residence and ask for Janet's hand, he ran into the wrath of Annie, who would hear nothing of it.

"He was scared to death," remembered Janet more than sixty years later. "'You want to marry *her*?' my mother said. 'She's a baby! She can't cook! She can't sew! She can't do anything! Go get yourself a wife your own age!'" Six months later, Annie had relented. Janet and J.S.L., who would go on to build one of the great lumber dynasties of the Upper Ottawa Valley, would live happily together for more than half a century, until J.S.L.'s death in the late 1960s.

Willie, too, had his own ideas of what he wished to do with his life. He was twenty years old when war broke out in 1914, and he fought immediately with Annie about his obligation to sign up. With six children and no husband, she needed Willie at home more than any of them, but again she relented to a child's wish and he signed up with the Canadian army. Impatient to see action, he soon transferred to the Black Watch of the Imperial Army and, in 1916, set off for England and the European front. He was made lieutenant, soon rose to the rank of major, and recalled once having to parade in the same line as Edward, the future king of England. It gave him cause to quote Kipling even more often, one favoured passage in particular striking his impressionable younger brother, Duncan, who was only nine years old when Willie left with the Black Watch.

If you can talk with crowds and keep your virtue,
Or walk with Kings—nor lose the common touch . . .
Yours is the Earth and everything that's in it,
And—which is more—you'll be a Man, my son!

Three times Willie MacGregor was wounded, the worst being in late 1917, when he was missing in action following some of the heavy fighting around Cambrai. For weeks the family pored over the harrowing newspaper lists of the war dead, never finding the name they were looking for but dreaded seeing. "It was awful," Dunc once told Tom. "Just name after name. You'd see 'Pte.' after most of the names. I remember a lad saying to me, 'There sure are a lot of guys named Pete in the army.'" Finally, news came that Willie had been wounded and was now a prisoner of war. Ken also enlisted, lying about his age, but when Annie found out she put a quick end to the younger brother's plans.

Willie's worst wound had come from a sniper, the bullet entering the back of his neck and exiting through the lower portion of his throat. Somehow the shot had passed through clean, missing his larynx entirely and skimming the vital ducts of the throat. The injury left scars the size of silver dollars on both sides of his neck, however, and years later, when he visited (now calling himself Bill rather than Willie), he would eventually give in to the children's begging, loosen his collar and show us what war can do—though we, of course, thought it glamorous and, for that matter, harmless.

He recovered from this terrible wound quickly enough to be

sent back across the Channel yet again, and that time was captured in Germany, where he spent the remainder of the war as a prisoner. When the war ended, the British government offered two years of university to such veterans, and Bill decided to stay on and study economics at the University of Edinburgh. He also studied briefly at Oxford and returned to Canada to take up law studies at Osgoode Hall in Toronto. He soon graduated and returned to Eganville to set up practice.

Throughout Duncan's life, his older brother was the hero. Willie had marched with the king, and even if the king hadn't quite worked out, Willie certainly had. He had been a war hero, his chest emblazoned with seven glittering medals. He had wounds to show off and had survived a dreaded German POW camp. Soon enough he was a magistrate, and then a judge, and before his death from cancer in 1966, a true Ottawa Valley legend.

Willie MacGregor's travelling court became one of the great sources of entertainment for local people, with his courtroom wit soon part of area folklore. He once asked a young man charged with being drunk and disorderly what church he belonged to, and when the young man said he was High Anglican, Willie calmly replied, "If you're not today, you sure were last night." Once another local, one with money, hired a big-city lawyer to defend him in the Killaloe court. When the cocky lawyer began citing precedent, Willie MacGregor's gavel came down so sharply that the man all but jumped out of his expensive suit. *"That may be the law where you come from,"* the magistrate bellowed out, *"but it ain't the law in Killaloe!"* The line gave him his first nickname, Willie "Killaloe Law" MacGregor, and it stuck. The *Globe and Mail*, which became so entranced with his idiosyncratic rulings that they editorialized him when he died, tried giving him another moniker—"The Man Who Wears a Velvet Glove on a Velvet Hand"— but it didn't have quite the ring to it, and failed to stick.

Still, the *Globe* was on to something. Willie MacGregor had a view of the law that hardly seemed in keeping with his own strict Presbyterian background and long military career. He was an imposing figure—a slightly older version of Dunc, with a white clipped moustache—but there was so much joy to his face that the *Globe* once compared his look with that of Santa Claus. He was so gentle, so kind in court, that at times his rulings astonished. When a garbage collector appeared before him and pleaded guilty to pumping four rifle shots into the vehicle of a man he was feuding with, the unpredictable magistrate fined him $40.50 and sent him home. The judge did not bother explaining to the court, or the wronged party, how exactly he had arrived at that amount of compensation. But no one ever challenged him. He had their respect—even that, often, of those he ruled against. Having once been a prisoner himself, he abhorred sending people to jail. When a woman, a recent German immigrant, appeared before him on a shoplifting charge, his gavel pounded down and he dismissed the charge without even hearing the evidence. People had to understand, he said, that this poor woman had been forced to steal just to survive during the war years, and as a new Canadian she needed to understand that Canada was a forgiving nation.

Perhaps the *Globe* was merely using code, for the Santa Claus look surely came from Willie's well-known habit of downing a bottle of gin, straight, on his way to court. Twenty-three years after Willie's death, his reputation was still renowned enough throughout the valley that the *Ottawa Citizen* did a long feature on "Magistrate MacGregor," and shortly after it appeared, I drove Duncan up to Pembroke so he could visit with Willie's widow, Mary, who was then ninety years old and living in an old-age home on the edge of town. She did not, however, act like a ninety-year-old. She seemed more like the feisty young woman Willie had first seen playing piano in the Eganville Theatre in the days before talkies. The first thing Aunt Mary did when Duncan walked in was hobble over to her closet and break out an unopened bottle of rum.

She was outraged by the article. "They said he could drink a whole bottle of gin between Arnprior and Renfrew," she said.

Dunc obviously had sympathy for her. *"Tch-tch-tch-tch-tch-tch-tch."*

So did I. Why drag the family name down by dwelling on drink?

"Wasn't a full bottle at all!" Aunt Mary said, stomping her cane. "It was just a *mickey!* Bill knew his limits—he had *work* to do!"

If Willie was destined to be the star, the others in Annie Mac-Gregor's family were also expected to shine, even if less brightly. With Willie helping to pay, the rest received the best educations Annie could suggest for them. Ken, the quiet one who would never marry, also headed off to Queen's, where he became an engineer, and would eventually work in Western Canada on many of the large highway and hydro-electrical projects of the thirties and forties. Marjorie, the musical one, seemed destined to become a teacher, as would the baby, Isobel.

And then there was Duncan.

If Ezra Pound's Mauberley could be "out of key with his time," then Duncan MacGregor could be out of key with his space. He was the youngest of three, once four, boys, rebellious and daring. The family was very nearly hit with two tragedies when, the second summer after Dan McGregor died, young Duncan, then only six, tried to prove to the older boys in Eganville that he, too, could dive under the length of the floating dock that sat in the middle of the Bonnechere River, near the bridge, and was a popular swimming spot. He took as deep a breath as possible, dived over, turned and began swimming beneath the long dock—only to catch his bathing suit, on a nail. When he didn't surface, the older boys panicked, but two of them found him, ripped him free of the nail and the bathing suit and tossed him, naked and choking, up onto the dock to dry out and recover. By summer's end, however, he had mastered the feat. And he might have been able to swim the length of the dock and back if not for the intervention of a small matter that he would soon come to regard as another nail that was trapping him from the air he needed: school. As much as Annie McGregor's other children took to school, her youngest boy took to the woods and the banks of the Bonnechere, where he wandered and fished before and after school and every Saturday. He cut his own alder poles for fishing. He set traps for rabbits. He hunted grouse with a small twenty-two. He liked, best of all, his own company.

The Old Man never wrote about the wilderness, so there are neither easy nor sensible comparisons to most people we think of when we talk about those who set off for the woods for two purposes; first, to be there, and second, to leave and tell about being there. In reading Thoreau and Service and John Muir and Aldo Leopold and so many other North American giants of, for want of another phrase, bush introspection, I have come across only one who felt much like Duncan, and that was the Minnesota writer Calvin Rutstrum. Perhaps it was because Rutstrum spent so much of his time in northwestern Ontario. Whatever, like Duncan he began life in a village and took early to the woods. Both lost their fathers when they were youngsters (Duncan was four, Rutstrum three), both became entranced with the life around water (Duncan along the Bonnechere, Rutstrum along the Minnehaha Creek), and both read whatever they found and found school not at all to their liking. "To be free as a wild creature," was how Rutstrum put it, "not having to shoulder human cares, able to climb, run, jump, swim, lie on an embankment in the sunshine—these gave a release to the young spirit that may perhaps be described as primitive, but nevertheless exquisite in the most elemental sense." Both had no use for intellectual posturing or bragging, and both lived to be three months shy of eighty-eight years old.

"I must have fallen out of the cradle and into the woods," Rutstrum once told a friend. "And enjoyed it." Succinct, but Duncan could reduce his chosen life in the bush to only three words: "It suited me."

School certainly did not. He was an educational oddity in that he appeared extremely gifted in certain subjects, extremely restricted in others. He could score 100 per cent in history, but zero in Latin, which he considered a waste of time. If something interested him, it had him completely. If it failed to interest, it lost him immediately and totally. The same troublesome blood flows through my brain, and I see it again in certain of our children. Perhaps if school were served up in five-minute blasts—with no prerequisites and not even a timetable—if noise and fidgeting were welcome and good weather a course, we would be scholars; but we are not, and school has no patience for the impatient. Back in First World War Eganville there were no resource teachers, no educational psychologists and certainly no pharmaceutical tricks to get one to focus in on the task at hand. Duncan knew all the countries and capital cities in the world. He knew the important battles and treaties, the significant rulers and politicians, and had read, and loved, most of the great books. And yet he was failing. Lost in Latin. Struggling in mathematics, which at that moment held no interest for him, in that no teacher had seen fit to apply it to board feet or timber hauls.

He loved the Bonnechere. He loved how this thin, iron-coloured river slid through town like melting glass, and how, a few miles downstream, this same lazy river would pound through a narrow chute, filling the air with its roar and a fine mist. At the side of the chute were limestone caves, and while they were mostly under water, particularly in the spring, there were openings where a youngster could twist down far enough to see fossilized snails and squid and sea plants. Hundreds of millions of years ago the heart of North America had been under a tropical ocean, and here, in his own backyard, was proof that this had indeed been the case. The caves and the thundering chute gave him as much respect for the power of time as for the power of nature. He believed from childhood that humanity was but a passing fancy in the universe, and if you could not be amused by reality you would more likely be terrified. To fancy that humanity was any more lasting or significant than a fossilized snail trapped forever—no, not even forever—in a limestone wall was the ultimate human conceit. And as soon as he no longer had to go to church to please his mother, he stopped going entirely, to please himself.

In his developing outlook on religion, he was again like Calvin Rutstrum, who was just beginning to find his own way about the bush. Organized religion, to Rutstrum, was bunk and hokum. Men and cockroaches die the same death. "The only promise you got of living forever," Rutstrum told the American journalist Jim dale Vickery for Vickery's book *Wilderness Visionaries*, "is that you'll be taken up into the ether to a platform somewhere and you're going to be allowed to strum on a harp all day long. I don't like music that well."

When the school was closed, life must have seemed near perfect to young Duncan. He hunted grouse and ducks in the early fall, deer when the first snow fell, and set traps for rabbits in the deeper snow of later winter. He fished for bass and pike in the Bonnechere, for speckled trout in the nearby streams, and portaged canoes into the larger lakes in the area to fish for lake trout, which immediately became his fish of choice and of conversation. In late spring, he would often help some of the German families who came to the Bonnechere dams to net the mysterious eel that somehow made its way inland to Eganville. Most of the villagers shunned the snake-like fish, cutting their lines when they caught one rather than have the long, slippery beast twist its sinuous body around their arms as they tried to pry out a hook, but neither he nor the immigrant families who remembered the eels from their runs up the Danube and the Elbe and the Ems had any fear of the strange-looking creatures. He helped fill burlap sacks with eels and often received bottles of jellied and pickled eel in return, which he carried home to Annie with great pride.

The eels intrigued him as much more than a culinary delight. He often talked about this annual harvest, amazed that the eel could somehow return to streams they could not possibly have known in any way other than in their troublesome bones. Settlers along the Bonnechere talked of the eels as creatures from another world, which indeed they were, but what some of these people meant was that the mysterious eel could "walk" on land if there was not enough water in which to swim. How they got over log dams and hydro dams and up dried-up creeks baffled those who found them twisting and writhing on the end of their fishing lines. Science at this time had still not determined that the eels came from somewhere in the Sargasso Sea of the mid-Atlantic, where they were born, and that half the fingerlings headed off in the direction of Europe and half to North America, where they would run up the rivers, the St. Lawrence to the Ottawa and even into the Bonnechere, where they would feed and grow and, one day, return by the millions to spawn in the deep Atlantic. Duncan might have preferred to believe, as Aristotle did, that the eel rose spontaneously from the mud, perhaps from horsehairs that ended up in the water when riders and wagons crossed over shallow streams.

He played baseball in the summer and hockey each winter, a scrappy little winger who seemed to love the corners as much as the front of the net. He played on town teams that travelled about the upper valley by train and cutter to play other teams in Renfrew and Pembroke and Douglas. Games in Eganville were played on a large, shovelled rink on the Bonnechere, the banks surrounded by fans who were more interested in keeping their backs to the wind than in who won or lost. Typically, his fondest memory of playing senior hockey for Eganville had nothing to do with scoring, but involved a match with the nearby Douglas team when the whistle suddenly blew as he chased a puck into a far corner. Convinced that a penalty had been unfairly called on him, Duncan turned to protest, only to see the referee skating hard for the far side of the rink, where no fans were willing to stand facing into the wind. With the game suspended and more than one hundred chilled, feet-stomping fans staring across the ice at his back, the referee proceeded to take a long, spraying leak into the wind, shook off, buttoned up, blew hard on his whistle and returned for a fresh face-off.

He was obsessed with sports. When the National Hockey League started up in 1917, it seemed as if half the players came from valley teams. Frank Nighbor, the Pembroke Peach, was from the area. "Fearless" Frank Finnigan was from Shawville, on the Quebec side of the Ottawa River. Duncan once fancied, as most young Canadian hockey players fancy, that he might follow, but it soon became apparent that he was a good river player, not good enough for the fancy rinks of professional hockey. Still, he could dream. He delivered the *Ottawa Journal* around town and spent hours poring over the sports pages, reading about the hockey and baseball stars of the day. He read about Knute Rockne and John L. Sullivan and Jack Dempsey and Jim Thorpe and remembered, as a twelve-year-old, pacing out the 587 feet that a Boston player named Babe Ruth had apparently hit a home run in a game against the New York Giants. He struck a deal with Mr. McFadyen, an elderly man who lived in a small house closer to the river, whereby he could come by in the evenings and pick up the sports section of the rival *Ottawa Citizen*. After reading the racing results and boxing stories and box scores of the *Journal*, he read them all over again in the *Citizen*. He remembers the shock he felt when the Red Sox suddenly, and mysteriously, sold Ruth to the New York Yankees for $125,000. From that moment on, he was a Yankee fan.

The more he read the Ottawa newspapers, the more he wanted to know about the rest of the world. When he could, he would read the Montreal and Toronto papers and every magazine he could find. He discovered the writing of Grantland Rice and, most important, of Damon Runyon, and Runyon carried Duncan's imagination into a world that included gangsters like Al Capone and grand incidents like the Lindbergh kidnapping. Horse racing became a magical world to him, a world where everyone talked like Runyon's *Guys and Dolls'* characters and where toughness was a certain walk and tilt of the hat. Prohibition came in in the States and the Temperance Act in Ontario, and part of being smart became a cigarette and knowing where to find a flask of whisky. Becoming an actual gangster in Eganville was out of the question, however, with an older brother who was opening up a law practice and a mother who believed carrying even a handkerchief on Sunday was an unforgivable crime.

In 1923, the year he turned sixteen, Dunc quit school. He was in grade eleven and would be the only member of his family not to graduate from high school and go on to further education. But he didn't care. He just wanted out. Annie MacGregor, anxious to help her youngest son and resigned to his leaving school, agreed to set him up in an ice-cream parlour that he opened up at the centre of the village bridge. He had grand ideas. He would have Protestant customers to the right, Catholics to the left. He put in phony palm trees to give the shopfront a "beach" atmosphere. But hardly anyone came. Perhaps the Protestants felt it was a Catholic business, the Catholics felt it was Protestant. Within a matter of months, he had closed up and taken on work hauling pulpwood out of the bush for a local jobber.

His life took on a pattern during the 1920s that must have worried his mother and older siblings. With everyone else excelling and getting on with careers or marriage, Duncan showed no such ambitions. He called himself the black sheep of the family, but this suggests more trouble than he ever got himself into. He was content to play ball and fish in the summer, play hockey and cut wood in the winter. The little town, the river and the easy lifestyle suited him fine.

He talked vaguely about heading out West and working the harvest, but it was more romantic notion than career assessment. He liked the idea of riding the rails and he wanted to see the places he had been reading about. He was ill-suited to farming, more taken with bush and stream than clearing, and utterly incapable of doing his own repairs. I once asked him how it could be that he could live his life around lumber operations and sawmills, surrounded by machinery that cut down trees and sawed lumber and drove boats and even generated the electricity that provided the light by which he would read his books, and yet not know how to use tools. He could change a spark plug in his outboard, but that was about it. He owned no tools of his own. "I had no father to teach me," he said. "I never learned how to use them."

In the late summer of 1925, he finally boarded the Harvester Train for the West. The fare was fifteen dollars to Winnipeg and a half-cent a mile for anything beyond. He took it as far as Regina, and then caught another train south to just alongside the North Dakota border, where several men, including one friendly fellow from the East whom he'd hooked up with, disembarked and set out to find work. It more often found them, for workers were in demand. They made eight dollars a day, a vast amount for men who, back home, were lucky to find work at all and lucky then to make a dollar a day. He had some familiarity with horses and often got to drive teams as they took off the wheat. "People were a lot friendlier out West than they were back East," he remembered many years later. "I liked that." It also gave him a new appreciation for other cultures. He met and worked for Ukrainians and Germans and Scandinavians, and liked them all. "The most miserable bastards were the Scotch," he remembered. "But I guess that's only natural."

Dunc and his "partner" began travelling around together. They never had to ask for work; they just showed up and started in. The families were friendly and the meals wonderful. He even thought, at one point, that there might be something between him and one English settler's daughter, but there was hardly any time for courtship. They worked dawn to past dusk, and as soon as one field was finished they moved on to another. His partner wanted to press on into Alberta, so they split up, the friend heading farther West while Duncan prepared for the journey home. Decades later, much to the wonderment of his children, Dunc would sometimes say he should have continued on, should have tried his luck and stayed West. He had hoped to see the land his father had once owned up around Biggar, but he got no closer to it than the Regina train station, and was soon headed back home for another winter of hockey and bush work.

He came back to a home where Annie MacGregor was excitedly planning the wedding of her second daughter. Marjorie had become engaged to a young man who had come to Eganville to work in the bank. Annie wanted the event to be something everyone would remember for a very long time. They would—but not for the reasons Annie imagined.

Marjorie had always been treated as "special." She had suffered from rheumatic fever as a child, and had always been more frail than the rest. She was the musical one in the family, the one who had mastered Annie's treasured piano from Ottawa, and she had turned into a beautiful young woman who planned a teaching career after marriage. She was in Ottawa for the final fitting of her wedding gown when, walking back from the dressfitter's shop to the train, she was stung by a wasp. An allergic reation set in and she died on the eve of what would have been her wedding day. She was twenty-six years old. They buried her in Eganville, wearing the dress that had been intended for celebration, not sorrow.

The twenties were often a rough go for the MacGregors of Eganville. Janet had married John McRae and the two had moved east along the Opeongo Line to Barry's Bay, then a supply stop on J.R. Booth's railway line and a rustic village without even the amenities of Eganville. J.S.L. was trying to establish himself in the lumber business. He was using a team of horses to draw logs out of a minor timber rights he had leased from the province and was selling the timber to the larger companies. He was anxious to have his own mill and was looking farther east, to the very end of the Opeongo Line and almost to the boundaries of the newly formed Algonquin Park. He was gone for weeks at a time. Janet was often alone in Barry's Bay with their first child, called Donald, after Janet's lost brother; shortly after their arrival in the tiny outpost she had a second, a little girl who died shortly after birth. A boy, Jackie, was then born. Bright, curly-haired and soon talkative, he was two years old when a strange typhoid-like fever struck the isolated community. The woman next door lost both her little girls, then Jackie came down with a fever that caused diarrhea so severe it punctured his bowel. He lived a tortured ten days, then died. One more baby, named Marjorie for the lost sister, survived, and Janet asked John if they could move back to Eganville. In later years, Janet McRae would always speak of that decade as "the Bad Times."

Duncan stayed around Eganville after his great trip West. His mother was still too deeply in mourning for Marjorie for him to dare suggest he take the Harvester Train again, but in the fall of 1928 he did take another trip, albeit a far shorter one, in the opposite direction. He and several ballplaying friends from Eganville headed off for Hull, Quebec, where Babe Ruth, who had hit those unbelievable sixty home runs the previous summer, was himself scheduled to appear. Ruth and his New York teammate Lou Gehrig were barnstorming around the continent following the Yankees' four-game sweep of the Cardinals in the 1928 World Series. It was the Yankees' second straight series sweep, and Ruth was now the most celebrated player baseball had ever known. Dunc had to be there.

The two Yankee heroes played their late October exhibition game at Parc Dupuis, which sat at the foot of what is today the Interprovincial bridge between Ottawa and Hull. Ruth and Gehrig had come up with a semi-pro team from Montreal and were mobbed at the train station. Because of the relatively new phenomenon of newsreels and the rising dominance of New York, the two were likely the biggest sports stars on earth at the time, Ruth having batted .625 against the Cards and hit three home runs in a single World Series game, and Gehrig having hit four himself in the series.

The *Citizen* headline read, "Babe Ready for Hull Swatfest," and the breathless prose of the reporter would have made Damon Runyon smile to realize the reach of his own style: "'The Potentate of Swat,' one George Herman Ruth, the sound of whose lusty wallops has reverberated through sundry ball fields recently, and whose performances with the willow have offset in point of interest even the question as to who is to be the next president of the United States, accompanied by his trusty henchman and sidekick, 'Larruping' Lou Gehrig, arrived in the Capital this morning."

"Tell the boys we are both glad to be here," the Babe told the paper, "even for such a short visit, and at Dupuis Park this afternoon we will try and provide our share of the entertainment." The event drew three thousand cheering fans, twenty-one-year-old Duncan MacGregor among them. The Babe, as had to happen, drove in the winning run with a screaming double that almost broke through the left-field fence, and the game was called early on account of fans having swarmed the field to touch their heroes. The two stars caught the late train to Toronto and Buffalo, the next stop on their barnstorming tour, and Dunc caught the last train back to Eganville and the coming winter. It would be his last hockey season as a player.

In the spring, when he again set out to do little but hike through the bush in search of new speckled trout creeks, his mother and sister Janet spoke to him about taking on a full-time job with John McRae. J.S.L. had purchased the old Mickle and Dyment mill on the shores of Galeairy Lake, where the Madawaska came out of the park and began its long, twisting run down to the Ottawa. The old mill was up and running again, and J.S.L. needed help. There was a job waiting for Duncan, if he was interested.

He was very interested. In the late 1920s, Algonquin National Park, as it was known at the time, was seen as the definition of wilderness for the likes of wealthy American tourists and the Group of Seven painters that followed Tom Thomson into the Ontario wilds. The Park had the mystique of Thomson, dead now a decade, and the certainty of cold rivers, deep lakes and large trout, as well as bears and wolves. There was not even a road to it— the only ways to reach the park were by Booth's railway or difficult canoe routes. Given the bogs and rivers and terrain and thick forest, it did not even seem possible for a man to walk to it. If Henry David Thoreau had been thrown into near hysterics by the "grim" and "savage" wild country he encountered on a well-organized hiking trip to the northern tip of the Appalachian Trail in Maine, he would have trembled and wept at the notion of heading into Algonquin Park to spend the rest of his life.

But the idea of real bush held no terrors for Duncan. He was well used to the woods and more comfortable in them than in towns. This was not the teacher Thoreau moving out to the little pond on the edge of town, close enough to civilization that he could walk back in for food and mail and family visits every second day. This was not the banker Robert Service setting out for the Yukon in a deliberate attempt to conquer his near-debilitating fear of being alone in the dark, threatening bush. This was merely another young man from the Upper Ottawa Valley headed for Algonquin Park, a chance at some permanent work and an opportunity to seek out some new fishing grounds. He never thought about it as a romantic notion. He never considered that those who didn't live there might find it interesting to hear about. Who would ever bother to write about it? Who would ever want to read about it?

There was no ulterior motive. There was nothing to prove. It was just a job, and he needed work.

Sixty-three years after Babe Ruth hit that screaming line drive to the left-field fence in Hull's Parc Dupuis, Duncan MacGregor was once again headed off to see the Big Bambino. We had been driving in silence for some time, the windows opened to let in the sweet smell of pine, the Old Man dozing in the warm, late spring sun. I tried to imagine all that had changed in those sixty-three years. The stock market had crashed. The Great Depression. The Second World War. The atom had been split. Babe had died. Jets had taken off. Man had circled the earth, reached the moon. Communism had collapsed. Colour movies, television, computers that fit in your breast pocket, cellular phones, microwave ovens, fast food . . .

We were coming up on Old Forge, and I was hungry. I could see the Golden Arches rising on the right and put on the ticker. He roused in his seat as we bounced over the first speed bump of the parking lot.

"We'll get some lunch," I said.

"This a McDonald's?" he asked, reading the huge sign.

"Yes."

"What do they have?"

I stared at him with some incredulity. He wasn't joking.

"Think I can get a drink?" he asked.

"They have Coke. Or coffee."

"Tch-tch-tch-tch-tch-tch-tch."

I could take the hint. We passed over the rest of the speed bumps and skirted by the take-out line. Back out onto Highway 28 and, a few blocks away, a diner out of the fifties presented itself. Sliced lemon meringue pie under glass. Metal containers for the milk-shakes. Burgers and bacon sizzling on the grill. A place he could handle.

"What can I start you fellows with?" the middle-aged waitress asked, pencil poised over her pad.

"Rum and Coke—a double, if you don't mind, dear. And one ice cube—just one, though."

"Right away, darlin'," she promised with a wink, as if there were some conspiracy between the two of them. And perhaps there was. A half-hour later I had finished my egg-salad sandwich and milk and he was sitting in front of his third rum and Coke, a new one magically appearing the moment an empty glass, one ice cube, landed on the Arborite.

"Aren't you going to eat?" I asked.

"Get me a chocolate bar."

There was no point in arguing diet. He was eighty-three years old. His favourite meal was overcooked beans and gristly bacon. His breakfast of choice was kippers, fried and fuming. Toast had to be burnt. Fifty shakes of pepper over each egg. Thirty shakes of salt over everything. Whisky straight from the bottle when you had it. Rum stained with Coke, one ice cube. Cold lozenges, Scotch butter candies, sponge toffee, chocolate bars, Tums. Cigarettes all day long for more than seven decades, roll-your-own whenever possible, with the strongest tobacco; pinch off the filter and toss it away if only filtered smokes were available. Eighty-three years old and he didn't need glasses for distance, didn't take a single pill. And counted himself forty-nine years old first thing each morning.

"Where are we?" he wanted to know.

"Old Forge."

"Not Valley Forge."

"No," I said, not sure of either what he was getting at or my history. "Old Forge," I vaguely knew, had the ring of American patriotism to it. Perhaps Valley Forge was the next small town down.

"Valley Forge is near Philadelphia," he said.

"Well, we're not," I said. This much I knew for sure.

"It's where Washington wintered his troops. The British held Philadelphia. Washington almost lost the war there, you know. His men froze to death. Horses starved. Two thousand of his men deserted. How he kept the rest of them from mutiny is hard to imagine."

Not as hard to imagine, I felt like saying, as how on earth you would know such things. How strange that he could have such an uncanny grip on history and geography, and yet have no real sense of where exactly those places were that he knew so much about. As far as real travel went, he had been stuck on his own equivalent of what Faulkner had liked to call his "little postage stamp of native soil." Faulkner had travelled everywhere, however, and had spent his imagination on the little stamp of Yoknapatawpha County. Dunc, who went nowhere, had to send his imagination travelling for him, and the mind has a faulty odometer. Having never travelled in the United States by car, how could he know that we were just now easing out of the Adirondacks, hard hours from Pennsylvania, 213 years from the Continental Army and Washington and von Steuben and the howling winter winds of the Shuylkill basin? I would have to look it up—as I just have—and yet, in those forty-seven years in which I listened to him go on about everything from Julius Caesar's campaigns to Abbot and Costello's routines, I have not a single memory of him ever looking up a single fact. Perhaps he didn't keep his books because he didn't need to.

At Alder Creek we joined the freeway heading south to Utica, caught Interstate 90 heading east, and then took 28 again as it headed south towards Cooperstown. He was wide awake now, fascinated with the trees along the Mohawk River valley, interested even in the radio news that kept bringing us traffic reports from New York City. Here was a link that neither time nor technology had changed, for Jim and I had first visited the world beyond Algonquin Park with our father through the various car radios he had owned during the fifties—at least in those years when we had a car.

On hot summer nights in the park, he would gather us up, light a lantern, and the three of us would head off through a long dark path to where his car—a '54 Chevrolet, then a '56 Pontiac, then a '58 Chevrolet—would be parked in a cutoff at the edge of Highway 60, which twists through the central corridor of the park. And here, when the clouds were kind, he would turn the key halfway and walk the radio dial through the static and the fading signals until he could locate the sounds of a distant ball game, the magical voices of Mel Allen or Red Barber or Vin Scully describing the field and the positions so perfectly it felt as if we were not only there, but also playing. We would sit, the windows often rolled up against the mosquitoes and the plastic seats sticking to our backs, and after he and Jim had debated, once again, who was the greatest player of the day, Mantle or Mays, he would take the lantern and head off to the tiny creek that ran along the road and return a few minutes later with two or three cold green bottles, the slightly skunky smell of beer cutting through the citronella as he cracked the caps off with his pocket knife. It was some time before I realized beer didn't grow wild in creeks.

A generation later we were on the outskirts of a town dedicated to such memories, the green shimmer of Otsego Lake periodically peeking through the pines and cedar to our left. The cottages were becoming more opulent. Grand homes were beginning to appear. There was a historical plaque in the distance, and beyond it the rolling green lawn of what appeared to be a very old, very wealthy, estate.

"What's that place?" he wanted to know.

I squinted to read. "Cooper House—it's the home of James Fenimore Cooper. You know, the guy who wrote *The Last of the Mohicans*."

"*The Deerslayer*," he added. "*The Pathfinder. The Pioneers. The Pilot. The Red Rover.* I read them all, you know."

I had read *The Deerslayer*, but I now imagine that it, like *The Last of the Mohicans,* was the Classics Comic Book version. Too many times in my life I had claimed full knowledge of classics, only to flush with the realization that my memory was of cartoon characters with dialogue bubbles over their heads. We were a comic-book family, and though he could never have been called a disciplinarian, from time to time he insisted that the fistfuls of comics we came to him with on our monthly trips to the Whitney store include one or two of the classics. To this day I am grateful that he turned me into someone who at least knows to nod when vaguely familiar characters and titles are mentioned.

"Do you want to stop?" I asked.

"All right."

We pulled into the empty parking lot, paid our admission and walked about the sumptuous home, which seemed far more art museum than writer's study. We learned that Cooperstown was named not after James Fenimore, as I had too quickly presumed, but after his father, William, a wheelwright turned shopkeeper who became a judge around the same time that George Washington was freezing his wig off at Valley Forge. It was here, however, where James had set his *Leatherstocking Tales*—the five books that included *The Deerslayer*—and it was the Otsego that had served as the lake he called Glimmerglass, which seemed a superior name for the long lake on this sunny, calm day.

There were samples of Cooper's writing at various stops, and a small shop in which all of his books were available. I scanned a few pages of several of the books. His style seemed weak and overwrought, but this was from the perspective of the jaded adult, not the impressionable child, and it was clear that Cooper had had a profound impact on a young Duncan MacGregor. Back in First World War Eganville, Annie had made sure that all of the *Leatherstocking Tales* were on her bookshelves, and young Duncan had become entranced with the descriptions of clean flowing waters and deep bush and good, strong, honest men like Uncas and Natty Bumppo. Young James Fenimore and young Duncan were even kindred spirits of a type, Cooper's family set on a grand education for him but the young James so rebellious and determined to wander the woods that he was kicked out of Yale.

I picked up *The Last of the Mohicans*, the unfamiliar words of the opening chapter merely confirming that my entire literary knowledge of Hawkeye's exploits came from a fifteen-cent comic book picked up in Whitney thirty-five years earlier:

A wide and apparently an impervious boundary of forests severed the possessions of the hostile provinces of France and England. The hardy colonist, and the trained European who fought at his side, frequently expended months in struggling against the rapids of the streams, or in effecting the rugged passes of the mountains, in quest of an opportunity to exhibit their courage in a more martial conflict. But, emulating the patience and self-denial of the practiced native warriors, they learned to overcome every difficulty; and it would seem that, in time, there was no recess of the woods so dark, nor any secret place so lovely, that it might claim exemption from the inroads of those who had pledged their blood to satiate their vengeance, or to uphold the cold and selfish policy of the distant monarchs of Europe. . . .

I doubted I could read much more, and I snickered to myself, arrogantly and unfairly. It would hardly be the first book retried— if a Classics comic and real text can be considered equal—and found wanting. I once doubled up in laughter rereading *The Greening of America,* a late sixties book I once carried around like a Bible and bookmarked with my own version of tobacco droppings. What would I think today of *Siddhartha?* Even *On the Road,* which Kerry, our oldest daughter, Dunc's granddaughter, now carried around in her backpack with reverence? Mark Twain once ridiculed Cooper better than I would dare, with my deep comic-book research. Twain claimed in a mean-spirited article that in less than a full page of *The Deerslayer,* "Cooper has scored 114 offenses against literary art out of a possible 115. It breaks the record." It would break Duncan's heart for me to show such cruelty to a book that obviously, at one time, meant so much to him. Cooper was merely a romantic, the American prose equivalent of the European poets of the time, and if Duncan MacGregor's young imagination was once swept away by such words, who am I—a man who can quote no one without looking it up, who relies on comic-book memories—to make jest of it? Would that we all had such lack of pretension about us, a reader who simply put value in books and would never lord a Twain over a Cooper, or, for that matter, Plutarch over Mickey Spillane. Never had anyone seen Duncan MacGregor cart a book around so that others might note what he was reading. The same, alas, cannot be said for those of us who followed.

From Cooper House we soon found our way into the town proper, and dropped down onto Main Street through a collection of old-money summer homes that left us both gasping. If there is a difference between Canadian wealth and American wealth, it is measured in square feet. We passed by one hotel that did not even bear checking, and moved along and down side streets towards the water's edge until we came upon the Lake Shore Motel, green, gaudy and sixty-five dollars a night.

"This'll do," I said.

"Can we get a room?" he asked.

I pointed to the sign: vacancy.

"Should be able to. I'll go in and check."

"I'll wait," he said.

He seemed uneasy, unsure of where he was and what he was doing. There was no one in the office and I had to wait, twice tapping the little bell that sat over the hand-printed Ring for Service sign. There was time to think, and I realized why he might have been so concerned. I had to presume he didn't sleep in the streets of Dallas when he went down to Texas over that hardwood shipment, but the rooms were likely taken care of by the national adjudicator who accompanied him.

The Lake Shore had plenty of rooms, and offered one with twin beds overlooking the lake. We couldn't have been happier. A quick meal at the little restaurant just up the street, and we still had the evening ahead of us.

"The Hall's open pretty late," I suggested. "Why don't we go now?"

We walked over to the Main Street in a light June breeze off the lake that rubbed warm as a cat against us, the Old Man hobbling and bobbing along with his cane, me always moving slightly ahead and turning slightly to wait, the way some people will walk an old dog. We passed by souvenir shops, windows filled with memorabilia, and restaurants serving up things like the Mickey Mantle Platter. There was red, white and blue bunting up everywhere.

"I met Mickey Mantle's sister once," he puffed. "Time I went to Dallas. She had a car dealership down there, you know. I went down about some lost wood. Flew down, too. Both ways. And it never cost me a goddamn cent."

My eyes were everywhere. People walking in the fine air. Expensive cars drifting up and down Main Street. More baseball junk in the store windows than it was possible to imagine. His eyes, however, were where they usually were: checking out wood.

"What's this?" he said, stopping and sharply rapping his cane against a skinny tree that seemed to grow right out of the sidewalk. He seemed bewildered. "I didn't notice any maples coming in here."

I checked. It was indeed a maple tree, but one with a plaque to the side of it. I read it aloud: "The Government of Canada, in conjunction with the Canadian Baseball Hall of Fame and Museum, is pleased to present this Canadian maple tree to our American baseball friends to commemorate the 50th anniversary of the National Baseball Hall of Fame. Presented by the Prime Minister of Canada, the Right Honourable Brian Mulroney, Toronto, Canada, May 1, 1989."

"Tch-tch-tch-tch-tch-tch-tch."

"What's that for? You think it's a waste of taxpayer's money?"

"No," he said. "But it should have been a white ash. It's baseball, after all."

We paid our money and entered the Baseball Hall of Fame. I felt like a father taking his child for the first time to the fall fair midway. Ty Cobb—or at least a mannequin of Cobb—was there to greet us at the doorway. A huge, charming Babe mannequin was just to the left.

"I knew them all," the Old Man kept saying. "I knew them all."

He had a million names and games in his head. Wee Willie Keeler and Home Run Baker and Walter Johnson and Rogers Hornsby and Honus Wagner and Hack Wilson and George Sisler and Casey Stengel. He could remember meeting the trains that came through the park in the summer of 1941 and asking if they had a newspaper he could have or if anyone had word about DiMaggio. Was the hitting streak still intact? He had his favourites from every era, Christy Mathewson to Mantle, and a special soft spot, as everyone should have, for Nellie Fox, the little White Sox scrapper who defied striking out.

"I knew them all," the Old Man kept muttering, as if they were the living and he the one being passed by.

He stopped for the longest time in front of Ty Cobb. "Jesus but he was a villain. Spike you as soon as look at you." I imagined the Cobb mannequin smiling slightly as Dunc said this. After all, as Cobb once said in a letter to a close friend, "My real weak spot is unjust criticism."

The Old Man himself had a bit of criticism for the hall's interpretation of where exactly the Grand Old Game had begun. A committee was set up in 1905 by Albert G. Spalding, of the sporting goods company, and chaired by Spalding's good friend Col. Abraham Mills. The Mills committee soon concluded that Abner Doubleday had "invented" the game right there in Cooperstown back in 1839. In 1916 the documentation that had been assembled in Cooperstown to "prove" this historical fact was lost in a fire. Doubleday's diaries survive, however, and it has been duly noted by scholars that nowhere in them does he mention anything remotely called baseball. The game, some scholars suggest, invented Abner Doubleday, not the other way around.

"Some people say a Canadian invented the game," the Old Man said. I expressed both surprise and doubt, but he knew about a claim, long ago made in *Sporting Life* magazine but conveniently ignored, that a game with a pitcher and batter and bases twenty-one yards apart had been played in southern Ontario back in 1838, a year before the much-disputed Doubleday claim. It was played, apparently, to celebrate the anniversary of the putting-down of the rebellions in Upper and Lower Canada a year earlier. How he knew this I have no idea, but a few years later he was tapping conclusively on an article that had just appeared in the fall issue of *The Beaver* and made the same points, in finer detail.

For two hours we toured the building. The Bambino's glove, Mantle's bat, Cobb's spikes, a photograph of Paul and Dizzy Dean the year they combined for fifty-one wins for the St. Louis Cardinals ("It ain't braggin' if you done it"), even a video of Abbot and Costello's magnificent "Who's On First?" that seemed to delight him as much as seeing the special exhibition on the great Leroy "Satchel" Paige.

"Nobody ever knew how old he was, you know," the Old Man said, staring into Paige's strangely sad but challenging eyes. "They once asked him what he'd say if he had to appear in court and take an oath on it, and you know what Satchel told them?"

"What?"

" 'I'd tell the judge the goat ate it,' " the Old Man chuckled.
" 'The goat ate the family Bible, and my birth certificate was inside
the Bible.' "

We stared a long time at the Paige exhibit. His mother had been
a slave. He hadn't even pitched in the majors until he was well into
his forties. He had to be almost sixty the day he pitched three run-
less innings for the Kansas City Athletics in 1965. Dizzy Dean, who
once lost an exhibition game to Paige, called him "the best pitcher
I ever seen."

"I used to be ashamed of my age," the Old Man said as we
walked along to the special section reserved for the Negro Leagues.
"Now I'm kind of getting proud of it."

No longer forty-nine, except for that first surprised blink of
early morning, he had been boasting ever since he passed eighty.
Eighty-year-olds are not supposed to be drinking double rum and
Cokes. They shouldn't be smoking. And they certainly shouldn't
be frying everything they eat (even old Satchel claimed that Rule
No. 1 for a happy life was "Avoid fried meats that angry up the
blood"). At eighty-three, Dunc was still two years from being
banned for life from the Huntsville Legion for disorderly behaviour. Too much fried meat, perhaps.

But it was not that age made him suddenly forward. He had
always been this way. His ability to walk up to anyone who happened to pass by and strike up a conversation had long astonished,
and at times alarmed, those of us who knew him best. He
enchanted tourists. He enthralled children. He intrigued lumber
buyers who came to the park and could never comprehend how a
man who seemed to know more about the world than they, who
was a marvellous bridge player with no one to play, who seemed
to know everything possible about Major League Baseball yet had
never seen a game, could exist in a place so isolated that even radio
reception was impossible. Perhaps he knew his own powers of

enchantment, for if a question formed in his mind, he rarely kept it from his mouth.

A large, middle-aged black man was the only other person in the room dedicated to the Negro Leagues. The man seemed almost in a trance as he moved from exhibit to exhibit—John Henry Lloyd, who could play shortstop as well as Honus Wagner; Josh Gibson, who could hit home runs as long as Ruth—the man's privacy almost a visible shield around him. It meant nothing, of course, to the Old Man, who hobbled directly over and stared at the same faded grey jersey at which the big man had stopped.

The Old Man looked at the big black man until the larger man looked up, wondering who was staring and why.

"It's a damn shame about Satchel Paige," the Old Man said. "Him not being allowed to play just because of colour."

I cringed. Colour? What would he say next? I slipped through the opening into the next room, not wishing to witness his humiliation. In a way, I knew he was innocent, naive, but no one in Cooperstown, New York, would understand how or why. Algonquin Park would mean nothing down here.

We children could still recall that day in the fifties when word came down from the rangers up at the Lake of Two Rivers campgrounds that "a family of Negroes" had set up tent in the back edge, along the south branch of the Madawaska. We had all been hurried out the path to the old ranger's car, where we joined a literal flotilla of other park workers who'd come to stare at that poor, patient family sitting around the campfire. None of the children had ever seen a black before. I doubt many, if any, of the adults had either. It was, for Algonquin Park of 1955, a sighting as rare and unusual and noteworthy as if a herd of caribou had showed up at the West Gate.

Time, however, has a strange way of bringing matters full circle. When Jim married in the late sixties, he kept both the upcoming wedding and the prospective bride a secret until the very last moment. He had met a nurse, Stephanie, and she was Jamaican. The wedding was for the coming Saturday afternoon, and everyone who could make it was invited down to Toronto for the church ceremony. Tom and I and our mother drove up from Huntsville into the park to let the Old Man know and see if he wanted to come to the city, which he did, much to her surprise. No doubt she was much worried about how he would react to the news. We were late arriving at the church, the traffic coming south worse than expected, and when we got there all of Stephanie's relatives and friends were already gathered on the bride's side; the groom's side was empty.

"Bride or groom?" a sidesman asked as we entered the doors, eyes blinking to accustom ourselves to the dim light and candles.

"It's pretty obvious where I'll be sitting, isn't it?" barked the Old Man, the entire church turning as he hiked up his old suit pants and started heading down the aisle.

But by day's end, as we should have known, he was the hit of the post-wedding party, our departure delayed while Stephanie and her friends hugged and kissed this funny old guy who had come down from the bush to tease them and kid them and, at one point, show a loud room of lively Jamaicans a touch of Ottawa Valley step-dancing.

I waited a while, then, when he didn't show, went back into the room holding the exhibition from the Negro Leagues. There he was, practically arm in arm with the large black man as they moved from display to display, both tossing new information at each other. The Old Man introduced us. "This is Errol," he said. "Once played semi-pro himself."

We shook hands, Errol grinning from ear to ear. "Your father sure knows his baseball," he said.

I nodded as if I'd known they'd be kindred spirits from the moment we had walked into the room.

Errol and Dunc separated and went their separate ways—but not before hearty handshakes that made it seem as if they'd soon be meeting up again—and off we went to the souvenir stand.

He was clearly tired, but I thought he should have something to commemorate his visit to the Baseball Hall of Fame. He had no interest in the caps or shirts or coffee mugs or any of the other overwrought souvenirs. I thought maybe a book, and carried over to him a lavishly illustrated copy of Ernest Lawrence Thayer's "Casey at the Bat." How many times had Jim and I sat out in the old Pontiac under the summer sky and listened to him quote snippets from this classic? "Ten thousand eyes were on him," he would say suddenly, as the broadcast out of New York broke up, "as he rubbed his hands with dirt; / Five thousand tongues applauded when he wiped them on his shirt. / Then while the writhing pitcher ground the ball into his hip, / Defiance gleamed in Casey's eye, a sneer curled Casey's lip. . . ."

And he would, of course, always say it with a nasty, exaggerated sneer. Much larger, in fact, than the small sneer that greeted my suggestion that I buy this fine copy of "Casey" for him.

"What do I need a book for?" he asked, tapping his temple. "I have it all right here."

It seemed to me a vain claim to make, and I put the book back on the shelf reluctantly. The cashier was doing up her cash. The security guard was waiting at the door. Dunc thanked them both, much to their surprise, and we headed out for the hotel.

The sun had gone down, but the air was still warm and easy off the lake. The streetlights were on, giving Main Street an illustrated look, but we seemed the only two there to appreciate it.

There was the sharp rap of a cane on concrete behind me. I turned. The Old Man had his cap off, held in the fold of his arm. He was going to prove that he did indeed have all of "Casey at the Bat" in his eighty-three-year-old head.

He stood there in front of the Baseball Hall of Fame, cap in hand, cane to his side, and he recited all of "Casey" without missing a beat, without missing an appropriate facial expression, his voice at times so light and singsongy I could barely hear, his voice at times so loud I wondered if the security guards would soon be out to check.

The outlook wasn't brilliant for the Mudville nine that day;
The score stood four to two, with but one inning more to play,
And then when Cooney died at first, and Barrows did the same,
A sickly silence fell upon the patrons of the game. . . .

I looked around, uneasy, and then realized that there wasn't a person on earth, baseball fan or not, who could come along and see this aging old man with the cane and not be taken in by the concert of words he was delivering. A chill of pride ran up my back.

Then from five thousand throats and more there rose a lusty yell;
It rumbled through the valley, it rattled in the dell;
It knocked upon the mountain and recoiled upon the flat,
For Casey, mighty Casey, was advancing to the bat. . . .

I stood, and waited. A car passed, but no one else seemed to notice. He had his eyes shut, his voice growing ever more thin and dramatic as he neared the end.

Oh, somewhere in this favored land the sun is shining bright;
The band is playing somewhere, and somewhere hearts are light,
And somewhere men are laughing, and somewhere children shout;
But there is no joy in Mudville—great Casey has struck out.

"Beautiful," I said.

"I knew them all," he said.

We walked back through the night air towards the little motel. He was tired, his hip and bad leg slowing us down. I walked slower this time, more patient. He was again the parent, I the child.

We sat up talking a while. He talked of life in the park and of fights in the mill yard and of the people he had known who were now gone. "All my friends are dead now," he said. "I'm the last one left." He didn't appear to be feeling sorry for himself. Just stating the facts.

He wanted to go to bed. He pulled back the cover and settled in over the blanket and sheets. I didn't bother correcting him. He was soon asleep and so, soon enough, was I.

Sometime late in the night I was awakened by a sense that something was wrong in the room. It would be some before I knew what Cheyne-Stokes breathing was, but having heard two dying family members go through it now, I realize that this is what had awakened me: the Old Man breathing so deep it seemed he was under the floorboards; lips, nose and lungs rattling like some ungreased mine-shaft hoist, then suddenly stopping dead, the air utterly silent for what seemed minutes.

That the Old Man snored was part of family lore. It was almost impossible to sleep through a night at Lake of Two Rivers without the thin cabin walls shaking until we could hear our mother's elbow slap against his shoulder, his grunts of surprise and her sharp "Dunc—you're snoring again! Turn over!" But this sound was not the snoring we all remembered. This sound was different, and frightening.

He rattled and sucked and rattled and expelled, and then, after I'd been lying there some time listening, he went completely quiet. A minute passed, then another, then it seemed five minutes had passed. The silence was almost overwhelming. I lay there thinking about what we had talked about, long life and death, and wondered if perhaps it had all been coincidental, if in a fluke that we would all one day say was poetic justice, the Old Man had died after reaching the Baseball Hall of Fame.

I sat up, moving to the edge of the bed, and waited some more. Nothing. The silence of the dead. I had never been with anyone who died before, but there was nothing frightening about it. My mind was consumed with the practical: what would happen? would there be any difficulty getting his body home? should I be doing something now?

The possibility that something had gone badly wrong and I had failed to react caused panic to set in. I got up and went to his bed, leaning over to see if he was breathing, but could hear nothing whatsoever from those nicotine-cast lungs. I touched his shoulder, but he did not move. He felt soft and warm, and I wondered if this was how he should feel if he was dead.

I went into the bathroom and washed my face. There was a small mirror there, the kind women use for makeup and men for bald spots, and I picked it up and carried it out into the bedroom with me. I leaned over him, placing the mirror directly below his hairy nostrils, but there was no light to see anything. I switched on the bedside lamp and tested again.

This I had done before—once. Our first-born had stopped breathing in her crib, or at least so I believed, and I had raced for a mirror to see if anything was coming out. The mirror fogged instantly, and I hurried to hide it so no one would know what a worrywart I was as a father. But that was an infant and this was an eighty-three-year-old man. I placed the mirror in as tightly as I could, waited a moment, yanked it away and checked it against the light.

There, on the bottom edge of the little mirror, was a slight trace of condensation: he was alive. He snorted sharply, and the snoring began again.

Feeling the fool, I could not sleep. The window was washing pink with the first light of day, and I dressed and went out and walked to the end of the docks, where I sat on a bench next to an ancient mahogany boat and stared out over the still, dawn waters of Cooper's Glimmerglass.

Knowing he was safe, I thought about him dead, and understood how terribly he would be missed. He had, obviously, never been the easiest person in the world to live with, but he would be harder to live without. No one to set you in your place with a sharp, gentle crack. No one to bring the past alive when you least expected. No one to ask when you needed to know things like Casey Stengel's managerial record versus his playing record, or who was behind the assassination of Czar Nicholas II, or, for that matter, why there are no walnut trees in Algonquin Park. Sometimes you want to know such things.

The sun rose high enough to begin baking the small bench I was sitting on. I stayed a while longer and then thought to go back and check on him one more time.

The bed was empty when I reached the room. The cover crumpled back, but the blanket and crisp sheets still untouched except for the crush of his weight. I wondered if the maid making up the room would notice. I also wondered where the hell he was. I the parent, he the child.

It is odd how little patience we have for our own parents when they have shown so much for us, but my first instinct was that he should have told me where he was going. I'd say *asked* if he could go, but I had not yet reached the level of offspring tyranny that is so often evident when we find middle-aged children with elderly parents. To call the Old Man anything less than his own person was to suggest you were something more than his own issue.

He wasn't on the street. He wasn't at the little motel office. He wasn't by the water. He was, however, sitting happily on a bar stool in the tiny restaurant just up the street, talking with the owner about the significance of Canadian baseball. It was just going on 7:30 a.m.

"Your father?" the waitress on duty asked as I stood just inside the front door, waiting.

"Yes."

"He always order a double rum and Coke for breakfast?"

"Whenever he can," I said. "Whenever he can."

CHAPTER TWO

J.S.L. McRae's first mill, at Galeairy Lake on the edge of Algonquin Park, circa 1920.

THE OLD MAN DID BUY himself a book that final morning in Cooperstown. After his breakfast of rum and Coke, he hobbled back up the street to the Baseball Hall of Fame gift shop, looked around for something appropriate and finally settled on *The Twenty-Four-Inch Home Run and Other Outlandish, Incredible But True Events in Baseball History.* It was exactly the sort of reading he enjoyed most. There was historical antecedent—a story about a Union regiment and a Confederate regiment playing "catch" during the Siege of Vicksburg. There was the incredible—the day in 1909 when the outfielder James Phelps made a dramatic leap to steal a sure home run and landed, ball triumphantly in hand, on a water moccasin that promptly bit and killed him. And there were, of course, the great, lasting lines—like the spring Yogi Berra was asked his cap size and snapped, "How do I know? I'm not in shape yet." For Dunc, the book was proof that sport does indeed have meaning, if only to prove life itself well beyond comprehension.

The Twenty-Four-Inch Home Run was one of the very rare books he kept. He wrote his name on the inside cover in his elongated, exaggerated penmanship—"Duncan MacGregor"—then thought to add: "Purchased at the Hall of Fame home in Cooperstown, New York State, U.S.A. Contains a few funny incidents that happened in my uneventful life."

Somehow, this book tapped into his desire, now well into his eighties, to record some of the anecdotes from his past. Whatever it was that so moved him, he read *The Twenty-Four-Inch Home Run* voraciously—this was obvious from the dog-eared reading marks and the squashed Player's tobacco flakes that spilled out as the pages turned—and from time to time he scribbled his own stories in the margins, sometimes running on for several pages.

"The first time I came up to Whitney was in 1929, August 30th," he began writing on page 102, opposite a story about ballplayers who had been given feminine nicknames like Lady and Little Eva and Daisie, Peaches and Baby Doll. "There was a picnic at Madawaska that day and Whitney was playing ball and of course they wanted to know if I played ball. Loving the game, I was quite happy to play for Whitney. The ball park faced the Catholic church, which was out in centre field. Anyway, the first time at bat I came up and I hit a line drive to centre field. The church door was open and the ball hit in front of the church and bounced right into the church. Result—home run, of course. The opposition teams complained and railed and ranted that it should have been a double. Anyway, the umpire ruled it a home run.

"I must say that the umpire was James Costello, a friend of mine. James was a great friend of John Barleycorn as well, and he was in great shape to decide on this incident. He used to take a two-ounce drink every inning and by the end of the game the ball was just a blur to James. Anyway, Whitney won and everybody was happy."

So, too, was Duncan MacGregor, who had turned twenty-two a couple of days earlier. He had just hit a home run for the winning side, which made him instantly known and popular in the little bush village. He was headed off to his first real job, working for J.S.L. McRae, and he had reached the very end of the historic Opeongo Line. After Whitney, there was nothing. When the poet and constitutional expert F.R. Scott looked down from that floatplane and decided to describe his country as a "huge nowhere, / Underlined by a shy railway," he could just as easily have been flying over Algonquin Park in 1929 as the Mackenzie River in 1956. Algonquin National Park was considered, at that time, the most significant wilderness park in all of Canada. More than twice as large as the province of Prince Edward Island and roughly the size of the state of Connecticut, the new park was, at its creation in 1893, the largest tract of dedicated bush in the world. When he got there, he was home for the rest of his life.

It is important to point out that it was *work* that took him there, not vacation, not adventure, not design, not romance. This is a significant distinction, in that there is a Canadian forest experience profoundly apart from the American one, the Canadian bush—as opposed to the American frontier, woods or even wilderness—opening to men and women who came almost exclusively because they had no other choice, and who were almost invariably so busy with survival that they had little or no time to intellectualize the experience. For the next fifty-one years, right up until that moment the chip truck slid backwards on the ice and took him with it, Dunc MacGregor would never have a vacation, so there would never be opportunity for comparison, for book-writing, for lecturing—for that matter, and much to his later regret, for much reflection on what it was he was doing. Dunc was going to work;

he was no John Muir, the Scottish-born American naturalist who set out to "plash into wilderness" and experience all that he could around the small farm he had moved to near Madison, Wisconsin. Unlike the philosophers with their books, the lecturers with their slide shows, even the well-off eccentrics with their family backing, the vast majority of those who headed off into the Canadian tangle did so without ulterior motive, without any future prospect other than a possible livelihood to be had from the bush alone.

"I went to the woods because I wished to live deliberately," Henry David Thoreau had written in the previous century, describing his experiences at Walden Pond, just outside Concord, Massachusetts. "To front only the essential facts of life, and see if I could not learn what it had to teach, and not, when I came to die, discover that I had not lived.

"I wanted to live deep and suck out all the marrow of life, to live so sturdily and Spartan-like as to put to rout all that was not life, to cut a broad swath and shave close, to drive life into a corner, and reduce it to its lowest terms, and, if it proved to be mean, why then to get the whole and meaningful meanness of it, and publish its meanness to the world; or if it were sublime, to know it by experience and be able to give a true account of it in my next excursion."

There is much good to be said about what Thoreau left behind: his observations, his pithy philosophies. But he spoke more to those who were not in the bush than to those who were. Men who had worked most of their lives in crowded, stinking bush shanties, who were barely able to keep their families, who froze all winter and fought blackflies and mosquitoes all summer, who had lost children and wives because of a total lack of, or inadequate, medical care—they might find just a bit much Thoreau's claim that "Most of the luxuries and many of the so-called comforts of life are not only not indispensable, but positive hindrances to the elevation of mankind." Fine, perhaps, for one who could walk to town and back each day, as Thoreau could, and who constantly had visitors dropping in with food and other gifts. In the chill of the Canadian bush, on the sharp edge of survival, philosophy could not be eaten, did not throw heat, keep out the rain and snow and wind, or clear the land, fell the trees or paddle the canoe upstream.

Concord was a fairly civilized town in 1845, when Thoreau built his little cabin out on Walden Pond. Town was but a short walk away, and if his well-off family wasn't quite in sight, it certainly kept an eye on him. He seemed, by his own writings, to be terrified of the sort of endless tangle that confronted those who arrived in the Whitney area nearly eight decades later. Walden, after all, was a "tamed" woodlot, and Thoreau was happiest rambling through cleared forests and found the greatest beauty in landscape that included gently rolling farmland. His preference for the cultivated countryside was apparent in notes he made from a brief sojourn in the Maine woods, which would have been much more accessible to hikers than the tangle of Algonquin Park. "It was a relief," he wrote once happily back in Concord, "to get back to our smooth, but still varied landscape. For a permanent residence, it seemed to me that there could be no comparison between this and the wilderness. The wilderness is simple, almost to barrenness. The partially cultivated country it is which has inspired, and will continue to inspire, the strains of poets."

Thoreau knew nothing of the poetry to be found in fast water; vicious, relentless winter; impenetrable growth; and the wear of isolation. For his most famous act—demanding to spend the night in jail because he refused to pay his poll tax—he would have found no sympathetic ear in the first lumber camps to open around the park, where no one ever paid tax, and could not have even if they wished to, because they were never given money for their work. As for respect for the law, his essay "On the Duty of Civil Disobedience" would have bored loggers with its lack of concrete action. As local legend has it, when the provincial police tried to send their first representative into Whitney, the man was found the next morning tied to a tree at the edge of the village.

Whitney's history does not follow the normal paths of Canadian settlement. Tourists today find it charming, a tiny and quiet village on the edge of Algonquin Park and approached, from the east, over high rolling hardwood hills. Spectacular in autumn, when the maple and sumac and birch make a dreamcoat of the landscape, Whitney is a comfort in spring and summer, when campers and canoeists have one last chance to pick up supplies and equipment and bug spray on the way into the park, and their first chance for gas and soft ice cream. After Bite itch lotion and Noxema cream for sunburn on their way out. In winter, however, it is a surprise, smoke rising from houses that haven't been seen for mile after barren mile in both directions, a spot of warm relief that seems, on first glance, to have been dropped accidentally into the great frozen bush.

Yet Whitney was no accident. The march into the Upper Ottawa Valley and its northwesterly offshoot, the Madawaska Valley, began in response to Napoleon's blockade of Britain, which started in 1806 and very soon cut off all European timber shipments to British ports. When Britain turned to the colonies for timber supplies, Canada was the obvious choice, the Ottawa Valley the natural beginning. Here was where the tall, easily felled and squared white pine grew. Here were the rivers that could deliver the timber to the mills, and from the mills to the ports of Montreal and Quebec City. The valley had tall and straight timber for masts and spars, and once the white pine was all but gone, there was still the hardwood and other pine and pulp. A seemingly endless supply, stretching on forever.

Once the shantymen headed into the bush, it wasn't long before the entrepreneurs and politicians began trying to see what lay beyond the next swamp or ridge. The brief 1812–14 spat with the Americans was still a fresh memory when talk first began of a mammoth canal that would bring grain shipments from Georgian Bay across the Ontario heartland to Ottawa, thereby avoiding the prospects of skirmishes along the two most vulnerable of the Great Lakes, Erie and Ontario. The idea was preposterous. If the Rideau Canal, completed between Kingston and Ottawa in 1832, had taken six years and cost, by some accounts, the lives of scores of men, mostly to typhoid, how much would it take to build a canal that spanned from Ottawa to Georgian Bay, with high hills and solid granite cutting off the connecting waterways?

In 1837 the most famous explorer in all of Canada set out on an expedition that is, mysteriously, rarely, if ever mentioned in accounts of the life and travels of David Thompson, the man *National Geographic* called the world's greatest land geographer. Thompson had already mapped a fifth of the North American continent when he took on this commission to paddle into the tangle of what was then known as Upper Canada. It was a job he desperately needed in order to keep his wife, Charlotte, and the younger of their thirteen children fed, as well as to pay off some of the huge debts his deadbeat sons had built up with their failed farms and blacksmith shops.

Thompson's orders were to find a canal route between Bytown and Lake Huron that would cut right cross the Precambrian Shield. It made little sense to anyone familiar with the harsh terrain of the Algonquin highlands, and Thompson, surely, would never have taken on the task if it could have been avoided. The little Welshman's place in North American history was solid. He had, after all, found the passage through the Rocky Mountains. He was then sixty-seven years old and in failing health. He had retired to Williamstown in Glengarry County and had written his autobiography, but had failed to interest a publisher. The British government had turned him down on his request for a pension, and he had been reduced to borrowing from friends, pawning his clothes and selling off his surveying instruments just to make ends meet.

The search for a canal was a job and he needed work, but the world's greatest land geographer was, in fact, a poor choice for the task at hand. He could then see only well enough to note the obvious, that the Algonquin route was all but impassable for such a grandiose enterprise, but he thought, through his blurred vision, that the land surrounding the rivers and lakes he and his men passed through would make fine farming country once the trees were cleared. He did not know that pine turns soil acidic, and that what little earth there is in the park is but a thin skin over ever more rock. Perhaps his last great exploration is usually expunged from the official record because it was so, well, embarrassing to his reputation.

Thompson's blind passage had fascinated the Old Man. He kept in his dresser a book on the explorer, *The Map-Maker: The Story of David Thompson*. In it, there is an account of how young Thompson, at age seventeen in 1786, had left on a cross-country trek with the Hudson's Bay Company and had broken his leg. While convalescing, he had learned to use a sextant, and since he had no ocean with which to find his horizon, he had come up with an ingenious method that allowed him to use the sextant as effectively as if he had been sailing the South Seas, not paddling the northern rivers. He carried with him a supply of mercury, which he would pour out into a small pan, thereby creating an artificial horizon that would ably reflect the sun and the moon and stars. Blind and perhaps even demented as he was when he journeyed through the park so many years later, I have often wondered since reading this if perhaps poor David Thompson wasn't suffering from mercury poisoning.

Fortunately, there was soon a fresh idea that made any talk of a canal superfluous. Railroads were suddenly the answer to everything, and in 1856 the federal Department of Public Works hired Walter Shanley to examine the Ottawa River and lands west for the purpose of building a railway through the Precambrian Shield rather than locks and a canal. Shanley divided his men into two parties, one heading overland from Georgian Bay and the other headed into the bush from the Ottawa River.

They would meet, Shanley calculated, at Lake Opeongo, where David Thompson had found such promising opportunities for settlement. Shanley found the truth and felt compelled to deliver it back, even if it meant the end of the hopes of putting through a railway. He and his men had crossed an extraordinarily harsh land, he reported back, one that was virtually uninhabitable. The Upper Ottawa Valley, he concluded, was "not a district into which emigration can be rapidly poured by any new process of colonization with the least hope of a successful issue to so hazardous an undertaking." On the contrary, Shanley believed, any attempt to force settlement in opposition to the natural laws that govern the colonization of all new countries would here be certain "to end in failure, and in the mean time to entail incalculable suffering and misery on the earlier settlers, to whose lot it would fall to act the part of pioneers."

Shanley saw accurately how difficult it would be to penetrate the Canadian Shield, but he wasn't much more successful than poor blind David Thompson when it came to serving as a visionary. Shanley argued, further, that the notion of suitable harbours along Georgian Bay was out of the question. Besides, he said, the true trade route of the future was bound to be up and down the mighty Ottawa River. He even foresaw a time when Great Lakes ships would travel up the Ottawa, cross over through the Mattawa River into Lake Nipissing and from there head out to Lake Huron—the *grand voyage* route the Récollets had taken to their doomed missions more than two hundred years earlier. Shanley could see a time when Ottawa, the brand-new name for Bytown, would serve as the trading heart of the country. Queen Victoria had only just selected the old lumber town as the new capital of the colony—by default, admittedly, in order not to upset the established centres of Montreal, Kingston and Toronto, and also because Ottawa was a defendable distance from the United States border— but no matter, in Shanley's eyes, the future belonged to Ottawa and its timber-rich valley. He could see settlement based not on farming, the usual method, but on logging, and he saw the railway as the key for getting settlers into the tangled forest and the squared timber back out. Lake Opeongo, with its deep bays, nearby rivers and rich timber stands, would be key to this grand scheme.

Not much of Shanley's wild plan for the Ottawa River survived, obviously, but the notion of a railway across the Shield did. The American Civil War, which began in 1861, four years after Shanley tabled his report, served only to convince all the more those who believed there must be a rail alternative to lower Great Lakes shipping. J.R. Booth, the Bytown lumber baron who made a fortune supplying the timber for the construction of the new Parliament Buildings, had picked up, for a mere $45,000, John Egan's extensive timber rights at an auction held after Egan's death. (To keep the bidding low, Booth had come to the auction disguised as a poor labourer so no one would suspect that the millionaire timber baron was skulking in the room with a limitless bid.) The sense of Shanley's vision was obvious to Booth. He began building a rail line into his timber limits, heading always towards the Opeongo depot that Shanley had suggested.

Booth was ruthless in completing his line. He hired children as labourers and ignored the laws that forbade this. He found an anchorage at Depot Harbour, near Parry Sound, and ignored the protestations of the Natives who claimed the property belonged to them. He shoved the Natives out of the way and built a logging community large enough to support three churches and several businesses. Crews built east from Depot Harbour and west from Ottawa, and by 1896 the remarkable Booth line was completed. Neither David Thompson nor Walter Shanley would have believed it possible. Called the Ottawa, Arnprior & Parry Sound Railway Co., it ran 396.6 miles, Ottawa to Parry Sound; it headed west through the Algonquin Park, running slightly south of Opeongo along the route Thompson had paddled a half-century earlier. It was an astonishing engineering feat, and involved filling in the swamps and dynamiting through the granite and passing over rivers on the largest trestles ever built entirely out of timber. Prime Minister Wilfrid Laurier took the inaugural trip through the park, swaying through the muskeg and trembling over the trestles.

Booth was no fool. Born into poverty on a Quebec townships farm, he would leave an estate worth $33 million. He saw immediately the value of the line. It could draw lumber from the area around the park and carry grain from the West. There were soon six trains a day running through the Park and by 1904 the little line had been folded into the Grand Trunk Railway system. By 1910 there were 120 loads of grain a day passing through, and by 1923, as Booth had imagined would happen, Canadian National Railways made a rich bid for the little money-making line.

Whitney became a community because of the Booth line. As Northrop Frye so appropriately pointed out many years later, Canadians essentially "made a nation out of the stops on two of the world's longest railway lines." Whitney, on the banks of the Madawaska as it began running fast out of Galeairy Lake, was perfect as a water stop and timber depot. A spur line was built up to Opeongo's Sproule Bay, fourteen miles into the park, where huge booms were holding the Booth logs that had been cut and skidded out during the previous winter. Booth, however, had no interest in encouraging settlement. Settlers to the aging lumber baron meant one thing—fire—and Booth had good reason for his well-known phobia. Fire had destroyed every business he'd had from the first enterprise, a Bytown machine shop, and he'd grown so obsessive about the threat of new fire that he would hire teams of men to follow the river drivers, giving them no other duties than to drown their campfires. He once estimated that twenty times as much Ottawa Valley timber was lost to fire as to the axe, and he fought his last fire at the age of ninety-seven, still wandering about his timber limits in a state of perpetual fear of lightning, careless smokers, hunters' campfires and, worst of all, the land-clearing methods of unwanted settlers. A year later he was dead, exhausted and sick from a cold, wet autumn spent fretting in the bush.

Had there been no J.R. Booth, there would be no Whitney. He built the railway line into the bush, and an American lumber company saw opportunity at the water stop where the line crossed the Madawaska. The St. Anthony Lumber Company of Minneapolis, Minnesota, bought some four hundred square miles of timber rights around Opeongo and the area, and immediately began building a large mill on the shore of Galeairy Lake, a mile from where the new Booth line crossed over the Madawaska. Isolated, distant and inaccessible by anything but canoe and the Booth line, the mill site allowed a business to do virtually anything it pleased to its employees. "It is the intention of the company," the magazine *Canada Lumberman* reported in 1896, "to build up a model community. . . . The business of the place will be kept in the company's own hands, and no outsiders will be allowed to locate on their property. The sale of whiskey will be strictly prohibited, and drunkenness or connivance there-at, will be punished with instant dismissal. The men are at present accommodated in the company's boarding houses, but cottages will be provided for the married men, to each of which a quarter of an acre of ground will be attached, which the men will be obliged to cultivate."

St. Anthony put up forty-eight similar houses, an office, a company store, a boarding-house, stables, warehouses, a post office, a school and both Catholic and Protestant churches. There was even, briefly, a doctor's office. But it sounded better than it was. There was no freedom of choice for those who signed on. The company charged rent for the houses and board for the boarding-house. The men were paid in trade at the company store. So powerful was the general manager of the St. Anthony Lumber Company, Edwin C. Whitney—his brother, James, became premier of Ontario in 1905—that the little village soon took on the Whitney name.

A few independent-minded loggers and businessmen tried to beat the St. Anthony system, but with no success. Little settlements sprang up in the surrounding bush, one called Jerusalem downstream from the mill, and a number of French families built there in the hopes that they could save on their rent money and grow and hunt their own food. Saul Holtein of Montreal even came and opened up a little supply store, which attracted business from the disgruntled logging families, but after Holtein's slab-wood store burned down three times, he gave up and headed back East.

Fires like the ones that levelled the little supply store may have discouraged Saul Holtein and caused J. R. Booth to lose sleep, but others, both more determined and more optimistic, poured into the new settlement. The St. Anthony mill was employing 150 men, and many of them arrived with their families. There were Irish and German and French-Canadian families. Polish immigrants who had come up the Booth line working for the railway stayed on once the railway was completed. They moved by the dozens into Sabine township, east of the mill area, and built their own homes and went to work in the bush, cutting and skidding timber. For generations the language of the park area mill yards was a mix of Polish and English, with a smattering of French and, inevitably, the valley lilt of the Irish.

St. Anthony was almost exclusively interested in pine, which was light enough to run fairly easily down through the rivers and leave floating in Galeairy Lake, but the deeper the cutters moved into Algonquin Park, the thinner the pine grew and the more they ran into vast hardwood stands. Heavy enough to sink at times, the hardwood was harder to move. The most effective, albeit more expensive, method was to draw it out on the ice and stack the logs at the mill. St. Anthony decided to sell out to the Munn Lumber Company of Orillia and was soon gone from the scene. Another mill, employing a hundred men, was constructed on the opposite shore by Mickle and Dyment of Gravenhurst, and a small village, named Bellwood—and later Airy—grew up around the new mill. Two other tiny communities, Slabtown and Paradise, flourished briefly in the hills around the mills, but soon vanished, the high hopes of the failed settlers with them.

It was the Mickle and Dyment mill that J.S.L. McRae, with the help of his father, purchased after the Great War. It was a time of lumbering lawlessness in and around the park, with the Whitney regime in the Ontario legislature having placed control of the province's vast forests entirely in the hands of the lumber barons. The Munn Lumber Company was particularly cavalier in its attitude. Owned by a member of the legislature, J. B. Tudhope, Munn felt it set its own rules and regulations. Munn felled hemlock in the park, stripped the bark for shipment to the Huntsville leather tannery and simply left the slash to rot along the trails. When Munn men moved in on Cache Lake, where the park superintendent had his headquarters—and where the earliest tourists were coming by train to stay at the grand Highland Inn—the two main uses of the park had their first clash. The tourists who had come to enjoy nature were appalled by what they found up from the shorelines and off from the portages; yet it was only when the Munn men began felling the high pines surrounding the superintendent's cottage that the provincial authorities decided it was necessary to act. Munn was ordered to surrender its licence. Tudhope, however, held out until he received $290,000 in compensation for the timber rights. The logging companies still had enough power to prevent Minister of Lands and Forests Frank Cochrane from convincing cabinet to ban lumbering entirely from the park, but at least from then on there would be regulation and supervision.

Law, or at least a minimal form of it, had come to the timber frontier. The original St. Anthony operation was, for a while, under the control of Dennis Canadian, of Grand Rapids, Michigan, but by 1922 this company, as well, had decided to move out. The white pine was virtually wiped out. A year later, when the big mill was being dismantled, fire broke out and completely destroyed the St. Anthony landmark.

The system had changed dramatically. Suddenly the lands and forests ministry had government cruisers on the timber rights to assess the lumber and control the harvest. Now the lumber companies required men on hand who could do their own assessments and count board feet and keep accurate books. John McRae, who had picked up extensive timber rights in the park, thought it might make ideal work for Duncan MacGregor. The call went out, and Dunc MacGregor had his first, and last, full-time job.

By the time Dunc arrived in Whitney that late August day in 1929, it had become a government town, literally. St. Anthony and Munn and Dennis Canadian were all gone, but the people, the houses, the store, the post office and, thanks largely to J.S.L. McRae, the jobs were still there. The Ontario government had to assume ownership of the little town—or whatever manner of beast Whitney was.

O.E. Post had come to Whitney as the last manager of the Dennis Canadian operation, and when the mill moved out, he stayed on and took over the company store that had been originally established by St. Anthony. Post had an entrepreneurial side to him, and proposed to the provincial government that Ontario "lease" him the town. A deal was struck for $1,100 a year, and Post assumed the omnipotent position last held by Edwin Whitney. Post, fortunately, was far more benevolent. Houses were rented out for $2.50 a month, $5 for the larger ones down along the tracks. He even sent one of his children, Gilbert, off to medical school on the understanding that "Gib" would come back to serve the poor logging families, which he did, setting up a small Red Cross outpost in 1928 and staying on as the only doctor in the area until his death more than thirty years later. O.E., landlord and storekeeper, dealt in vouchers and often traded in goods—chickens for flour, venison for yeast—and for the next two decades the little town of Whitney was entirely his concern.

It made for a rough, frontier-style town. Apart from the railway, there was no way in and no way out, except by walking or water. A very rough corduroy road—thin logs piled and laid side by side through the mud and swamp—was built through more than twenty miles of bush to the railway yard at the village of Madawaska, and Madawaska was then joined by similar rough passage to Barry's Bay by 1930, meaning it was now possible, in theory, to travel by wagon or cutter through to Ottawa. On the driest days of summer, when the muck had hardened and the ruts filled with corduroy wood and branches, a car might attempt the trip, but it was still an all-day journey, with passengers forced to walk and push up the hills and often sick from the hard jolts and endless bouncing. When they made it to Whitney, they were immediately struck, as Dunc's sister Janet would remember many years later, by how pathetically "ugly" the little community was. The buildings were poorly constructed, with no foundations. No one painted; yards and gardens, once demanded by the St. Anthony management, were let go.

There was no one but Post to serve as law and order and justice. Weekend dances were notorious for their brawls. Unwanted strangers were tossed out of town on the first scheduled train. When Phil Roche, who would become a great friend of Duncan's, arrived in 1935 to take up his new job in Post's store, he was greeted with the snapping whip of Sam Bowers, who was then droving supplies and wood about town with his team of oxen. "What the hell do you want here?" Bowers growled. Roche wasn't sure. Decades later, however, once the community had become a real town, with telephones and electricity coming in in the 1950s, Phil Roche would still be there, as proud reeve.

Duncan had come to Whitney on a beautiful August day, when the sun sparkled on Galeairy Lake and he shone at the plate. It wasn't long, however, before the games and good fishing changed to the harsh realities of life in the bush. Word came that fire had broken out near Cranberry Lake, and men were needed to fight it. He joined in, though he had no proper workboots for being in the bush, and ended up helping to bring the fire under control but in the process badly burned his ankles in his low-cut shoes. He ended up in the little Red Cross outpost that the new doctor, Gib Post, had built up from his father's store. It was a fortuitous meeting. Gib Post was a large, shy man with a deep literary bent—a lover of the classics, a reader of Shakespeare—and he was astonished to discover a logger who had similar tastes and who was, if anything, even better read than he was. They shared other passions as well: trolling for lake trout, bridge and strong drink. They were lifelong friends from that point on, the doctor who worked more often for eggs than money and the young logger who could get lost in a book faster than others could get lost in the vast bush that surrounded Whitney. When Gib Post and his wife, Jay, who also served as his nurse, came down with tuberculosis and had to enter a sanitarium in Ottawa for nearly two years, it was the long, weekly letters from Dunc that kept their spirits going. "They were the most wonderful letters I ever read," Jay would say more than a half-century later. "Duncan told stories so funny about the Whitney characters that Gib would lie there in tears while I read them aloud." The letters, unfortunately, were lost when the Posts—Gib one lung short and never to recover fully his health—were released from the sanitarium and allowed to head back to Whitney.

Duncan was more fortunate with his health. He worked six days a week for the McRae mill. He was miles back in the bush when they felled the trees and skidded them out by horse over treacherous ice roads. He helped them move the huge log booms from the Madawaska into Galeairy Lake, and down the lake to the bay at Airy, where the mill was located. He was in the mill yard when the timber was cut, and began to learn from an American scaler how to grade the lumber for shipping. He was good at tallying, and liked it, which was a bit unexpected in that he had done so poorly at mathematics while in school. Even when he worked in the bush camps, he would do the "clerking" in the evenings just for something to keep his mind active while the other men smoked and talked and played cards.

He got back to Eganville only rarely. The mill broke for Christmas and sometimes a long Easter weekend might allow for enough time to catch the train home and back again in time for work. But The Boss, as J.S.L. was called by his men, "never believed in holidays." They were rare indeed, and allowed only when John McRae figured he had no alternative but to give his workers an extra day off. Once back in town, Dunc would hang around with his old hockey and baseball friends and, eventually, with a new, younger crowd that included several women, one of whom was Helen McCormick, the daughter of an Algonquin Park ranger who had moved out of the park so the five McCormick children could attend school. They were friends, and skied and skated and picnicked and went to dances together with a larger gang, but nothing more, not then.

Apart from the bush camps, he lived the majority of his time in the large bunkhouse at Whitney, reading in the evenings or visiting with Gib Post. In the summer the mill shut down at noon on Saturday, giving the men who lived some distance away time to catch the afternoon train east and the men staying on a chance to fish or play sports. When summer came, Dunc was expected to carry the Whitney colours on the local ball team. He and Gib Post would stay up long into the night, a bottle of rye or rum between them, as Dunc told the stories of that day's game. When Gib and Jay fell ill, he told the stories by letter.

"Whitney was playing Barry's Bay down at the Bay," he wrote in the margins of *The Twenty-Four-Inch Home Run,* "and Alfie Fox [the station manager of Whitney] was playing at outfield. Alfie liked a few shots before the game and, as a result, he pulled off the greatest catch I ever saw. The Barry's Bay batter hit the ball, and Alfie made a one-handed grab at the ball and missed it. However, it landed on Alfie's head and bounced into the air and Alfie gloved it on the rebound. It was a wonderful catch and received great applause from the Whitney fans at the game."

They must have been memorable games, because he never tired of telling the stories. He talked lovingly of James Costello, the "well-oiled umpire" who was almost invariably the star of every game he officiated. With Whitney playing against Killaloe one game, Costello's calls became so odd that, finally, the Killaloe pitcher refused to throw any more. Costello kept calling "Ball!"

as he crouched back of the plate. When the Killaloe pitcher protested, Costello switched to "Balk!" and began sending the batters to first base. For a while, Dunc's cousin, Alexander "Sandy" McGregor, joined the team, but Sandy's weakness—the same as Costello's—soon did him in. "Sandy had quite a few drinks," Dunc wrote in his book, "but he still hit the ball somehow and took off for first base—only he didn't go to first, he cut immediately straight across the diamond for second and slid in. Of course, the umpire called him out. Sandy put up a hell of an argument and we had a hard time convincing him to leave the base and go back to the bench. He was convinced he'd run to first base first."

It was cheap fun, and a welcome diversion, for times were not good and certainly not getting any better. Dunc had been in Whitney only two months when Black Friday hit the New York stock market. The financial failure would not for some time be recognized as a depression, but the effects in Whitney were almost immediate. The automobile and building industry was in trouble, which meant the mills were in trouble. Men who could land jobs with the only mill in operation—J.S.L. McRae's sawmill—counted themselves lucky to make thirty-eight cents a day. Duncan considered himself a favoured employee, in that he was getting fifteen dollars a month, but it was soon dropped to ten dollars. As the combination of stock collapse and crop drought became known as the Great Depression, it had the unexpected effect of opening up the park in ways the lumber barons would never have wanted. Relief work crews arrived from all over the province—often including lawyers and accountants in their number—and they began building a road into the park, following the blaze of ranger Tom McCormick, Helen's father, who selected a route that would, roughly, follow that of Booth's railway. The work crews—earning ten dollars per month per man—pushed through the park for most of the Depression, building as well an emergency airstrip at the west end of Lake of Two Rivers, where the railway skirted the lake to the south and the highway passed it to the north.

The push into the park changed the face of Whitney. For the first time, there were different skills than lumbering required. New rangers were taken on by the park. Construction workers for the road came, and stayed. After decades of virtual feudal-type conditions, Whitney was changing. The Catholic priest, Father Hunt, led a battle to "Free Whitney," as he called it. The community, he said, was nothing more than a "shack town," and the reason, he argued, was a system that perpetuated poverty and discouraged enterprise. He hired, at his own expense, a lawyer to study the legality of an entire town being leased by the provincial government to a single man, who also controlled the commerce of the isolated little community. It was not a popular battle. After so many years of having their entire lives—work, school, church and store—controlled by company managers and, lately, by O.E. Post, many of the people were terrified to fight for change. Worshippers stopped going to Hunt's church. He was even shunned by his parishioners. "For months," the priest claimed, "I was deserted by everybody. . . . The public, by and large, did not wish to be considered on my side when actually they were, but the feudal system under which they lived alarmed them and clouded their mentality."

The priest was stubborn enough to persevere, however, and eventually the unusual case of Whitney, Ontario, became a simmering political issue that the provincial government wisely decided to dampen by the simplest method available: the Department of Lands and Forests cancelled Post's lease and put the houses up for sale. Many people bought their homes for $50. Aubrey Dunne, a park ranger, bought one of the finest and largest homes in town for $240, having talked the department that employed him down from the government starting price of $400.

Even if Duncan had wished to invest in a bargain house—though by then he had no interest whatsoever in possessions—he would not have had any use for it, for he was soon gone from Whitney and living deep in the Algonquin Park bush. A spark started a fire in the machine shop of the old Mickle and Dyment operation at Airy—the mill now owned by J.S.L. McRae—and spread faster than water could be pumped from the lake. The McRae mill was completely destroyed. McRae now moved operations directly into the park, twenty-five miles up the Booth line from Whitney to Lake of Two Rivers. With the new timber rights he had picked up from the disgraced Munn operation, McRae was moving gradually from softwood to hardwood, from the pine that had created the Ottawa Valley logging industry to the maple, ash, beech, oak, white elm and birch that, with controls, would sustain it. It was more expensive to produce hardood lumber, but it also sold for more. The market for all wood was weak, especially in the States, but the quality of Algonquin wood was so superior that McRae was able to sell most of what a pared-down Depression workforce could cut and ship. Much of it went to Detroit, where hardwood was being used in the early assembly-line manufacture of automobiles.

The park was opening up, even if only slightly. There were people around now, usually in good weather, but they were different from the loggers. Tom Thomson had brought in Lawren Harris, A.Y. Jackson, Arthur Lismer, J.E.H. MacDonald, Franz Johnston, Franklin Carmichael, who would form the famous Group of Seven artists, and their art had inspired others to come. Algonquin Park, it was said, was virtually weed-free, perfect for those who suffered terribly from allergies. The outdoors were said to have great recuperative powers, and the wealthy came to the park to recover from everything from the Asian flu to tuberculosis. "There is virtue in the open," the Canadian poet Bliss Carman wrote in 1920, "there is healing out of doors; / The great Physician makes his rounds / along the forest floors." A nice sentiment, but hardly deeply held by the privileged. When Carman came down himself with tuberculosis, he checked into an expensive sanitarium.

For the urbanized wealthy, this was heady stuff. It combined, somehow, the romantic notion of the painters with the harsh realities of the real bush. When they boarded the trains headed north from Toronto's Union Station, they may even have been carrying their Thoreau, convinced that they were about to step beyond the known garden into "the unhandselled globe. It was not lawn, nor pasture, nor mead, nor woodland, nor lea, nor arable, nor waste land. It was the fresh and natural surface of the planet Earth, as it was made forever and ever—to be the dwelling of man, we say—so Nature made it, and man may use it if he can." By the time they got there, however, staring from the luxurious passenger cars into the dark skirt that high pine draws over the bush, into the black swamps and high rocks, with everything fading into shadow and every shadow leading to dark, they were perhaps not quite so brave. For Canadians, Northrop Frye wrote in *The Bush Garden,* there is "a tone of deep terror in regard to nature. . . . It is not a terror of the dangers or discomforts or even the mysteries of nature, but a terror of the soul at something that these things manifest."

This *frisson* of danger was perfect for the lodges that went up at various railway stops across the park. The lodges offered safe rooms and soft beds, with a garbage dump and live bears within walking distance, a guide to bait your hook at the end of the dock and deer coming up to the sprawling porches in search of bread. With landscape the only art form it is possible to step into, and be a part of, even briefly, the attraction was enormous, and the lodges—particularly Highland Inn, at Cache Lake, and Mowat Lodge, on Canoe Lake—continued to do brisk trade in American and Toronto tourists who didn't seem affected by the Depression.

They were called, and are still formally called today, park visitors. They almost invariably arrived in good weather and left quickly in bad. Ranger families were here to stay, in all weather, no matter how cold or bleak or lonely it would get. The loggers, too, were now year-round residents, no longer merely walking into the camboose bush camps for the winter cutting and riding out with the logs in the spring run-off. Now they felled the trees and drew the logs and ran the rivers and set the booms and sawed the logs and shipped the lumber—and never left the park boundaries.

But people were not the only new species to be introduced to the park. There was still some confusion as to what, exactly, a park should be. Was it a "game preserve"? A logging management area? Was it open for settlement? Or should it be a wilderness reserve, as first envisioned nearly a half-century earlier by Alexander Kirkwood, the Ontario chief of crown lands who had somehow convinced his government that the head waters of these four key rivers—Muskoka, Petawawa, Bonnechere and Madawaska—needed protection. Kirkwood himself, however, was all for settlement and "a system of forestry," and at one point even went so far as to imagine "a million or more of people" sustaining themselves in this wild terrain.

The confusion led to tinkering, which had been tried before in Algonquin Park. More wild creatures, the theory went, would mean more visitors, and more visitors, more prosperity for the lodges and summer camps that the government then believed would be the future of Algonquin. At the turn of the century, five hundred smallmouth bass had been brought into the park and released into the Madawaska watershed; they had thrived, giving great pleasure to those tourists who had not the skill to fish for, and catch, the more elusive, deeper-running lake trout. To attract waterfowl—the natural flight routes to the north being the Ottawa River valley, not the park highlands—the government decided to plant wild rice, which took only intermittently. The rice, however, did much better than the fruit trees that were brought in, planted, bloomed once and promptly died off. Concern that the hardwood might one day go the way of the majestic white pine, the lands and forests ministry brought in bushels of acorns and planted them all over the Park corridor, with very little success. They brought in pheasants, which failed, and then large European grouse, which soon vanished into the thick woods, never to be seen again. They brought in ten elk in 1935, which looked promising at first but, by 1949, had all died out. They talked about bringing in caribou but, with the failure of the Algonquin elk herd, decided against it at the last minute.

Such ideas struck the men who worked there as absurd. They saw deer constantly, and often moose. There were bears around, and marten, otter, fox, mink, and ermine. Wolves slipped through the trees at day and howled long into the night from the hills high above the camp. For those who came to Lake of Two Rivers to work, they couldn't have found a more pleasant site for a new mill. There was a meadow between the tracks and the high hills heading over towards Provoking Lake, perfect for building a camp on and running a spur line over to the mill itself. The Madawaska River emptied into Two Rivers at this spot and also, on another branch, closer to the blazed ranger trail where they were going to put the first road into the park. The Madawaska was swift enough and wide enough to carry logs down from Cache Lake and Tanamakoon Lake. There was even going to be a landing strip built nearby, and already some of the fine straight hardwood McRae was cutting deep in the park was heading for England, where it was prized for fine structural work in the new, light fighter planes the British were building.

Duncan was doing extremely well learning his new trade as grader. He had a remarkable eye for hardwood, was able to identify a cut board by eye quicker than most woodsmen could tell looking at the whole tree and leaf. The mill began producing on-line in early 1934, and Dunc took up his new duties grading the wood for shipping. He was paid twenty dollars, a nice raise from the fifteen dollars a month the regular mill workers were being paid. So pleased was John McRae with his young brother-in-law that one evening, over a bottle of whisky, J.S.L. made Dunc a partner in the business, guaranteeing him 6 per cent of profits for as long as Duncan stayed on with the operation. John McRae wrote out the deal, signed it and then had two of the men witness his signature. It meant nothing at the time. It would have meant hundreds of thousands of dollars eventually, but the only use Duncan ever made of the contract was to pull it out in his later years, stare at it and shake his head. He showed it several times to his children, but never for a moment suggested he intended to collect. The piece of paper was missing from his few worldly goods when he died.

"I worked ten hours a day, six days a week," he once scribbled out on a notepad when a granddaughter asked him to write down a few of his early park memories for a school project she was doing. "There was no road through the Park at the time, only the railroad to Parry Sound. Most of the employees lived in Whitney and Barry's Bay and Wilno. The ones living in Whitney went home on Saturday evening on the railroad. We had good meals. Tom Cannon from Whitney was the cook. At that time you could buy a 150-pound pig all-dressed for five dollars and a quarter of beef for three dollars. Eggs were fifteen cents a dozen, and milk was ten cents a quart.

"The only good price was beaver or mink fur, and a large beaver skin would get you sixty dollars—at least two month's wages! Some fellows were trapping and doing quite well at it. Of course it was illegal to trap in the Park and if you were caught you paid a large fine and you'd be banned from the Park. The government started building airports around the country to give employment to the unemployed. They picked out Two Rivers right beside the mill and across the creek. The army ran the project army-style and suited the men with army issue.

"We had to build a bridge across the creek before they started building the airport. It was a godsend to the McRae Lumber Company as we supplied all the lumber for its buildings and teams of horses to do the work. It wasn't too long until the lads at the airport started selling clothes to McRae's men and in a month's time we were all decked out in army clothes same as the airport men.

"You could buy the following: army boots, two dollars a pair; shirts, twenty-five cents; pants, two dollars; underwear, fifteen cents; and socks, twenty-five cents, sometimes cheaper. They sure ripped off the government. The bosses at the airport used to sell the beef and pork at Barry's Bay, and sometimes the work gang went hungry. Also, they would put anyone's name on the payroll as working a team of horses and then pocket the cheque.

"There was all types of humanity there—former convicts, ex–RCMP officers, real down-and-out characters. Most of them came from Montreal, Quebec, but very few of them were French-speaking. We had one hundred men and at the airport there was about the same number. Just to give you an example of how they employed their men, we had one bull cook for all the men. The bull cook's job is to carry all the water, clean the camp, keep the fires going and bring in all the wood for the fires. They had fifty bull cooks for the job. They'd make home brew in their spare time, and they sure used to get pretty high at times."

He obviously cleaned up this history somewhat for his grand-daughter's class. The story of trapping beaver is true enough, but the trapper was Duncan MacGregor himself. With an axe over his shoulder and a couple of traps hidden in his coat, he would set off down the tracks until he came to the swampy area between Lake of Two Rivers and Cache Lake. Once there, he would hunt out a beaver lodge—the "chimney" a sure sign that it was inhabited—locate the entrance and chop a hole through the ice. A trap would be set on a branch, the branch set over the tunnel heading into the lodge, and a few days later he would be back chopping away in the hopes of a little extra money to pay for the books he was ordering by mail and the odd train trip home to Eganville.

Trapping was so lucrative in the Depression that poaching became an impossible problem for the few rangers the park employed year-round. When the price of marten went to nearly one hundred dollars for a good pelt—and the best pelts came from the park—native trappers from Whitney and Golden Lake began hopping trains going through the park and dropping off at random, moving through the bush until they came across the marten's distinctive tracks and trailing the animal for as many days as the weather held. They would then smoke it out of a stump or a tree, shoot it cleanly through the head, if possible, and head back to catch the next train with as much money as a logger could make in two months. Rangers Tom McCormick and Jerry Kennedy were often out for weeks at a time on snowshoes, sleeping in snow-packed lean-tos when they weren't fortunate enough to reach one of the many small rangers' cabins that were built throughout Algonquin. It was on one of these trips that Jerry Kennedy first froze his feet, and subsequent freezing in later years led to gangrene poisoning that ultimately caused him to lose both legs to amputation.

So desperate to stem poaching did the park rangers become that the authorities took the extraordinary step of trying to co-opt one of their suspects. Norman Bowers was a well-known Whitney trapper whose success suggested to the rangers that he was also working the mammal-rich park trails, so the park superintendent decided to offer Bowers a full-time job as a ranger with specific responsibilities for poaching. Bowers, a gruff man who had an equal love for poker and preaching, was only too happy to have the steady paycheque, and he took to his new work with evangelical fervour.

"Norm was on their side now," Duncan continued in his account. "And he was a very diligent ranger. Norman had a Ranger cabin right close by our Two Rivers camp and he used to preach to the boys whenever possible. If you didn't listen to him, he'd roar and rant hell fire.

"Anyway, I used to go down to the railway tracks to visit a girl [at Cache Lake]. It was four miles down the track. There was lots of snow and I didn't know that Norman was at the Ranger cabin, so I went on the track and on the way down I saw a mink trap. Of course everyone was trying to trap fur then, because a mink was two month's worth of wages at that time. I went off the railway track to check the trap for mink.

"In the meantime, Norman came down the track. He was going to preach at the girl's house and so he followed my track right to the trap for the mink. It was his own trap! And he figured whoever had been there had taken his mink. He knew it was me, because he soon found out that I was the only one ahead of him. That night we had a religious meeting and Norman in all his glory was attacking sin. The text of his sermon was 'Thou shall not stray off the path of righteousness.' Of course he was looking right at me. And of course I was guilty. But he never pinched me, because he was so fond of playing cards he didn't want to lose that pleasure. Anyhow, when he'd finished I whispered to him about how thankful I was, and all he said was, 'The Lord forgives.'"

So adept was Duncan at cards that Norman Bowers, fearing he might lose his best card partner, turned a blind eye to Dunc's poaching. They played at the mill, at the ranger's cabin and even at Bowers's rundown little house out along Hay Creek, east of Whitney.

"I went out to his place one winter at 35 degrees below zero," Dunc remembered in his notes. "It was freezing. Norman still wanted to play cards, but I said, 'It's too cold.' Norman said, 'We'll fix that.' So he went to the back kitchen and took the axe and he started chopping up his floor, and he kept the fire going with the floorboards so that we could play cards. Norman was in his glory.

"Next morning we went in to Hay Lake where a few people lived and where I used to go once in a while when we needed extra workers. A man named Eddie was staying in a trapper's cabin. Eddie had a team of horses and we could use them in the bush. He was asleep on the bed when we got there and I told Eddie to come to work. Eddie said, 'Okay.' He wanted to get his socks on and they were frozen to the floor it was so cold. We wondered that he never froze to death, but he was quite healthy and cheerful."

Dunc, too, was cheerful in the bush, even if, sometimes, "It was a day's work just to get to work." He had variety: clerking in the camboose camps during winter, tallying in the mill yard when they cut, shipping the lumber when the orders came in. Sometimes the work was exceedingly tough—he would always remember being sent with other men to establish a winter cutting camp at Mosquito Creek. When they set up camp, the wind came up so high that it ripped the tents and they huddled through the night as freezing rain and sleet pounded over them. But it turned out fine. He tried Mosquito Creek after spring breakup and took some of the finest speckled trout he ever caught, and Mosquito Creek from that point on was his vision of heaven rather than hell.

In those early years in the park, he got lost only once. He had been out cruising timber, deciding which trees the bush operation should cut, and he lost his bearings briefly between two similar-looking hills. It can happen easily in such bush. There are few vistas for the simple reason that once you climb a hill, there is still nothing but trees around you. There are outcroppings, and much can be seen from them until the point at which you turn and go back into the thick woods. Unless you have your bearings, and some sense of the lay of land, it seems next to impossible to disentangle from the deep woods. It was mid-December and dark was quickly coming on. He built a small shelter and a fire, and tried to stay awake all night. "I almost froze," he claimed. "But I made it through the night and once I found the creek I was all right. I found my way back to the camp." He always made sure after that to have his bearings, and to keep in mind how quickly darkness can fall in the northern bush.

But he liked being deep in the park, no matter the obvious dangers. There was always the possibility of a mink or a beaver on the winter weekends, a bit of baseball on the landing strip that was going up across the creek, and from ice out to ice in there was what he liked best; fishing for trout. Almost every summer there would be fires breaking out—lightning more often the cause than campers—and the men were always immediately dispatched to protect the timber rights. It was tough, dangerous, exhausting work—but not without its unexpected perks.

"We went up to this place and there was a big forest fire," he told his granddaughter Kerry, in 1992. "There might have been sixty men, sixty-five men. The fire was just in or out of the park. Our timber limits anyway. We all had to go to the fire, so I went, too. I was there for a while fighting the fire, and then it started to rain and that was a great thing. This fellow came up to the camp one night and started to fish for speckled trout, and by God he was just dragging them on the ground he had so many fish. The next day we all went up there to fish and there was a hole there, a pond, a little bigger than a house, and all we had was salty pork for bait. Just imagine—we caught 295 speckled trout out of that hole. And some of them were more than four pounds, five pounds—there was no way of weighing them or anything.

"We ate them all. Shantymen can eat like hell, you know. Trout just like that, you've never seen the likes of it. All you had was an alder rod, everyone had an old rod with a piece of string or any god-darned thing with a hook on it. As soon as you put your line in, there was a trout on it. I don't know what the hell drove them all in there, but it must have been the fire. It had been all along the creek, you see. There was a pond there, and that's where all the trout went, the cold water, and they were hungry as hell—295 trout! We counted them, just for the hell of it. The lad, I don't know how many he caught the day before. Sixty-five men were there that day. Some of the fellows in the camp could eat—oh, you've no idea—eight eggs for breakfast, nothing unusual to tell the truth.

"It was tough work in our time, you know, when you worked. Just imagine, ten hours a day and you worked steady six days a week. You had to work like hell.

"But I didn't mind it. I liked it."

CHAPTER THREE

Roy, Jimmy and Ann at Lake of Two Rivers, 1950.

THE SUMMER I TURNED seven, the Old Man turned, briefly, to fly fishing. The fly rod, a ten-foot bamboo pole in three sections, complete with carrying bag and a selection of dry and wet flies, was a gift from one of the buyers who dropped in periodically on the McRae Lumber Company. There were different buyers, of course, but they seemed singularly exotic to the park people: white shirts and dark ties; wide-brimmed fedoras; store-bought cigarettes; silver- and gold-plated lighters; long, clean overcoats; shiny toe rubbers; long, new cars; and disdain for pocket change. They came up from the cities, checked the winter draw of timber and placed their orders for shipment. They invariably came bearing gifts, but whether it was because they thought a bottle of five-year-old whisky might get them a better grain of bird's-eye maple, or because they just liked the bush characters they met in the park, I then had, and now have, no idea. Nor am I interested in knowing. That was the way they did business, and better a fishing rod than a case of whisky, our mother would have said.

Duncan was forty-eight years old that summer of 1955, one year away from the age he would forever consider himself first thing in the morning. He was forty-eight years old, had fished since he could walk and had, by his count, outfished everyone from the apostle Simon to Izaak Walton. Yet he had never felt a fly rod in his hand, never felt that bewildering lightness and admirable balance, never felt the extraordinary delight that comes from both hands working to perfection, the line snaking out, seeming to settle and suddenly snapping one more time to sail again, slowly and weightlessly until dropping with the click of a soft kiss precisely where you imagine the trout is waiting.

He had grown up in a world where there were four ways of fishing and two types of fish to go after. He had cut long alder poles and tried to sneak up on the timid speckled trout, crouching down so as not to cast a shadow and trying to drop the line quietly into the dark pools of cold creeks. He had trolled for trout with soft twill line from a canoe, though never embracing that favourite park guide trick of running the line through one's bare toes for better feel. Although he found light-line trolling exciting, since it involved the larger lake trout and better fights, he also found it restrictive, working best in the week when the ice goes out but impossible by mid-June, when the trout seek deeper waters. He had still fished and cast for the likes of bass and pickerel, but neither the technique nor the fish had captured him as they have so many. Too easy, he had long since concluded. Pickerel are fussy and stupid; bass tough and simple. And while there is a great difference in bringing them in—the bass yanking and leaping, the pickerel essentially bored with the whole process—the act of pursuit was roughly the same: worm on hook, line over side, wait. One of the few books he did keep around was Boswell's biography of Johnson, who wasn't much of a fisherman himself but who at least could see that fly fishing held some challenge. The alternative, according to the witty doctor, was to fish "with a worm at one end and a fool at the other."

Like so many Canadians, Dunc departed from the American fisherman on the point of pike, or Great Northerns, as the U.S. fishing magazines call them; the Indians call them hammer handles and, for the really big ones, axe handles, and treat the pike with such contempt they will feed the fish only to their dogs. Perhaps it is merely an indication of Canadians being slightly closer to the land, to the bush, to the original imperative than Americans. Most Canadian fishermen still regard fish as food first, game second; the American fisherman is consumed with game and measurement and the *baseballing* of all sports (a statistic for everything, whether it be chances of faceoffs won and lost in hockey, or girth of a fish the people of Northern Ontario prefer to bury in their gardens to promote tomato growth). For Duncan, the pike offered only nuisance, no challenge. A pike meant lures lost, stinking slime, nasty thumb and finger cuts from the miniature shark teeth and wasted time. It was a sentiment he shared with Walton, who claimed to have known a man who caught a pike with a mule. The man, a farmer, had taken his old mule down to water in a pond that had, apparently, been cleaned out of minnows by a ravaging pike. When the mule bent down to drink, the pike latched on to its lips, startled, the mule bucked back, throwing the pike up onto the grass, whereupon the farmer clubbed it to death.

What Duncan had found perfect to his temperament was trolling with steel line. While somewhat possible in canoe, it was best done in a boat with a small two- or three-horsepower outboard that could crawl along at prime trolling speed. He liked to sit and think while he fished, drifting in his mind as the little motor took him over the shoals and past the islands in a carefully planned and executed route. And he liked to know that no matter how deep the trout were, he could let out three or four hundred feet of steel line to reach back and down to tempt them. He would use one lure, always a William's Wabler, though sometimes silver and sometimes half-silver, half-gold, a thin, slightly curved lure in the shape of an alder leaf with a treble hook at the end, the lure and line heavy enough to tap bottom in even the deepest of the park lakes.

Steel-line fishing is easily criticized. There is no give, and getting snagged on bottom can sometimes feel like being rear-ended at an icy stop sign. The line, especially since there is so much of it, can be difficult to control, and a tangled backlash in steel line is almost impossible to clear. The wire kinks easily and can suddenly break off and drop out of sight, line and lure lost forever by a troller who has failed to pay attention to what is forming at the end of the rod. When a trout is caught, it is not played as much as it is pulled, a smaller fish sometimes being hauled up so quickly by an excitable troller that it is drowned by the time it surfaces.

But such problems belong to those who have no appreciation for the art. The best steel-line trollers have soft hands, just as the best goal scorers do in hockey and the best singles hitters do in baseball. Dunc's hands were perfect for trolling. Somehow, they could *see* what was happening three hundred feet down and away from the rod tip. He knew when he was passing through silt, knew when he had tapped bottom and should reel five or six turns up, knew precisely when the lure clicked over the first rock of the coming shoal and even knew when a trout had, as they sometimes will, slipped out of the shadows and nose-bumped the lure out of curiosity.

Others were not so lucky. "I just had a bite," I would say.

"Bottom," he would say.

"There! Another! I've got him!"

Sitting one seat back, one hand on the motor, the other cradling his own rod, he would reach out to touch the end of my line, not unlike a doctor feeling for fever, and smile and shake his head. *Tch-tch-tch-tch-tch-tch-tch.*

"It's a branch."

"Can't be! It's fighting!"

And I would crank and yank and haul and churn the big reel so fast the steel line would assemble in lopsided layers—only to stare back in astonishment as the water behind the boat broke to reveal a dark, slimy, waterlogged branch that the tough wabler had broken off.

"The first one was a real bite!"

Roll-your-own cigarette hanging from mouth, hat pulled down tight from the sun, he would stare at me with those blue eyes, wince and shake his head as if there must have been a mistake. This could not be his child. There must have been a mix-up at the hospital. Good theory, except there was no hospital back in June 1948 and I'd been the only one born that month at the Whitney Red Cross outpost. No mix-up. Just bad hands.

None of us had ever seen a fly rod. There was good reason for this. Fly fishing, with all its poetic glamour, with all its panoramic beauty, came about because of space. If Norman Maclean had written *A River Runs Through It* about Algonquin Park, Robert Redford might have one day found himself directing a movie about a family setting minnow traps. While fly fishing is so perfectly suited to where it was developed, along the quiet, open banks of English streams, and even to where it is now so celebrated, along the wide, shallow rivers of Colorado or even from the flat, open river boats of the Miramichi and Restigouche, it is a challenge to behold in Algonquin Park, where the tangle hangs out over the riverbanks and the trout waterways are often so narrow a fisherman must learn to paddle forwards and then backwards to enter and exit a promising stream. Here there are none of

Walton's "cowslip banks." Here there is no gorse, no meadow, no permission to ask of an understanding farmer. Here there is only bush, branches in your face blocking your path to the water and, for those persistent enough to break on through, branches now at your back, trying to push you in.

But Duncan was determined to use his new gift. The buyer who gave it to him would be insulted. He must master the technique, and the next time the man pulled his big-city Buick into the McRae mill yard, there must be pink-fleshed speckles in the freezer to greet him and thank him. Dunc's dilemma was the opposite of most ambitious fishermen: he knew exactly where the trout were, and he was already there himself, but the equipment posed a problem. There were no fly fishermen in the park. He had known none growing up in a world where they filled burlap sacks with eels and buried pike in the backyard, where a good lake-trout strike was more like getting whopped on the back of the head than delicately letting the tingling line run out between thumb and fingers. If a fly fisher seemed at times to be letting out line like a cotton spinner at the wheel, then a troller was more like the winch at the top of a steel lift.

What little he knew of fly fishing had come from reading. He knew his Walton and all those references to honesty and poetry and God's approval. He knew—and we knew, because he sometimes mentioned it—that the great irony of the ludicrously male world of huntin' and fishin' is that the first treatise on the sports was not Walton's *Compleat Angler,* but far more likely the work of a woman, Dame Juliana Berners. If she did indeed exist—and some scholars say she did not—she was claiming, more than five hundred years before Duncan held his first fly rod, that the activity was good for heart and soul, best enjoyed in solitude and capable of developing in one the "good spyryte" that leads to a long, flourishing life.

But what use was "good spyryte" when it came to cross winds? What good was solitude when the fly was twenty feet up in the trembling aspen laughing behind your back?

"You want to come along tomorrow?" he asked one night as I still-fished, futilely, for smallmouth bass off the rocks of the point on Lake of Two Rivers.

"Where?"

"I don't know. We'll try out the new rod."

"Sure. Great."

He woke me early the next morning. The cabin was barely rinsed with the first light coming over the high hills to the east, beyond which lay the mill. We dressed and ate as the full wash of the morning spread down the point and along the bay. He collected his rod and flies, packed a few sandwiches for later, set his straw hat with the Anzac single fold on one side and we set out on the walk to the road.

No one else was stirring. The lake had taken on that syrupy look that is found only at dawn, as if during the night someone had switched the water for mercury. Not a ripple, not a shimmer— then suddenly, out towards seagull rock, the unexpected splash that says fish, the circle that indicates size, the remainder left to the imagination. It was going to be a good day. Low as a missile, a loon passed over the high pines, its long neck and anxious call searching the bays for others. It was so still we could hear the wind passing through its wings as we walked under the tall cedars and took to the path heading out along the rocks and raspberry patches to the road. The beaver grass was soaked with dew, the spider webs in the spruce wet and shimmering and reminding me of what I had suspected for some time: the only ones who dare sleep at night in the bush are humans. Without the cabin walls, without my older brother in the bunk above and our parents on the other side of the thin wall, I wouldn't even think of it.

There were two cars at the end of the path, Duncan's green 1954 Chevrolet and the old ranger's blue 1955 Dodge. One morning—one morning out of, say, fourteen or fifteen years, it should be pointed out—they came out here to find that neither car would start, both having been relieved of their batteries during the night by some highwayman, but it had been passed off as such a park aberration that they still refused to lock their vehicles. Duncan started up the Chevrolet, used one swipe of the wipers to toss off the dew, and let the car idle while he completed one more necessary morning task: he dropped down into the creek, waded up to the first gentle turn, reached in under an outcropping root and yanked free a rope strand onto which were tied three glistening green bottles.

We drove west, the sun at our backs as he headed along the north shore of Lake of Two Rivers and past the public campground. There was no one stirring, thin smoke still trickling off campfires that had been let die. He kept pretending that he, too, was falling asleep, letting the car weave down the empty road foolishly while I screeched and he pretended to suddenly awaken and drive on seriously. The road dipped through low wisps of fog, then rose back into clear light before Mew Lake. He left the road and pulled onto the dirt path that headed into the abandoned airport strip and the ruins of the old McRae mill, where he had come to work during the Depression. He slipped the Chevrolet in under some hanging alders and we got out, the blackflies and mosquitoes already upon us. There was a small bottle of 6-12 in the trunk, and I slapped the oily, fetid liquid all over my neck and face and arms and legs. It was like bathing in diesel fuel, but I had no choice. The flies of Algonquin Park like their meals young. Duncan, as always, used nothing but his smoke and his disdain to fight them off.

We were headed to a small branch of the Madawaska where he knew there were speckles. It required going down a steep sand bank, filling your shoes with irritating gravel, and then climbing and crawling and jumping and stumbling through a thicket that not even Br'er Rabbit would ask to be tossed into. But that, unfortunately, is the nature of speckled-trout fishing. The books all talk about the technique of catching them; the book that shows you how to get to them has yet to be written.

With one running shoe soaked and black with muck from the bog, the other feeling like it was filled with blood from the grinding gravel, my face and arms and legs scratched and bleeding from the hawthorn swords, raspberry vines and black spruce suckers, my hair caked with blood from the mosquito and blackfly and deer-fly and horsefly blitzkrieg—I pushed through, the Old Man charging ahead happily while I followed, jumping and twisting out of the way of the limbs and branches that whipped back into place once he had passed. He was singing a song about marrying some girl named Mary-Anne. I didn't know whether he should be saying such a thing, already being married to a woman named Helen.

He was the only one in the family who could sing. Ann belonged to the Anglican choir but because they needed bodies to fill the cassocks, not voices to fill the church. I was about to enter Miss Parker's class and would, before the school year was out, strike a secret bargain with her. If I agreed only to mouth the words and our class won the music competition, she would send me up to receive the trophy. There is a photograph somewhere of me walking back, plaque in arm, mouth cemented shut, while the others in Miss Parker's winning class stare in baffled envy.

He held up a hand as we neared the creek, a location we could hear more than see through the heavy cedar, spruce and tamarack cover. It, too, was singing, that lovely constant gurgle that says, in a place like Algonquin Park, cold, clean water and possibility. The Old Man stopped the moment he heard this. He wanted noise from the creek, but not from us. No sound, no shadow, no ripple.

When I grew a bit older, I thought for a long time that this had merely been an affectation in him, a little unnecessary drama to make the taking of the trout seem all the more impressive. After all, what could they hear down there under water, with the gurgle probably a roar in their ears, if they could hear anything at all? And even if a shadow did spook them, where could they go in a creek so narrow that a man, if he could ever find a clear run, could probably leap over? But later, once I'd read Hemingway's Nick Adams stories as a young man and Roderick Haig-Brown as a middle-aged man, and long after I'd come away from creeks empty-handed too many times to count, I came to understand that method doesn't exist for ritual's sake alone. The catching of the speckled trout is fishing's equivalent to catching a falling star. You have to be lucky, but luck is only part of the mix. You also have to be at the right place at the right time, and you have to concentrate on nothing else.

Dunc knew this arm of the Madawaska well enough to know where the twists formed the pools, and where there were large enough rocks to give the speckles the still and dark little canyons from which they prefer to launch their feeding attacks. He had fished here often, but never before by fly, and now it was necessary to find somewhere, anywhere, where he would have enough room to work the line.

We came to a sharp turn in the creek, the water burbling as it rounded the bend and rolled over a long shoulder of sand and small stones that barely broke the surface. Back of this small half-sandbank relief was a red pine, its lower trunk twisted so it angled, slightly, out over the bank and then straightened again high over the tangle. Between the lower trunk and the water was a sheltered clearing of soft needles and earth, and here he laid down the bag containing the sandwiches, beer and warm pop for me, opened up the rod holder and twisted together the new rod.

It was, for him, a surfeit of equipment. He had no waders for the water, no tube in which to strap himself for the float downstream—which would have been quite an accomplishment in water that barely reached the knee. He had no tackle box, no knapsack, no fly-fishing vest with its ten thousand pockets and soft flap of lambswool in which to hang the flies. He opened his pack of Players, and the tiny hooks Mr. Stark had given were pressed to the back of the 1955 calendar, the only use I ever saw him make of a cigarette-pack calendar in the forty-seven years I kept expecting the next smoker's cough to be the end of him.

With the smoke from his cigarette keeping the blackflies at bay, he kneeled over the rod and threaded the coarse line from the reel through the seven or eight eyes that led to the tip. He then tied on a long, thin leader and, finally, threaded the tapered end of the leader through one of the tiny dark flies he plucked from the back of the calendar. He stood and took the heft of the rod, if heft is a word that can be used to describe something that weighed less than any of the tiny trout it was expected to catch.

This was not exactly the first time he had ever held a fly rod. He had practised with it in the open grounds along the point at Lake of Two Rivers. He could nurse the line with a roll of the wrist, snap it with a flick back of the wrist, and haul back just as it seemed the fly was about to drop like a feather over the water. The beauty of fly fishing is that, like tennis, it is the simplest thing to do functionally, almost impossible to do perfectly. I had never seen anyone fly-fish before, but it looked beautiful, the line, once wetted, so fluid and shimmering in the sunlight, the arm and wrist moving more like a painter's than a lumberjack's as the line snaked out, threatened to settle, snapped back and snaked out again.

But that was there and this was here. Just poking the rod through the underbrush and over the water was going to be a challenge on the north branch of the Madawaska. He stepped carefully through the overhang of the pine and out past the poplar barrier, the low bushes and the stones until he could tiptoe in his workboots onto the crest of the half sandbank. The large, brown steel-toed boots—the steel glistening through the right toe from kicking the fresh lumber over when grading the wood—sank down, then held. He moved in slow motion, partially to ensure his footing, more importantly so as not to alarm whatever trout might be around.

"Can you do it?" I asked from back under the pine.

"Shhhhhhhhh."

He eased out the line, the reel buzzing with fine parts and oil. It fell in loose drops over his boots. He kicked the line out into the water. Working his wrist back and forth and back and forth, tempted but not daring, he finally flicked the line upstream, but the folds of it caught in the tongue of his boot and stalled. He flicked again, the fly landing about twenty feet away and immediately drifting back to rest on the edge of the sandbank nearest the water. He repeated the cast, again and again and again.

This wasn't much fun. I was itchy and hot, sand and needles stuck to the scum of stinking 6-12 that covered my legs and arms, I was getting hungry and thirsty. I knew I couldn't drink from the creek. It might scare the speckles—presuming they were still there. I went to the base of the tree, opened a warm can of root beer and felt it fizz over my mouth and down the neck of my shirt. I didn't need that; it would only attract any wasps that might be stirring in the morning sun. The drink gave me hiccups.

He cast the fly upstream and let it float downstream. He tried to get up to the nearest eddy, but couldn't quite reach it. There was just no room for a second haul, no room for a full sweep of the arm. He shifted and tried flicking the fly downstream and reeling in, but nothing happened.

"There's nothing—*hic*—here," I said. I was ready to give up.

"How do you know?"

"No bites."

"You didn't get any bites last night, did you?"

"No."

"Are there no fish in the lake, then?"

"No. *Hic!* That's different."

"How?"

"The lake's big."

"This stream goes all the way to the ocean."

I giggled. "*Hic!* What?"

"All the way to the Ottawa. And the Ottawa River goes into the St. Lawrence. And the St. Lawrence goes into the Atlantic Ocean. How do you know there's not a whale working its way up here?"

"You're being silly."

He was often silly. With kids he was completely unpredictable. He would grunt and screech and spin around like an ape. He would burst into song. He would offer smokes all around. He would act as if he couldn't hear. He would do something deliberately stupid—like making animal sounds while walking along the street—and act as if it were the most normal thing on earth to be doing. He would let fly his imagination, making the impossible seem probable and challenging the child to one-up him.

"Or maybe a—*hic!*—shark!" I shouted.

"Ak-ak-ak-ak-ak-ak-ak!" He squealed, pretending to be stuck in the sand and doomed to die, twisting in the jaws of a great white shark that had made three wrong turns and ended up jammed, fin to boulder, in the north branch of the little Madawaska.

He pulled his line free, switched the one fly for another from the cigarette pack, and nursed the line until it shot out in a rolling loop and landed farther downstream than he had yet reached. He fed more line out, letting the fly tumble ahead through the rolling water to the darkened area where the creek turned under an overhanging jack pine.

He worked the line between thumb and forefinger, pulling, releasing, tightening, feeling. And then he released outright, the reel buzzing smoothly as he quickly caught up his slack. Firmly but gently, he pulled the tip of the rod up until the line sizzled up from the water, stiffened and caught.

"Got one!"

"*You do?*" I said, forgetting my scrapes, my bites, my stomach. My hiccups cured.

The Old Man set his mouth. It did not matter the equipment—fly rod, trolling rod, casting rod—or the place—lake or stream—he always set his mouth the same when he tested the hook with a firm, steady tug before playing the fish and bringing it in. With his lips folded over, pressing the mouth tight in a grimace, he looked, momentarily, like a man lifting a car from a snowbank or a gunfighter about to have a forty-five slug removed from his shoulder with a hunting knife. It was an expression of extraordinary, superhuman effort, whether it was expended for a twenty-three-pound laker or a six-ounce speckle. The mouth had to set just so.

I saw then the breathtaking beauty of taking a trout on the fly. The rod bent like a bow and then seemed to bend again. The tip danced like a conductor's baton. The reel gave a sweet mechanical sound coming in, screamed quietly giving out. The line danced in the sunlight, water dropping like clothes pegs from a line as he wound in, the line stabbing oddly as it wound out on him.

"It's a big one!" he grunted. His lips were still so tightly pressed together it was a wonder the cigarette hadn't been pinched off. But it burned on, the ash sagging off the far end and breaking up softly in the light breeze.

I scrambled down as close to the sandbank as I dared. Looking downstream, I could see the line straight as a pencil, then sagging, then the water breaking into foam as white belly flashed and turned, dark side glistening and down again.

It didn't look that big to me.

Dunc worked the speckle patiently. It didn't seem to concern him in the least that he might lose it. I, of course, would have yanked it so hard the fish would have been airborne until it wrapped itself around the topmost branches of the big red pine. He seemed more interested in the fight than the triumph, and would appear, at times, deliberately to feed out the line so the trout could run again and have another chance.

Eventually, however, the fish tired. It broke surface, flipped to show its belly, flipped back and seemed to relax. He reeled it in smoothly and bent down to pluck it out of the water as it gave one last flick and conceded. He inserted his forefinger into the gill, using the grip to hoist the speckle up into the sunlight. The fish was beautiful: black back, sides like scattered rainbow, orange and blue and red and green and black and hints of pink. It wiggled once, hard, in his hand and then sagged. He plucked out the little fly and flipped the fish towards me.

It landed in the sand and slid onto the pine needles, flopping now in terror. As always, I was half appalled to see such a beautiful creature out of water, but at the same time half desperate to get it back to the point and show it off to the rest of the family. Perhaps, as he sometimes did when we went out trolling for lakers, he would let me claim it for my own. We would eat it and everyone around the big table in the log house would compliment me on it, and I would be both honoured and heartsick as I realized the fish was gone forever.

I stayed there on my haunches, watching the beautiful fish die. It would flop, then go quiet, then flop some more, but it was not the dying that so enthralled me. I had seen fish die hundreds of times. I had never, however, seen a speckle die so closely and in the sunlight. It is a phenomenon that knows no comparison. Its colour goes out like the lights on a Christmas tree. The fish alive is the most exquisitely beautiful creature I have ever seen; the fish dead is a fish—dead. Perhaps that is the true lure of the speckle. Like a snowflake on an open hand, it begins to vanish the moment it is caught.

I wanted to see another one, fresh and rising from the water. I wanted to see those colours again. I left the paling fish on the pine needles and worked back to the opening.

The Old Man had stepped farther downstream. He was up to his knees in the water now, his workboots and socks completely under, his rolled pant legs slipping down and the black rise of the water working its way up his thigh.

He had caught the knack. He was working the line quite well now. He was more daring. The line higher above his head, the rod tip high and his arm high over his shoulder. I stood there watching, admiring, as he hauled again and sent the hook back for one mighty cast that would take him all the way down to the pool.

I never felt the hook until it whipped back. And then I screamed as if shark and whale and lumber truck had suddenly rounded the corner and all three were crushing into my face.

"*AAAAEEEEEEEIIIIIIIIIIIIIII!*"

He turned so fast he stumbled on the rocks, dropping down onto one knee and losing his hat. He tossed the fly rod so it landed like a child in the arms of the overhanging bushes and was running as soon as he again found his footing.

All I could feel was the searing pain. It was in my left hand. I was screaming and screeching and bawling and sobbing—all at the same time. I grabbed at my hand, but it only made the pain sharper. I screamed again, louder.

I had no idea what had happened. It was like a wasp sting, only worse. It was like a cut, only worse. I didn't realize until he was almost to me that it was the hook, and that it was embedded deep in the fatty tissue below my thumb. It was bleeding now.

The Old Man was already there. The fly rod was thrown to the ground and the line was coiled in the bushes and on his arms and around his legs. He stepped free of it and lifted me, leaping up the bank and in under the red pine.

The line caught in his feet, and yanked again on my hand.

"NNNNOOOOOOOOOO!"

"Just hold on," he said in a voice so calm it struck me that he had no idea how serious this was. I howled again. "Crying won't do it any good. Give me your hand."

I was crying, sobbing and shaking as I held my hand out. He looked at it, touched the hook, and I screamed again.

"It'll have to come out," he said.

"DON'T TOUCH IT!"

"It has to come out," he said.

He laid me down on the soft pine needles. He grasped my wrist and squeezed, deflecting the pain, but it only made me howl more. He wiggled the hook, but it would not give. I screamed. He let go of my wrist.

"Can you tough it out?" he asked.

I was caught off guard. "W-wh-what?" I sobbed, gasping for breath.

"You're going to have to be brave," he said. "I've got to take that thing out of your hand. Can you be brave enough?"

I was crying helplessly now. "I don't know. I don't know."

He had his knife out. *He wasn't going to cut it out, was he?* But he wanted the knife to cut the line. He cut it once, then a second time, so he had a short piece of line.

"This'll hurt," he said. "But it'll be over fast. Are you okay?"

"I-I guess."

He looped the line over the hook and snugged it in tight to the shank. The barb was deep in the skin, which was why the hook wouldn't come out. He put my hand flat on the ground and, just as I was preparing for pain, whipped back suddenly with his right hand, the line ripping the hook free and away.

It happened so fast I forgot to howl.

He had me up in his arms. He carried me back to the creek, where he placed my hand in the cold, cold water. The effect was immediately numbing. I was choking but no longer crying. I could feel the tears drying on my cheek. I could taste citronella; the tears had washed the 6-12 down onto the corners of my mouth.

The hand was still bleeding. The blood was washing away in the water, thin as it left my hand and disappearing as it broke up in the water and headed downstream.

"We got to get out of here before the blood brings the shark," he said.

I started to laugh. I couldn't help myself. Laugh and cry at the same time. He had me up and tight to his shoulder now and lifted me back onto the bank. He felt around in his pocket and brought out a red-and-blue handkerchief. He bent back down into the water and wet it, then tied it around my hand.

"My fault," he said. "I should have been watching."

"It's okay," I said, sniffing. I was already feeling better. The hankie in the stream made it feel as if we were in a cowboy movie and he had just yanked out an arrow or dug out a bullet. I was already thinking about the reaction I'd get when we got back to the point, where the rest of the family would now be up and wondering how we were doing.

"If you don't think about it," he said, cinching the hankie just a bit tighter. "It will go away."

I wasn't sure now I wanted it to. I wanted, instead, to have the cut forgotten and the wound remembered. I wanted him to tell everyone how brave I'd been—and I knew he would, too, even though I had squealed and wept far more than the hook had deserved. But I wasn't crying any more. I was seven years old and in the bush with my father, and I had a huge wet hankie wrapped around my cut hand and everything was going to be just fine.

He made sure I was sitting all right and went back to retrieve the rod and reel in the loose, flopping line that he had cut away from the leader and fly. He worked quickly, put the rod away and pushed everything—sandwiches, unopened beer, pop can—into the bag and then turned and broke off a branch, which he ran through the speckle's gill until a sucker caught and he had a way to carry the fish back. He carried everything, leaving me the heft of the hankie and the pampered hand.

I never knew him to fly-fish again after that. It left him with a curious tally: one day, one speckle, one boy.

The following summer, the last year that McRae had a mill operating down on Hay Lake, just to the east of Whitney, the Old Man decided to test my courage. It may have been accidental, it may have been intentional. He never said, and I never asked. Perhaps he knew what an eight-year-old was going through when it came to spending so much time in the bush. Outwardly, I adored it, was never so happy as when the morning sun hit the high rocks on the point and I could lie, warm as toast on the granite, and stare over the drop to the sheltered bay below, three or four large bass lounging in the clear waters before the winds came up and rippled and distorted them from view. Inside, in my imagination, I was typically eight: frightened of the dark; terrified to go to the outhouse alone at night; hesitant, even, to strike out the path to the highway on my own to gather worms from under the boardwalk.

No one else seemed afraid of anything. Our grandmother would charge a bear head-on if it dared show its face anywhere near the log house on the point. Our mother, who had been born in the park, seemed alarmed only when driving into town. Brother Jim would happily head off into the bush on his own and sometimes portage over to the little lakes on the other side of the hills on the far shore of Lake of Two Rivers, thinking only of the fish he might catch and never, it seemed, of the wolves that howled in those hills every night as we tried to doze off in our bunks. Sister Ann was eleven years old and slept happily in her own cabin at the edge of the high rocks. Younger brother Tom was barely walking, but seemed fearless of water and bush.

The old ranger, our grandfather, was retired now, and refused to let a week go by without a day-long hike as deep into the woods as his seventy-three-year-old legs would permit. Because of my age and availability, I usually went along, always under strict orders from our grandmother not to let him push himself until he had another heart attack. I lived more in terror of his heart giving out on the trail than of running into an angry mother bear or a pack of wolves. He took me farther back into the Algonquin Park bush than I had ever been, his ranger shirt blackened with sweat as he blazed, for what would be the last time, a dozen overgrown trails into lost camboose camps and magnificent rock outcroppings and spectacular little lakes too isolated to portage into and too small for a float plane to land on. We saw moose and marten, otters and fox, a few distant wolves and bear; we listened to the lonely song of the white-throated sparrow and fed the whisky-jacks; we found deer antlers and wild leek and tiny square nails where, once, a hundred men had slept and eaten and worked from dawn to dusk felling the white pine—but all I ever listened for was his wheezing, all I ever saw was the way his shoulders would heave when he plunked down on a rock or log to catch his breath and all I ever tried to remember was the way out.

There would be no such confusion at the start of the gravel

road that led into the mill at Hay Lake. Straight ahead one way lay the mill. Back the other was the road to Whitney. Not even an eight-year-old could get lost there.

"I'll just be a couple of hours or so," Duncan said. "You can fish the creek."

It was a pickle of my own creation. Dozens of times, while heading on the gravel road to the Hay Lake mill, I had talked to him about the creek we first crossed over. It ran black and swift below a log-and-rough-board bridge, and he had always claimed it was teeming with speckles. The family had stopped a couple of times to see if we could see any, but the water was roiling and dark with iron, and though we had seen shadows we still had no proof. If the thin black torpedoes we sometimes caught firing across a sun spot were fish, they might just as easily be suckers. He claimed to know they were trout. The locals often took trout here, he said, and there were apparently some good-sized ones hiding among the rocks and cedar roots. He had eaten speckles from this creek himself, and they were pink and beautiful. Every time the Chevrolet rattled over the board bridge, I stared down longingly into the water and asked when we were going to try it.

"Find some worms," he said. "We'll be going as soon as you can get ready."

There was no backing out. Yes, I had desperately wished to fish the little creek. But no, I had never imagined doing it by myself. I tried to talk Jim into coming along, but he was headed off with an older cousin and their hand-made bows and arrows. Ann was reading. Everyone told me to have fun.

We drove out of the park, through Whitney, and turned onto the Hay Lake Road. It was so hot the open car vents made it feel like the heater was on. The backs of my legs stuck to the seat plastic, but my sweating was not entirely due to the heat. He had the no-drafts cocked full open, the warm outside air roaring in on us, and we barely talked. He was singing, as usual, and driving madly down the gravel roads, a thick mustard-coloured rooster tail of dust rising behind us as he drifted recklessly around corners. I sat, wondering how I could possibly bail out of this, but soon realized there was no out whatsoever apart from getting through it. Nothing would happen. Nothing *ever* happened. *But . . .*

He crossed the bridge and pulled over into a small gravel pit. It had been dug out during the construction of the road many years earlier and then abandoned. It was a place I liked: the low-ground holding ponds of frogs and pollywogs and mosquito larvae, the banks covered with raspberry bushes. The main face of the gravel pit looked as if something had been taking small bites out if it. A cottager had probably used a spade to fill a trailer. There were fresh tracks where someone had taken several different runs at backing in and up as close to the sand as possible. Perhaps there would be people around after all.

Dunc was pulling my little casting rod out of the trunk. I grabbed the tin of worms, wondering if they'd already perished in the heat, but they darted in fine health as I lifted the top strands of broom moss. I had my tackle box, an old cigarette box with a half-dozen rusty hooks, some split sinkers and a couple of badly twisted leaders. Mercifully, he had never been one of those parents who says, "Take care of your equipment, and it will take care of you." I was already ahead of him in equipment terms, even if I would never reach him in fishing terms. But then, who ever judged a painting on the price and variety of the artist's brushes?

"You okay, then?" he asked.

"Yeah, I guess."

"I'll pick you up on the way out. Shouldn't be more than a couple of hours."

"Okay."

But it wasn't okay. Two hours to an eight-year-old is a very long time. Two hours to an eight-year-old with a wild imagination is eternity. I knew I had trapped myself. I knew I had to stay and fish and forget that I was there alone. This, after all, was exactly where I had dreamed of being a hundred times.

He started up the car, pulled the gearshift towards him and down, and moved away, the tires spitting rocks back at me. A hand came out the window and waved me good luck. I waved back, ducking away from the rising dust.

I listened to the car fade away. The roar and clatter of gravel gave way to a distant hum, the dust rising over the trees, and I could hear him downshift to climb the first big hill, but soon there was only silence, the dead silence of the bush, and the growing sense of being surrounded by that same bush.

The creek was gurgling as it passed through several large boulders at the bottom of the bridge. It reminded me of the Laughing Brook of the Thornton W. Burgess books our mother read to us before we could read ourselves. But here there was no Chatterer the Red Squirrel or Reddy Fox or Sammy Jay or Jimmy Skunk or Jerry Muskrat (I never could identify with Danny Meadow Mouse or Unc' Billy Possum). There were only red-winged blackbirds calling from the alders along the creek and a huge raven speaking in tongues in a pine high above the little gravel pit.

I had loved those Burgess books and would never forget the pleasure of our mother sitting on the edge of my bed and starting a fresh one. "Billy Mink ran around the edge of the Smiling Pool and turned down by the Laughing Brook. His eyes twinkled with mischief. . . ." They played and talked and got in and out of trouble, in my mind, all around the old ranger's log home on the point. Eventually, of course, I moved on to other animal books—Jack London's *Call of the Wild* and *White Fang*, in particular—and from there into other writers who had an extraordinary feel for the bush and the woods and the wilderness. Hemingway's Nick Adams stories. Ken Kesey's *Sometimes a Great Notion,* which felt, to me, as if it could just as easily have been about a logging family in Algonquin Park as about one working and living in the Pacific Northwest. It was some time before I realized that the better feel, for me, came from American writers, and that so many of those *Canadian* writers we had met in school along the way had next to no feel at all for where we were living and what we knew and felt of the bush.

It strikes me now as odd, or perhaps even telling, how often those who wrote here were frauds in their real lives. Grey Owl, whose *Tales of an Empty Cabin* is actually quite lovely and certainly the best of the lot, was, of course, not the "full-blooded Red Indian" the posters promoted on his European speaking tours, but a full-blooded Englishman named Archibald Stansfeld Belaney. He dyed his hair black, used henna to redden his skin, flattened his nose by endlessly rolling a spoon back and forth across it, performed "Apache" war dances while singing gibberish and wore an Indian headdress he'd picked up in a London souvenir shop—but at least he had spent enough time in Northern Ontario to have developed a real sense of the deep bush, in all seasons, in all weather and alone enough that he clearly came to know it well.

The Canadian nature-writing tradition is strange indeed. Ernest Thompson Seton was also an Englishman who changed his name several times and who ended up preferring that strangers and friends address him as Black Wolf. A strange man whose eyes would cross whenever he became nervous and who was so terrified of nocturnal emissions that he slept on boards and splashed his private parts from a bowl of cold water, he seemed rather justified in telling his siblings to put only one word—"misunderstood"—on his grave marker. Seton, unlike Grey Owl, liked to have some comfort when he entered the Canadian wild, preferred to stick to the less-intimidating woods and farmland of Southern Ontario and almost always moved about with a guide in good weather. He was also a bit of a dreadful role model for nature writers, in that he was once arrested for using baiting traps and also for the illegal shipment of hides. His other great crime against animals, however, was to personify the creatures in his tales, which sold marvellously in places where the animal in question could never be questioned. This wasn't Burgess writing for little children. This was a highly successful author writing for, and selling to, adults in other countries who took his cockamamie tales about North America at face value. *Tito, the Coyote That Learned How* is only one example. His most successful book, *Wild Animals I Have Known,* so enraged President Teddy Roosevelt, who fancied himself a bit of a bushman, that Roosevelt launched an angry campaign against such "Nature Fakers." Roosevelt had it right. Seton's animals have intelligence, intuition, emotion; they are cute, kind and thoughtful. He called himself Wolf, yet had he ever bothered to ask the Natives he met for their stories of the deep bush, he would have heard of death, violence, terror and monsters—the work of the imagination, the effect of reality. Tito meets the Windigo.

Frederick Philip Grove was also a fake, a great Canadian nature writer who managed to keep secret his entire life that he was actually Felix Paul Greve, the rich son of a Hamburg merchant. Grove died in 1948 and wasn't found out until 1972—despite the fact that he'd much earlier published an autobiography called *In Search of Myself,* in which he somehow forgot such details as his real name, his true background, his running off with another man's wife to Italy and his spending a year in prison after being found guilty of fraud. In Canada he was the bestselling author of *Over Prairie Trails* and considered himself the Canadian reincarnation of Thoreau. He wasn't, much to his regret, anywhere near the writer that either Seton or Belaney was, and he so bitterly resented his poor sales that he invented yet another story that his books were being banned out West, hoping to pump up Eastern sales. He was, however, much ahead of his time in one significant aspect: he thought that as a Canadian author, he should be paid by the government to write. "I do consider," he once said, "that Canada owes me a living."

Such a strange heritage of words. Frauds who came from other countries, wrote about this one and then sold the words in books and lectures back in the countries they had left. People of privilege, like the Strickland sisters, Susanna Moodie and Catharine Parr Traill, who came, in Moodie's case anyway, thinking the bush could be tamed into some new society where she would rediscover her natural social standing—only to have it not work out. Traill, at least, had fewer expectations, as well as a much harder time of it, and her wildflower and plant-life books speak of a genuine love of the natural world she found in Canada. Not so her sister. "The farther in the bush, the farther from God, and the nearer to hell," Moodie wrote. She and her husband so utterly failed to survive as settlers that she lucked into a sinecure for him that allowed them to stay on, essentially, as Canada's first hobby farmers. Meanwhile, she continued to write as if she were, in fact, struggling as much as those who had no such connections. But even with government help, she couldn't bring herself to like what she was selling. "If," Moodie wrote, "these sketches should prove the means of deterring one family from sinking their property and shipwrecking all their hopes, by going to reside in the backwoods of Canada, I shall consider myself amply repaid for revealing the secrets of the prison-house and feel that I have not toiled and suffered in the wilderness in vain."

Such writing had validity for the authors and their audiences, people usually far removed from where the research had taken place and the writing had been done. Seton was more summer tourist writing for armchair travellers. Such writing, however, had no connection to those who came to the bush and stayed and worked far too hard to write and usually too hard to read—if indeed they could read. In all the years I knew him, I never caught the Old Man with a book on the bush in which he had spent his entire life.

I knew that if I lost myself in fishing, the time would go faster. I unrolled the thin, threaded casting line, tied on a leader and attached one of the smaller hooks. I reached into the can with a finger and forced a worm up the side, catching it tight between finger and thumb as it rolled out the top. I hooked it twice, leaving the tail loose to attract the trout.

I tried first from the bridge. I could feel minnows nibbling at the bait, and lost two of the worms, but knew from the action that this was not the trout I was after. The pulls were tentative and weak, the way shiners and chub feed. The creek immediately below the bridge was too shallow. I would have to go down and find a pool.

The banks were steep. I scratched my legs getting down through the raspberry and nettles, but easily reached the banks and worked my way, careful to keep my shadow down, upstream to where the creek curled dark and calm on the surface, a sure sign of some depth.

The alders and loosestrife and sedge made for heavy going, especially with a rod in one hand and a can of worms in the other, but I eventually made it to within casting distance of the pond. I fitted a fresh worm, cast short, cast again and let the sinkerless hook settle on its own.

A tug, quick and sharp—*a speckle!*

I yanked back—for once not too hard. I waited, my breath

quickening, and very gently, very surely, pulled the tip of the little rod up and felt the hook set. *I had him!*

The little trout darted upstream, then down, straight towards me. I reeled furiously, afraid that it would use the slack to slip away, but the line caught again and in an instant the speckle was shuddering out of the water, flashing in the light and vanishing into the high grass and whippy pussywillow that surrounded the tag alders. I could hear it thrashing, the flipping loud and desperate but futile. I followed the line down and pulled the little trout up by the leader, the hook barely caught on the inside of its lip, its gills reaching desperately for water.

I knew I had to get it away from the creek before I took the hook out. I had lost too many fish already to slippery hands and rock crevices and thick grass and the unfair way in which all slopes lead to water. I climbed back up the bank and placed it down in the sand, each flip covering the trout in a soft dusting that made it look, strangely, like it was being prepared for the frying pan.

The hook was easy to remove. It flopped some more, and I was torn, as always, between showing it off and letting it go. The moment's indecision, however, made the decision. The trout was too far gone. A few more desperate flips in the hot sun and it lay still, flipping only as if in afterthought, shimmering as death arrived.

Such a gorgeous fish. I picked it up and tried to clean off the speckle with my hands, but I only spread the dust. I could see some of the brilliant colours sparkling through, and wished that the Chevrolet would suddenly appear in a dust cloud from around the first corner so I could show the fish off before the colours died as well. I listened, but there was no sound of anyone coming.

I left the fish by the tackle box and fished some more. I tried the pool again. I tried below the bridge, behind the bridge, even once ventured around the first bend, so that I was for a moment completely surrounded by bush, but not even a bite. All that activity must have spooked off whatever speckles there had been.

Soon I was back on the bridge, the rod resting on the flimsy wooden railings, the line hanging in the water with not even a shiner to bother the worm. I had lost interest in fishing. I could think only how close it was to two hours. I tried counting sixty steamboats to make a minute pass, then another minute, then found the word "steamboat" was no longer making any sense in my brain. It didn't sound right. I couldn't say it right. But I couldn't stop saying it, no matter how nonsensical it sounded.

It was no longer so quiet. So much for Grey Owl's "calm and silent presence of the trees." A squirrel was moving about in the bush down by the creek. It was so hot that, every once in a while, it seemed my head was filled with cicadas, the buzz beginning low and rising to a scream that seemed to come out of the earth and sky at the same time. There were two ravens now, one in the high pines over the gravel pit, one in a tall elm back of the creek, and they were calling back and forth in that impossible Tower of Babel garble that separates raven from crow.

It would be wrong to say I was afraid, but not wrong to say I was uneasy. How I longed for that plume of dust to appear up the road! How I wished a car or truck would come along from Highway 60, heading into the mill, and perhaps stop and offer a ride in. We had relatives—an aunt and uncle on my mother's side, cousins on my father's—living farther down the gravel road, nearer the mill and lake, and perhaps they would come along and rescue me from this terrible heat and thickening loneliness.

I could, of course, have walked. The thought had crossed my mind several times, but it seemed too far and hardly worth the effort, if the Old Man was coming back this direction anyway. All I had to do was wait. Even if I was no longer going to fish, I could sit and wait.

I tried it. I sat in the shade, but there were more noises in the bush. Another squirrel. A chipmunk. Several birds fluttering about the low branches.

And then a thud!

My heart leapt, drumming like a partridge's wing. I could hardly breathe. I turned, thinking whatever it was was close by, but there was only the bank, then the bridge, and on the far side of the bridge more gravel road and deep, dark bush. Whatever the sound was, it had come from over there.

I let my breath out, grateful for the bridge. I had no idea what it was, but I couldn't imagine a bear or a wolf or a moose coming across the narrow bridge. They wouldn't dare. *Would they?*

For the longest time, I sat there listening to my own heart thumping and the silence of the bush. But there was no second thud. The squirrels began chasing again. A white-throated sparrow whistled. The ravens started up again, their sound now like a bubbling chemistry lab in a Boris Karloff movie. Were they doing this deliberately? Were they teasing me?

I decided to start walking. The more distance I could put between myself and the bridge, the safer I would feel, even though I had already half convinced myself that it was only a dead branch finally falling off, or maybe a deer. Whatever it was, it was no threat to an eight-year-old with his wits about him and a casting rod held out like a sabre. I abandoned the worms, but broke off a small poplar branch, peeled away the leaves and suckers and left a "Y" so that I could push it through the gills of the speckle and carry it by the end that stuck out the dead trout's mouth.

The sun beat down, with no relief at all along the gravel road. It felt like my shirt was being ironed with me in it. The bushes were yellow with dust, the raspberries sagging, dust-covered and overly ripe, the leaves folded in on each other for protection. The cicadas were screaming. I could hear my feet dragging in the gravel, dust scattering behind. I could hear my own breathing. I could hear, or perhaps feel, my heart pounding against my ribs, a marching drum, a death march, the beat suddenly picking up.

Up over the first hill and along the run where we sometimes came to pick chokecherries. Dust everywhere, the forest almost grey with it. A thick garter snake was sleeping up ahead on the road and slithered off only after I had poked it with the end of my rod. I could hear him rubbing against the small gravel as he made his way across the road. It sounded like he was frying.

Up and past the bog. Along and past the cedars. Up and along the bluff. Down and past the pin cherries and the little creek where the forget-me-nots were in bloom and where the Old Man sometimes stashed a few bottles of beer.

Thump!

What was that? Whatever it was, I had heard it clearly. A thump, a thud, a fall, a *step.* I paused and moved to the far side of the road, stopping entirely, listening so hard it felt as if the cicadas were buzzing from somewhere inside my inner ear.

Leaves. Moving! I heard that for certain. I stared into the bush, praying for a squirrel. But nothing—nothing but the forest darkening into black, then deeper black.

Thump!

My heart felt like a woodpecker was trying to break through. I choked down breath, stared again, and still could see nothing. But there was definitely something there. Something moving.

My mind was racing almost as fast as my heart. It *had* to be a squirrel. It *might* be a deer. It *could* be a moose. . . .

No, it was a wolf, stalking. That would explain the sound and then the silence, then the sound again. No, no, it was a bear, wounded. Gathering itself for the charge.

Thump! Thump!

That time I saw a branch sway. But what was behind it? No

animal. A *person?* A *madman!* A bearded, filthy, drunken, sick, demented, insane *murderer* with an axe in his hand. With a fish knife, ready to skin me alive! With ropes, ready to *tie me up and leave me to die!*

I began to walk. Steady, keeping to the far side of the road, then quicker, moving to the centre. Head down, pumping straight ahead, trying not to think of death, then spinning, panicking, to see what might be slipping up under cover of my own dust to grab me by the throat and drag me off into the trees and rip my entrails out the way the Old Man cleaned his fish.

The fish! Of course—I hadn't been thinking! I still had the fish in my hand. I could smell it from here. I lifted it high and turned my face towards it and the smell of fish and death was overpowering. An animal would be able to smell that for miles. A wolf pack might have sniffed it! Or a mother bear and her cubs! Bears had been known to break into packs to get at fish. They'd climbed trees to get them. Never, ever, we'd been told, carry your fish in your jacket. If a bear wants them, let it have them!

I held the fish out—the fish dead, the eight-year-old trying to breathe. It had lost its colour. It had lost its attraction.

I took the branch in my throwing hand, spun twice and hurled the fish and stick as far back into the bush as I could, sending it in the direction of the sounds.

Thump! Thump! Thump!

There was more in there than just a little speckle crashing through the trees! I had done the right thing, I figured. I had at least bought a little time. I hurried on, driving myself up the next hill, the sun so hot I worried I might die of thirst before any wolf got the pleasure of ripping out my throat.

I passed the first of the houses, old and abandoned, an upside-down stove on the broken steps, the roof caved in and the windows shattered. An old half-ton stood halfway to the road, orange lilies growing up through the open hood, the engine missing. *Here! This is where a madman could live.* Perhaps there were graves of eight-year-olds all through the back.

I was running now, the casting rod swinging out in front of me, the tip sometimes bouncing on the gravel. It was only about a quarter-mile to the other houses, and someone would be there to let me in. Hopefully.

I heard a roar—but not, mercifully, of an animal! It was the Chevy coming up the far hill. I saw a light yellow sprinkling of dust rolling above the far trees. And suddenly, around the corner, came the sweetest sight I had seen in eight lonely years lost in the woods.

I could see his face through the dusty windshield. He seemed at first puzzled, then smiled. He must have known. He stopped and reached over and opened the passenger door, the dust roiling all around the car. I threw the casting rod over the seat and myself in, slamming the door.

"You look hot," he said, smiling.

"I walked all the way," I said. I tried to make it sound like I had done something special, not something humiliating.

"What happened to the fishing?"

"I ran out of worms."

He nodded and pulled out a cigarette to light. He said nothing as he poked in the lighter and waited for it to pop. He pulled it out and held it up to the cigarette, drawing deep. The flame looked like the sun I had just walked through.

"No luck?" he asked.

I think I paused a second. I wanted so much at that moment to show him my trout. I wanted him to look at it and admire it and for the both of us to race it back to Lake of Two Rivers where we would clean it and show it off and take it into the ice house. There we would clear off enough sawdust to uncover a clear ice block, leaving the fish to cool until supper, when grace would immediately be followed by giving larger thanks to the one who had provided the magnificent speckle that came curling and sizzling out of the oven.

But I had no fish. Not even a fish story I could dare tell.

"No," I said. "Nothing."

"Too bad," he said.

He put the car in gear, dragged on the cigarette and stretched his arm out the window as he released the clutch. The Chevy bucked away and back down the road.

"You sure are sweating," he said.

"It's hot," I explained.

He smiled, bringing his hand back in for a deep drag that said, as loudly as possible, that my secret was safe with him.

Two or perhaps three weeks later, he announced that the two of us were going fishing again. It caught me off guard. I had thought we were just driving down to the mill for the day, but no, he said we were going fishing. Going fishing without fishing rods. Going fishing without a canoe on top of the car or a boat and trailer behind. No outboard, no tackle box, no life preservers, no live well, no downriggers, no scented lures, no electronic fish finder, no wraparound sunglasses, no baseball caps, no fisherman's tool, no electric trolling motor, no net, no sponsors' jackets, no track suits, no expensive sneakers, no bait. But going fishing, all the same.

"Where are we going?" I asked.

"L'Amable," he said. He pronounced as everyone around Whitney did—*la-mabb*—and I would not know for years that the little creek that twisted north off the Madawaska east of Whitney, tumbling down a lovely falls and through some quick rapids and under the road had been named for the magnificently christened

L'Amable du Fond, an Indian hunter and trapper who worked the area around the time of Alexander Shirreff's 1829 trip into the Algonquin highlands.

"We're going to meet people there," he said.

"Who?"

"You'll see when we get there."

It was early morning when we left Lake of Two Rivers, and it took us the better part of an hour to reach the dirt path that headed in off Highway 60 to the creek. It was a place we kids loved to go. The path died at the falls, and there the water rushed over a wide, stooped stone so smoothly and swiftly that it looked more like a mass of blown glass than a small river. The flow was so even it gave the water added substance. It seemed as if you could step across the back of the water as it folded over the rock, and yet immediately below it broke and exploded into churning white foam and bubbles, dancing wildly off through jagged rocks and disappearing into the fold of the tag alders.

The falling water gave off a permanent haze, rainbows within reach, water crystals sparkling in the sunlight. On a hot day it was cool and refreshing, and the permanent drizzle filled the crevices alongside the waterfall. There we would find crayfish and mysterious stick bugs that moved around like toy soldiers as you watched but seemed to vanish into tiny, thin, soggy branches when you scooped them up and tried to examine them.

But the Old Man wasn't interested in exploring. He parked the Chevy in the shade, rolled up the windows and slammed the doors shut, not bothering to lock them. With his hands in his pockets, he started walking. We were, he had said, going fishing.

There were trails heading back from the waterfall. He moved easily through them, knowing exactly where he was headed. He showed me the place where, many years earlier, he had stepped over a badly torn log and almost onto the paw of a little black bear cub. The bear squealed, the sow rose in the nearby raspberry bushes and Dunc turned on his heels and ran for the nearest trees, climbing the first one on which he could get a hold and staying up there half the day, until the old mother bear had tired of rocking the tree and the cub had convinced her to wander off in search of more grubs and berries.

It was hard going. We had to push through branches. We had to climb up hills using roots and rocks for purchase. We had to jump and slide down the other sides using branches and tough dogbane for balance and support. I was hot and sweaty, but hardly worried. Unlike the old ranger, Duncan never carried an axe or a hatchet to blaze a trail. He never seemed to map out where he was going, never even seemed to be all that much aware of where he was going. But because he was my father, I trusted him implicitly. He had to know where he was. And if he knew where he was, I knew where I was. With him.

We came back to L'Amable on higher ground. There was hardly any trail at all, here, but then, just after I had seen the creek again, deeper and wider and darker, we broke through into a small clearing, and here there were people waiting.

It caught me completely by surprise. I would more have expected moose or bears or a pack of wolves. But I had expected nothing, having heard nothing. And yet it seemed as if they had been there for some time. There were several women, an old man, a couple of younger men, and five children, three boys and two girls. They were all dark-haired and deep brown with summer sun. There were picnic baskets and blankets and a large wooden box, the handle of a huge frying pan waving out the top. The younger men were sitting flat, their legs splayed, and they were using their jackknives to clean the suckers off long alder saplings.

The noise when we broke through the bush was like a cranked radio coming on with the turn of the ignition key. They had clearly been waiting for us. There was shouting and joking and laughter and introductions, even though I recognized the older man, Joe Lavalley, and his wife. The Lavalleys were a Métis family who lived on the edge of Hay Lake. We had often been there before, we kids fascinated by the chickens and geese and turkeys that ran freely in the yard, hypnotized by the traps and snowshoes and pelts that hung in the workshed, and worried that the Old Man and his great friend Joe would get so deep into the whisky that we'd end up in the ditch on the way home.

This man was known as Hay Lake Joe Lavalley, though there were several Joe Lavalleys and, in fact, several different spellings of the Lavalley name. Some Lavalleys had worked at the mill. Some had hauled logs that the mill bought. They all hunted and fished. And they all seemed to like the Old Man.

Dunc always said that his Joe Lavalley was "the only man I knew who could go through the bush in the middle of the night." He was famous for his ability to strike out for anywhere without a map or a compass and reach his destination, seemingly, in the most direct line possible. "He was amazing," Dunc's nephew, Donald McRae, says. "Absolutely amazing."

Dunc had also been a long-time friend of the man who must be called the original Joe Lavalley, an Algonquin Park guide who had been such a renowned character that the British writer Bernard Wicksteed once wrote an entire book about him after a fishing trip. His *Joe Lavally and the Paleface*—the missing *e* is either Wicksteed's error or, more likely, the incorrect spelling offered up by the guide—had been published in 1948, and there had always been a copy about the house.

Wicksteed had become entranced by the park in 1945, when the war had finally come to an end and he found himself in New York City with a dozen days of leave, after which he would return to civilian life in England and retire from his duties in the Royal

Air Force. He found himself sitting in a bar with a whisky and an Algonquin Park brochure spread out before him:

"*Game is abundant,*" *I read.* "*Bear and moose are occasionally encountered. Beaver, mink, marten, muskrats and practically all the fur-bearers are fairly common. . . . Speckled trout run four to six pounds and are best in the Petawawa-Oxtongue River system. . . . Lake trout up to 35 pounds are caught in Opeongo and Smoke Lakes. Black bass . . . up to five pounds in the waters of the Madawaska. . . . 2000 lakes and nearly all of them them contain fish. . . .*"

Even if you're no fisherman, isn't there music in those names? Don't they make you want to bring out your boyhood copy of Hiawatha and read again of the Big Sea Gitche Gumee, of Pau-Puk-Keewis, the fool, and Mudwayaushka, the sound of water on shore?

I read on: "*Guides are all old-timers with as much as 25 years' experience in the park and in bush life generally. They know the best fishing-grounds, when to fish them and how, the best types of lures and tackle. They know how to cook and make the camp comfortable and some of them are Indians. . . .*"

Wicksteed was entranced by the very wilderness fantasy that had wrapped its magic around the imaginations of John Muir and Robert Service, the bush and the wild something beyond North America at the same time that it was within North America. An old world deeper than the New World. If the streets of New York were paved with gold, the pathways of the North American wilderness were richer still with whatever a boy's imagination wished to place there. "A schoolboy in England can only dream of these things," Wicksteed had written, "and as he grows up the fetters of civilisation thicken and dull the resolve to escape." He would escape for eleven days, and he would do so with his imaginary Hiawatha—who turned out to be no other than Joe Lavalley.

A day later, Bernard Wicksteed had stepped down from the train onto the little station boardwalk in front of the Highland Inn on Cache Lake. Ed Paget, the manager of the hotel, didn't seem much amused to see this Brit arrive, unannounced, wanting both a room and an Indian guide, but he gave him a room and, eventually, found a genuine Indian guide. "He's about the best man in the park," Paget told Wicksteed, "*and* he's the most amusing. You could write a book about Joe."

He did just that. For five dollars a day, Wicksteed hired on one of the most delightful, if unknown, characters in this country's literature, a Métis guide whose original French name, Lavallée, had been altered to Lavalley, and who turned out to be, in Wicksteed's account, a bit of a Satchel Paige in his ground-level wisdom and his mangling of the English language. A wild storyteller who claimed, it seemed correctly, to have been a First World War sniper for the British and, incorrectly, a guide for the Royal Canadian Mounted Police, Joe told the British visitor that he'd quit his job as a flying ranger because "my system inquires exercise." He was a legendary park character: once jailed for knocking out a fellow ranger; once quit a good job at one of the Jewish summer camps because they wouldn't serve him bacon for breakfast; and forever maintained that he had once set out for China as a volunteer to build airfields, only to have the ship he was to sail on torpedoed. "The people was saved," he told Wicksteed, "but all their tools and machinery was drownded."

Joe and the British writer headed off for eight days of fishing, Wicksteed furiously taking notes. Joe fished with a silver lure he claimed he had made out of a cigarette case he took off a dead German. Joe refused long portages on the grounds that he would "drownded" if he had to hold a canoe over his head for two miles.

"I only swim when I change my underclothes," he told Wicksteed when the British visitor went for his evening dips. Joe dispensed his wisdom—"a trout don't like warm water any more than you like warm beer"—without even thinking that perhaps there were some oddballs in the world who drank their beer warm.

It is a charming book and, in parts, tells more about what the bush means to those who did not grow up around it and in it than anything ever written by the likes of Thoreau and London—simply because of Wicksteed's unbridled ingenuousness.

"Last time I was here," said Joe, "I paddled straight across the muskeg."

The muskeg! To my English ears the word just breathed adventure. In boyhood I knew it as well as any in the language. I read it a score of times in those hours with Jack London in the hay loft and during those illicit candle-light sessions in bed. Now, for the first time in my life, I heard it actually spoken, and spoken in casual passing conversation, as if it was cheese or a pair of boots, something I was supposed to know all about. And, of course, I did know all about it—everything except what it meant. You didn't have to know its meaning in the days when I came across it in my reading, for it was an atmosphere word like billabong and pinyon, carrying its own message without need of further explanation. Now, I thought it time to make further inquiries.

Joe waved his hand in a lordly gesture, taking in everything in sight.

"Do you mean that's muskeg?" I said, pointing to the nearest bush, something like a lavender.

"That's right," he answered.

"But Joe," I said, "you told me only an hour ago that that was a Labrador bush."

"So it is."

"Well, then, what's muskeg?"

"That is," he said, and this time pointed to an entirely different plant that he had previously named beaver bush.

"I don't get this," I said. "Do you mean that Labrador bush and beaver bush are both muskeg?"

"Course they're not," he said. "Why'd they have those names if they was something else?"

"Well, then, we're back where we started. What (pause) is (pause) muskeg?"

"This is muskeg," he said. "This and this and this. It's a word they use, that's all. They talks about 'walking through the muskeg,' but just which Jeezly bit it is I don't know."

It makes you wonder. Did William Shakespeare use phrases like "interior monologue" and "pathetic fallacy"—or did he just write? Could Renoir name all the flowers he painted? One of the oddities of those who live in the bush, rather than visit it, is that when pressed to name a plant, a moth, even many birds and trees, they rarely can, and yet they know what the bird sounds like, what the wood burns like, which plants to avoid and how to survive, effortlessly, in the wild. Years later I would read, and greatly admire, Margaret Atwood's northern bush novel, *Surfacing*, but I was struck, continually, by the almost clinical description of flora and fauna. She knew her surroundings the way a scientist would, the way her father, the scientist, would have described them. Most other fathers would have called the surroundings "bush." And if you want something different, there's "water," and up there, "sky." Be damned careful, however, of "fire."

What little we knew of the Algonquin Park plants and animals we got from our mother and her father, the old ranger, who was unusual among the park people in that he cared, deeply, about the science of life. He collected, and labelled, larvae—usually the dreaded spruce budworm—dropped them into little cardboard cigar-container type tubes, twisted on tin lids and mailed them off to the lands and forests laboratories in Toronto. He read books on plants and their uses. Perhaps it was as much to help him with the crosswords he worked on late at night under the coal-oil lamps—perhaps it was merely out of curiosity—but he himself was a park curiosity because of his interest. Still, even then we didn't fare all that well. What we and everyone else we knew called partridge were, in fact, ruffed grouse. I would grow up to write about nature and, in one magazine article, refer to an exquisite Algonquin Park moss called princess pine, only to have a fact-checker call and tell me that there was no mention of this in any book she had consulted and, in fact, the biology experts in the provincial natural resources department knew of no such thing. Well, I said, I could walk them to as much as they want, any time they wish. The magazine changed princess pine to club moss, which I had never heard of and prefer to think I could not identify.

Duncan was no more entomologist or ichthyologist than was Joe Lavalley, yet both knew which insects might attract a trout, what time of year it was just by the type of insects hovering around the top of the water, which ones bit the worst and which ones you could safely ignore. Just don't ask them to name them.

The original Joe Lavalley had been dead eight years the day we walked to L'Amable creek. He and his brother had been setting up their camps for the trapping season, and Joe had complained that he couldn't eat. "It's my innergestion botherin' me again," he had told his brother, and had taken to bed early in order to be ready for the next day. He never woke up. His brother, Mat, lifted him in a fireman's hold and carried him out of the bush and back to Whitney. It took him all day and all the next night. Mat Lavalley's arrival with the body of the town's most famous guide over his shoulder stunned the little village. News flew up the Booth line to the mill at Lake of Two Rivers, where Duncan MacGregor and the men refused, at first, to believe it possible. Joe had apparently been fifty-six years old but had looked, in Wicksteed's estimation, about thirty. He had claimed his family lived almost forever—father, 104; mother, 101; and her Algonkin father, 115—and he said he had a ninety-year-old aunt "who looked twenty." They had obviously avoided the curse of "innergestion."

The Lavalleys who awaited us on the banks of L'Amable creek were of the same family as the trapper Bernard Wicksteed made famous. They shared his thick dark hair, deeply tanned skin, ready smile. They must have arrived there only slightly before us, for they were just beginning to set up a small camp. Branches were cleared, blankets laid, a fire set but not lighted—which seemed silly to me on such a hot day—and lines and knives and small fishing spoons and single hooks laid out on a smaller blanket. I hardly felt in a position to point out that everyone had forgotten their fishing rods.

"You come wit' me," one of the older boys said, tapping my shoulder. I looked at the Old Man, who was smiling and nodding. The older man was walking towards Dunc with a green bottle of beer, opened, the foam rushing out the top and over the back of his dark hand. I could smell the beer, warm and sickly. How anyone could drink it, cold or hot, I had then no idea.

With the other young men, I headed back into the bush. They had jackknives, long, with thin blades fading with sharpening, and I wished I had brought my own little Mountie knife—except, perhaps, they might have laughed. Dull and poorly made, it tended to separate if I pushed too hard on the little cedar kindling we liked to carve into knives. One of them had a hatchet, and they all waded into a thicket of tall, thin, green saplings—I now know them to be alder—and carefully selected a couple of long, thin ones that the young man with the hatchet clipped off with one quick swing along the ground. They hauled out the tiny trees bottom first, the branches hissing and clicking on the other trees. They threw them down in the clearing beside the saplings they'd been working on and worked quickly up each sapling with their jackknives, thumbs alarmingly close to the action as they clipped the suckers and ended up with several long, flexible poles, the shortest about seven feet, the longest closer to ten. We now had rods.

The older ones drank their stinking beer and talked and laughed. The young men set up the poles with line and hooks and I was off with the younger ones in search of bait. They turned logs and rocks and broke off bark and kicked the grass, and came back with two tins filled with tiny worms and little grubs and even a couple of slim grasshoppers. We now had bait.

When the rods were all set up and the bait gathered, the older ones finished their beer—the Old Man slapping the bottom as he turned the bottle upside down—and joined us. Everyone who was going to fish selected a rod.

"Go ahead," said the young man who had taken me off to cut the saplings. "Take your pick."

I pretended to know what I was doing. I took one of the shorter rods, checked it for flex and set off to join with the gang headed for the creek. It took only about a half dozen steps, however, before I realized that this was not going to be a case of tramping to the water and slamming a floater down on the rippled surface. They were *sneaking* up, as if the creek could somehow run away with its water. They were now silent, no one speaking, everyone stepping softly, spreading out, slipping into the bush in both directions and quickly out of sight and sound. It was as if they had never been there.

"We'll try here," said the young man who seemed to be in charge of me.

"Okay," I said, and moved closer to the water.

He grabbed my shoulder. "You'll spook 'em," he said.

I let him lead. It was, to me, an astonishing way to fish. Not only had we come here without any equipment, now we were moving up on the creek in a manner I had seen the Old Man use only when hunting for grouse. I almost giggled, imagining L'Amable Creek suddenly taking flight and our pounding hearts with it. It was amazing to watch the young man. He held up his hand to identify exactly where the shadows were falling, then circled around to ensure that he came up on the creek's edge in such a way that no shadow would betray him. In fact, he didn't even go to the very edge, stopping well back from the water and kneeling to set his line with bait. I did the same, trying unsuccessfully to look as if I knew exactly what I was doing. Bernard Wicksteed had tried the same trick with, I suppose, this young man's relative, but it hadn't worked for him either.

We went on trolling for more than an hour without feeling anything on the line. Joe tested the tension with his hand and said he thought I had dirt on the hooks. It took some minutes to wind in the 150 feet of not very pliable copper wire, and when the lure came in sight it was heavy with old leaves and sticks. How long they had been on I do not know. Most of the time the line had been out, perhaps. Judging by the look Joe gave me that is what he thought. He was the man doing all the work. My part was but to sit in the canoe with the rod in my hands and hook the fish when it took the bait. Not only had I been unsuccessful, but, in Joe's opinion, stupid as well.

Without a word or even a look of condemnation, the young man then set up my rod, even putting a small worm on as bait, which I took as a deep insult. But I said nothing. He was in charge, and even if I could bait my own hook, I was out of my element here. This was not the bridge on the road into Hay Lake.

When we were set up, he led the way in, creeping closer but carefully keeping bushes between him and the water. He had the line spun high on the rod tip, so that there was only a foot or two between tip and worm, and it hardly seemed enough to me. He stabbed the rod carefully through an opening in the bushes, held it steadily over the black water of L'Amable, and then began spinning the rod in his hands so that the line slowly worked its way down and onto the surface of the creek and in. He indicated that I should do the same at the next opening to his right, and I moved quietly to do so, copying him exactly.

We were in the water only a moment, it seemed, before he very steadily, very quietly, lifted his rod and pulled it back through the woods, a flipping, silvery, rainbow-splash of speckled trout rattling through the leaves of the bush and flipping wildly on the ground. He plucked it off the hook, snapped its neck deftly and used his finger to hook the little worm out of the shivering fish's gaping mouth. Quickly, he broke off a pussywillow sapling and stuck it through the fish's gills, tossing the fish far enough back that even if it miraculously came to life again, it couldn't make it back to the water. He threaded the little worm back on the hook, spun the line closer to the tip and stabbed it back through the bush.

I was watching all this when my first trout hit. It felt odd, the alder rod not nearly as sensitive as the store-bought rods I was used to. But there was no doubt it was a fish. I had no reel, however. I pulled up, panicking, and bumped the rod on an overhead branch, dislodging the little trout which fell back into the creek with a loud slap.

"Take it easy," my fishing partner hissed. He didn't seem cross. But he did seem firm.

I let the hook dip down again and waited. Another fish was at it almost immediately. I waited, felt the line pull tightly and lifted steadily, the hook catching. I immediately hauled back, drawing rod and line and fish through the opening, and dropped the wet fish wriggling into my lap. I had him, my foot keeping him down. I took him off the hook and tried to snap his neck the way I had just seen it done, but I couldn't do it. I placed him on the pussy-willow string and left him flapping and jumping far enough away that he would expire long before he'd ever drag stick and dead companion back to the water.

My companion already had another out and on the ground. A larger speckle this time, its colour stunning in the light that dappled down through the trees. He had it off and on the stringer—all three necks now broken—and his line back in the water as fast as I could get mine in. A moment later, we both had trout on.

It was the most incredible fishing I had ever seen and remains the most amazing day of fishing I have ever known. Because I was eight years of age, I committed the number of speckles caught to memory: 121. And I still marvel to think that a few people with rods they had all but invented on the spot could accomplish so much in so little time.

We had three pussywillow strings of speckles to carry back. Some people were already at the clearing; others came behind us. They placed the speckles in a pile, everyone standing back, admiring and laughing. It remains, as well, the only great fishing success I have ever witnessed where no one had a camera, but no one even expressed regret at not having one. Taking photographs of lunch and dinner seemed to be something not done by the Lavalleys. Perhaps it was because the speckles were so small; most of them were only six inches long, a few as long as perhaps ten.

The women cleaned the little fish, tossing guts into the fire and, from time to time, farther away in the clearing, where already gulls were circling overhead with their anxious calls. The fish were cleaned, but with the tails and heads left on and no effort made to remove the bones.

The older man, the one Duncan had had the beer with, had the huge skillet out and over the fire and was dumping in a large tin of butter. The butter sizzled and bubbled and blackened and hissed. It seemed to me as if he had accidentally put too much in the pan, for it seemed a cauldron of butter, but this, apparently, was exactly the way he wanted it. He dropped in several of the speckled—head, tails, bones and all.

The women had large loaves of bread out and were slicing them on a board, thicker slices than I had ever seen. They looked big enough, and soft enough, to sleep on. There was pop out, and black tea boiling in an open pot. And boiled eggs to crack and eat whole. There were plates, real china, and everyone took one and lined up with their sliced bread and empty plates. The older woman came and pasted butter all over my bread. She said it would make the fish taste better. But all I could think about was the bones. When we ate the larger lake trout, I always claimed the tail, which held none of the little bones that had once caught in the old ranger's throat and almost sent him to the grave much earlier than turned out to be the case. The panic that swept that day through the log house at Lake of Two Rivers had terrified me. They stuffed bread down him. He wheezed and coughed and choked and spit up and went outside and sat, buckled over, on the kindling block, spitting and choking and hacking and looking pale as the fish's belly, until, finally, with one last hack, the bone dislodged and flew out onto the grass. Ever since, I had been as afraid of fish bones as I was of the wolves that were lying in wait beneath the outhouse seat.

When my turn came, the older man placed four or five nice-sized speckles on my bread, the grease and burned butter staining the bread black as he spooned them in. I looked at Dunc.

"Go ahead," he said. "Indian style."

The other man howled with laughter. Over the fish and fire smells, I could smell more beer.

I placed the other piece of bread over my death sandwich and turned to see what everyone else was doing. They all had the same sandwich I did, heads sticking out one end, tails the other. And they were all staring at me, waiting for the guest to begin.

I picked up the huge sandwich and bit in from the side. I do not believe I had then, nor have I since, ever eaten anything that exploded with such desire in my mouth. Never had bread or butter or fish tasted so good. I chewed long and carefully. *Where were the bones?*

I could hardly wait for the next bite. I bit in, my eyes closed, and felt the grease and butter and fish run out my mouth and down my chin. I chewed, aware now that there were small bones, but they had all the substance of sardine bones and were instantly forgotten. I ate the entire sandwich, carefully avoiding the heads.

"You can eat them, too, you know," my fishing partner said, jabbing at my plate with his knife.

"I know," I lied.

I scraped the heads into the fire and took a second sandwich, each bite as good as or better than the last. There were pies out now, large sweet-smelling raspberry and blueberry pies, and they were being cut into huge slices and dumped right onto the same plates that were still black and slippery from the fish. I took raspberry, and it seemed the mixture made it even more delicious.

We stayed in the clearing all afternoon. I—and, it seemed most of the others—had a little nap in the sun. The fire kept away the mosquitoes. I could hear the women cleaning up. I could hear the old men talking about people I vaguely knew and laughing, and every now and then, a beer cap would pop and hiss and bubble with hot foam coming over. I could even hear them blowing it off.

Finally we gathered up the stuff they had brought in. The young man I had fished with took the skillet to the creek and cleaned it out with coarse sand, the skillet as clean as if it had been done with soap and a copper sponge. They doused the campfire and packed up the cooking supplies and the uneaten food and the empty beer bottles and started to head back down the long trail to where the cars were parked.

The young men were snipping the fishing line off the poles and rolling up the lines and leaders and hooks. The poles they tossed back under some wide spruce skirts.

"Aren't you going to keep them?" I asked.

"We'll keep 'em here," my new friend said.

It struck me that he was storing them. Not tossing them, but putting them away as one might set something in a garage. They knew where they had left the rods. And the rods, of course, were where the fish were.

The bush was taking on a new face for me. We had taken nothing in, yet everything had been there when we got there. The bush had provided fun and friends and fish; we had eaten and been warm; no one had been worried or frightened, or wanted to be anywhere else apart from exactly where we were. And we could come anytime and find the poles where we had left them and the fish where they should be. From that moment on, and still today, I have always been more content in the bush than anywhere else.

"How'd you like your day?" the Old Man asked as we rolled the windows down to cool off the seats.

"I loved it," I said.

"Did you learn something?"

"Yeah, lots," I said.

We could have been talking about cutting poplar poles or catching trout. We could have been talking about other things we never did actually talk about—then or ever again. Perhaps because there was never again anything to say.

Bernard Wicksteed had come here with another Lavalley and had, evidently, cherished his time in the bush. Still, he was glad to be out of it when the fishing trip with Joe Lavalley came to a close. "I sat there with a stiff neck and soaked to the skin," the Englishman wrote. "The rain splashed through a hole in the roof and fell in cold drops on my face. I had an eight-day beard and hadn't had a hot bath or a drink for a week." He was delighted to return to Highland Inn, where he moved quickly in out of the rain and fell into conversation with a couple of railway men who were also waiting out the weather.

'Curse the bush,' said one of the railway men. 'I hate every minute of it. I won't be happy until the company sends me back to a section in the city. Any city, so long as there are houses and not trees.'

Old Joe Lavalley, of course, heard none of this. He was already busy chatting up his next "client," telling him he used a lure that he'd made from a cigarette case he'd taken off a dead German. He was getting more supplies and was already packing up for his next trip into the bush where he would very soon die of "innergestion." *Praise the bush,* he would have said, *I love every minute of it. I won't be happy until I get back to the portages and trout streams. Anywhere in the bush, so long as there are trees and not houses.*

The way I have felt since the summer I turned eight.

CHAPTER FOUR

Duncan MacGregor and Helen McCormick on their wedding day, January 27, 1943. In the days before that interfering third party—money—came between them.

On a warm summer's day in 1996, Don McCormick, a cousin who is much more a brother, and I took Helen back to that rocky point on Lake of Two Rivers. It was, she said, her eighty-first birthday present, and she was going home. On August 5, 1915, Helen McCormick had been born at Brûlé Lake, Algonquin Park; born, according to her older sister, Mary, in a summer tent on a day so sweltering that their father, the park ranger, dipped blankets into the cold Algonquin Park water and hung them from the tent struts to cool down the birthing area. Many years later, when Helen had to apply for a birth certificate in order to obtain a Canadian passport, it had proved almost impossible. There had been no registration; there were no documents, nothing. Eventually, after several submissions and the discovery of a faded baptismal certificate, she had been issued one stating that she had been born Helen Geraldine McCormick somewhere in sprawling, unpopulated Ontario Township, precise location unknown. It was all proof, she felt, that Algonquin Park is indeed a world apart.

She wanted, one more time, to sit under the high pines that sing over the long and narrow point that cleaves the north shore of the lake. There was no longer any clearing to pull into, so we had to park on the shoulder of the newly paved Highway 60, which heads through the park corridor. There was no longer the tiny corduroy bridge over the creek; no longer, for that matter, the little creek where once beer grew wild when the Mick's Yankees were playing the Duke's Dodgers and the crackling, fading-in-and-out call of Mel Allen could be heard against the rumble of the bull-frogs, the rhythmic, four-note hoot of the barred owl along the bluff and the random howl of the wolves on the far shore. The path was gone now, overgrown and lost to all but those who knew every stone and root by memory. It had been more than sixty years since the old ranger had put up the first of three little cabins on the perfect point that lay at the end of what had once been an idyllic, perfectly groomed trail. Back then, it was a trail with a log bridge over the creek; a boardwalk over the marshy spots; a long, slanted rock that took you down the last hill and past the rasp-berry stand to the tall white spruce, where the path opened up to a view of the stunning two-storey log house the old ranger had built with his own hands in the late 1930s and finished on another August day in 1940.

They had lived at Lake of Two Rivers through the late 1930s and 1940s and spent half of every year there until 1962, when the old ranger's heart gave out in his eightieth year and on the very day of his and Bea's fifty-first wedding anniversary. Bea tried to keep on during summers, but it was the most awkward time possible. Tom and Bea McCormick's five children, Helen included, were all busy with young families, and apart from a stretch of a few weeks here and a few weekends there, the log home and cabins were unused. The children squabbled over what to do with the property. All had need of money, some desperately. Helen, who had lived there most, both before and after her marriage to Duncan, wanted to keep it in the family, but she had no money to pay off the others. None of the fourteen grandchildren was old enough to step in, which certainly would have happened if this crisis had only come a decade later. The old ranger could not, it turned out, have picked a worse time to die. His children argued over what to do with his Algonquin treasure until, finally, those who wished to keep it going gave in and the place was hastily sold to a retired manufacturer from Erie, Pennsylvania, for five thousand dollars. A similar summer home on an equivalent point and southern exposure in nearby Muskoka would go for millions today.

The spectacular location had been Tom McCormick's reward from the Department of Lands and Forests for work well done. He had been in the park since 1907, working for the McLaughlin Lumber Company and running the log drives down the Petawawa and the Ottawa Rivers each spring. He had married in 1911 and taken his new bride, Beatrice O'Dowd, a tiny, energetic Irish Catholic who had married into the Anglican Church, off to live at Brûlé Lake, a Booth line depot deep in the heart of the park. All five of their children were born there—Mary in 1912, Helen in 1915, Roy in 1917, Irvine in 1918 and Tom in 1920—and all survived. In 1917, Tom McCormick joined the lands and forests and rose to become head fire ranger and, eventually, chief ranger of Algonquin Park. He had blazed the trail that became Highway 60. And the old ranger, with his great love of walking, had planned out and cut most of the hiking trails for which the park would eventually become so famous. As a small bonus after the highway had been completed, he was given permission to build a home in the park proper. He knew immediately where he would choose.

The property, however, had never been deeded. Like all other cottages in the park, it was held on a yearly lease, the land remaining the property of the Crown. The leases were cheap, but not without worry. At the time the old ranger's log home was put up for sale, there was already a simmering movement to rid the park of its few leaseholders and return the cottage properties to pristine nature. The new American owner took over a lease that would run out in a few years; he panicked and took the log home down, numbered the logs and moved them out of the park to Muskoka, where they were reassembled on a new property that bore not the slightest resemblance to the rocky point at Lake of Two Rivers. No sooner was the building reconstructed than the park authorities reconsidered and decided to extend the leases until the year 2017. The cottagers, the government seemed to decide, had a value not previously recognized. They were, after all, like a free summer police patrol in the park, quick to report and act on abuse and determined to keep the paths and portages clear of garbage and damage. It was too late, however, for the American, and far, far too late for the grandchildren of the old ranger, several of whom continued to come to the rocky point each summer for a day of swimming and pretending. So long as they kept staring out over the water, nothing had ever changed.

In fact, so long as one's line of vision kept to the water and rocky shoreline, little had changed since David Thompson made his way through the park in the fall of 1837. "East-southeast wind," Thompson recorded in his journal on October 10 of that year, "dark, cloudy. This appears a place of Indian resort. Came to a young Indian watching for deer in crossing the lake. He informed us that a tent of Indians was near hand. To the Indian tent—here we found an old Indian of the name of Cha Unde. He told us we were on the middle branch or proper Madawaska River, that no white man had been on it, that it was the shortest, best and had the most waters of the three branches, which form the main stream. I wanted him to give me a sketch of the north branch, which he declined but procured from him a sketch of the river lakes and [places to set up camp] for some distance. He advised us to be careful in the rapids, adding that when you are below them there is no more danger." Thompson had crossed the Algonquin watershed and was now paddling, effortlessly, into Lake of Two Rivers. "Current going with us, thank God," he wrote. It felt that way then, and still feels that way today for those of us who come here and sit and think about those things that matter more than others.

On the day my mother, my cousin and I walked in through the tangle, there had been no one living on the point for more than a quarter of a century. The logs on the creek and boardwalk had rotted away. Trees had fallen and never been cleared. The undergrowth had spread and tangled until the path itself had vanished into memory. Fortunately, memory recalled the steps, and partly on instinct, partly by invention, we pushed through, slipping on moss and rotting timber and, yes, princess pine, our breath gagging on broken fungi and overturned rock moss and churned bog, branches in our faces and raspberry bushes scraping our legs and spruce and cedar limbs blocking our every step. A few times Helen's bad leg—she had broken her knee in a fall several winters before—refused to work for her, and Don and I had to carry her, one gripping her legs, one under her arms, beneath leaning trees and over rotting logs. She laughed at her own helplessness, but insisted on pressing on, perhaps sensing it would be her final visit to the place she cared about more than any other on earth.

We came out at the shoulder of the reaching point, and there it opened up enough to walk normally. We could trace, partly by rocks, largely by imagination, where the workshed and the nearest sleeping cabin had once stood. We could trace the foundation of the log home by the rocks and pilings it had once rested on; and by the rubble left, we found where the fireplace had once stood. We had not been there for years, but it was far from our first time rooting around in the debris. We had all previously taken home stones from the fireplace—exquisite quartz stones flecked with mica, hand-selected by the old ranger from the shoreline of the lake—and we had once found lying at the root of a new cedar, in perfect shape, his blue shaving mug. Not a chip on it. And after a bit more rooting about, we had come up with a piece of trim from the roof, a cedar board on which, at the end, the builder had taken a sharp pencil and written, "Thomas I. McCormick, Sept. 10, 1940." The day the artist finished, and signed, his great masterpiece.

We spent more time kicking around the abandoned grounds. Up by where the outhouse had once stood, I found a long, coiled pipe, the exhaust from the old gasoline-fired washing machine, and I carried it back like a happy retriever and dropped it at the foot of Helen, who was sitting on a rock, resting. She recognized it immediately, but with mixed feelings. Proof that she had lived here, yes, but proof, as well, that her memories were coupled with work while ours were of play only. When she wasn't cooking she was cleaning. Every Monday she had had to drag out the old washing machine, carry the water in splashing pails up a steep rise from the lake, mix the oil and gasoline, funnel it in and choke and fire up the burping, roaring engine so she could wash and squeeze the clothes and bedsheets and then do it twice all over again for rinse. Work, and worry that somewhere hidden in the noise of the awful machine, a baby might be crying, a child might be calling for help off the deep end of the high rocks. When the washing machine ran, no one was allowed near the lake, except to load water in pails and carry it up the hill to the burping machine and the sweating, fretting woman who had the impossible task of keeping her own four children and usually another four or five of their cousins clean. No wonder she didn't laugh that day when she dipped her hand in to clean out her husband's pockets and came up with a writhing garter snake.

It had been thirty-five years since the old washing machine had rattled the silence and the sighing winds of the rocky point. She smiled weakly at the old exhaust pipe and then I carried it back into the bush and hid it in a thick spruce tree where, slowly, it would grow out of reach and beyond memory. Perhaps a future generation of tourists will be puzzled when, one day, a giant spruce falls here and a long, twisted exhaust pipe from a washing machine tumbles out of the crown. Will anyone know that once there was a family here? Would they believe that life went on here in the dead of winter, as well, when a young woman and her mother could be stuck for a month at a time with only their own company while the old ranger went out on patrol? Would these park visitors, who shiver together two thousand strong each evening during the ranger-conducted wolf howls, believe that each day in those winters, simply to fill the time, that young woman would strap on her skis and head out alone to strike seven miles through the bush and hills to Cache Lake, where she would wait for the mail train and the chance of a letter, and then ski home again in the failing light, sometimes not arriving back at the lonely point until dark had fallen and the yips and yelps were just beginning along the bluffs? Would they believe, when today's rangers talk about the noble and misunderstood wolf, that there was a time when the Algonquin Park rangers were instructed to shoot wolves and even poison them and would often, for mere sport, prop up the frozen bodies of the animals in the snow, leaving them in attack position to startle any trapper, ranger, logger or unsuspecting cross-country skier who might happen along?

We spent a lot of time being quiet after that, alone with our thoughts. In the last year, Helen had lost her husband and her only daughter. At eighty years of age, she had nursed Ann, at home, to the very last breath, the way both had wished it to end, and not once had anyone seen either of them cry. They say there is nothing worse than losing a child. They can say it, but saying so doesn't come close to describing what it must feel like, certainly not at the moment of death and likely not in those moments that follow, when memory is forced where it is not quite sure it is ready yet to step. This rocky point, after all, held so much more than a difficult washing machine that neither mind nor book could contain all at once. Here was where Ann had been a baby in the late 1940s. Here was where she learned to swim off the massive floating dock the old ranger had built with logs he hauled across the lake from the McRae mill. Here was where Ann had built an entire village, then country, then world, out of moss and small stones and a protected pool of water where she kept crawfish and dragonfly larvae and perch minnows so tiny and transparent you could see right into their organs and needle-thin spines. Here was where she would lie under the hissing Coleman light and read Lucy Maud Montgomery. Here was where we played Monopoly and cribbage and put together thousand-piece puzzles. Here was where she learned her lovely crawl stroke and where she would dive from the high rocks so elegantly and precisely that when she struck the water, it was more like a knife nicking it than, as it was in my case, legs and head and arms tackling it. Here was still the huge, flat rock where Ann had held her family-famous tea parties. Here were the shallows where, one summer day in 1956, she heard a splash just off the boardwalk out to the floating dock, went to see if it was a large bass or just the big snapping turtle rolling off the logs and found our two-year-old brother, Tommy, dancing in slow motion along the bottom. He would have drowned had Ann not dived in and pulled him to the surface in time.

Drowning was always the great fear. I once fell off the slanted rocks on the other side of the point, and Jim rescued me as I grabbed and slid helplessly on the slippery, moss-covered rocks. There were often canoers from the nearby campgrounds tipping over and calling for help, and someone would have to go out and haul them out of the water and tow their canoe back in to set it right and send them back off again, this time at least sitting in the correct position. Once, in a terrible wind, the old ranger had watched through binoculars while foolhardy paddlers on the far side of the lake tried to cross to the east branch of the Madawaska River, where they could continue in shelter. They went over and, lifejacketless, clung to the overturned, bobbing canoe while they screamed for help. They most certainly would have drowned had not Dunc and an older cousin, Hugh McCormick, braved the high swells in the little fishing boat, Dunc ploughing through the waist-high waves while Hugh bailed. They very nearly went down themselves, but returned, somehow, with two terrified, shaking canoeists that we dried out and gave coffee to. Then Duncan and Hugh, who would die shortly after in a car accident, drove them and their canoe back to the campgrounds. Nothing was ever made of the rescue, though today they likely would have been given special medals. Nothing was even said of it, for that matter.

Dunc himself had almost drowned, for the second time in his life, in these early years when the McRae mill was located at Hay Lake. He had struck out one foggy morning before dawn and, in the dark and fog, had caught the shoulder as the gravel road passed by a small lake. The car was thrown into water more than ten feet deep. He remembered reading in a book that people drown in their cars because of panic and exhaustion from trying to push doors that cannot open against the force of the water. He sat peacefully waiting for the car to fill up with water before opening the door and swimming up and out to safety. Having put his trust in books, he lived to read again.

It had been years since Helen was back on this point. But I come every year, usually with Ellen and the four children, and we all swim and dive from the high rocks out into the cold, tea-coloured waters, Ann's elegant, splashless style found in the one who would one day win a provincial championship in diving. They would use the same toe- and handholds that Jim and Ann and Tom and I once used to climb out and dive back in, and that before that Helen had used in the long summers when she had lived here with her mother and father. Family tree be damned; this family can trace itself through rock. After diving for an hour or more, we all swim out to the first rocks that surface in the lake—the shoal we called the Duck Rock—and there we tread water in a circle, catch our breath, hold hands and sink down together, down, down into the darkening Lake of Two Rivers water until our natural buoyancy catches and we stare at each other and shout and try to guess what each one is saying. The words don't matter. The shouting does. It signals that we are still here.

The last time I came here had been at the end of a long visit with Ann in Huntsville. She was slipping. It was long past the stage of denial or hope or wishing for miracles. It was mid-September, a magnificent Indian summer day in the park, with the birch and poplar leaves already yellow and the maples just beginning to take fire. The park was emptied of tourists—school back in, the camps closed—and I had taken my time travelling through. There were two moose at the Cache Lake turn and a white-tailed deer on the long hill heading down towards Lake of Two Rivers. I stopped and walked out along the rocky shoreline to a point where I could climb up, using roots and old, familiar footholds, to the descending crest of the long point.

I came out to the point to look for Ann's rock world. I knew where she had built her first village back of the old ice house, and I wanted to gather up a handful of memories for her. We had been talking a lot about Lake of Two Rivers, and several times she had mentioned the magical village she had built over long summers in the mid-1950s. The area, however, was now stunningly overgrown, thick cedar and scratching pine making movement difficult, but I kicked the thin pine-needled soil until a few small coin-like stones turned up. Once, I presumed, they had been steps to a castle where everyone was supposed to live happily ever after.

With my pockets bulging with the little stones, I headed back out to the tip of the point and stood listening to the wind in the high pines and the lake soft and slapping beneath the granite over-hang where we used to dive. It has always struck me as not quite accurate when it is said that taste and smell are the most acute memory triggers. For some of us, anyway, it is sound. From here you could sometimes hear the Scot at the far end of the lake who liked to play the bagpipes under a full moon. You could pick up the three-horsepower Evinrude as it roared to full speed at the end of an evening troll along the far shore. Sounds that will forever hurl me back to that time, that place. The slam of a screen door. The snap of burning spruce and the entirely different snap a flag makes in a wind that is forever out of the west. That sound seems to linger on at the foot of the point where the old ranger erected his flag pole by painting a long, trimmed cedar white and locking it into the rocks with wooden supports and long crib bolts. Here was where he would bring one of us just as the sun set, the old ranger in uniform; we would be expected to stand at attention as he lowered the Union Jack each night and then, one on each side, carefully fold it in military fashion, God be with you if you dropped a corner and it happened to kiss the rocks. There is no sign of the pole any longer, but the snap and shudder of the flag will always be in the air.

I was hardly alone in my memories about this very spot. In one of the many books that Duncan had left behind in that upstairs bedroom in Huntsville, he had scribbled a story he called "The

Interloper" down the margins of a couple of tobacco-flecked pages. "Jim and I were at the point watching five loons, three male loons and two females," he wrote. "They were raising the devil about something. Anyway, all at once two male loons turned on the other male and attacked him savagely. They killed him right there while the two female loons watched the fight. We were very close to them and saw the whole fight. Then the two couples went on their way apparently quite happy that they had got rid of an unwanted suitor. You see, loons have their laws, too, just the same as we humans do, and they seek justice in the wild world."

I remember the moment, if not the year. I remember how Jim and Dunc already had the boat down the roller and into the water by the time Ann and I hit the dock, and how we had to leap into the bow as Jim pushed off. They hadn't even bothered with the outboard. Dunc rowed, hard and deep, the locks groaning and the water splashing Jim in the stern as one oar slipped. We could see the one loon floating while the other four kept their distance and called angrily and rose on the water to flex their wings and flash their white bellies in defiance. Dunc rolled up his sleeve and dipped in and pulled out the loon by its limp neck, dropping it in a splash and a thud on the floorboards of the boat in front of where Ann and I were sitting. None of us had ever seen a dead loon before. I grabbed it by the neck as the Old Man had, and pulled, but could not even raise it. It was two or three times heavier than I had ever imagined, a huge, thick, heavy bird with the loveliest, smoothest, whitest feather covering along the breast. Its eyes were wide open and it looked to be sleeping, except for the fact that the neck had no support. If we raised the bird's head and let it go, the neck fell back onto the body like the sleeve of a dropped shirt. We could not speak. Loons, with their perfect little families, their single, sometimes double chicks on their backs, their constant calling and worrying, had always seemed the perfect creatures to be around. We had watched them dive after minnows, sometimes lying on the high rocks on a clear day with our heads over the edge so we could watch them "fly" underwater as they fished the shallows. We had never imagined cruelty or violence a part of their makeup. We were too young to see, as Duncan had obviously seen, that they were merely reacting to invasion—perhaps not so differently than little Bea McCormick would have done when she saw a black bear or, worse, an uninvited tourist walking down the path towards the log house on the end of the point.

It was to this very spot I came that September day to think about Ann. The wind was blowing hard, but the day was warm, the water surprisingly like summer when I plunged a hand in up to the forearm. I stood, feeling more sorry for myself than I had any right to, when suddenly the wind plucked off my baseball cap and flung it, spinning and swooping, off the end of the Duck Rock. It immediately began to drift, well out into the deeper water.

I hated to lose that hat. A good friend had mailed it to me, a souvenir of a minor-league baseball team in which he had purchased a small share, a moment that meant to him what buying a home along the Maine coast must mean to others. It had barely been worn, and I wanted it back. In a foolish moment, all alone in the middle of Algonquin Park with fall coming on, I decided to go after it. I took off my shirt, sneakers, socks and pants, careful not to spill my pocketful of castle steps. Since there was no one around, and the drive through to Ottawa was still three hours to go, I quickly dropped my underwear as well, to keep it dry, and stood, momentarily wondering if I had taken leave of my senses, buck naked on the end of the point.

I dove out, thinking of Ann and trying to travel in that lovely, graceful arc that was her own signature. Crashing into the light ripple of deep water that lay in the protection of the rocks, I stayed low and deep for as long as I dared. I was struck by the familiarity of the water, every molecule with a certain feel, the taste and odour of the lake as remembered as a mother's arms. I kicked, delighting in the startle of nakedness in September waters, and surfaced gasping, the blue cap bobbing in the higher waves beyond the natural breakwater of the long point. I began swimming, hoping for Ann's or Jim's practised crawl but living with my own flailings, and gained quickly on it, diving under at the last moment and attempting, unsuccessfully, to come up under the cap so it fit my head perfectly.

The hat in one hand, I made my way back towards the point, the current going with me, as Thompson had said, and thank God. I came to the rocks and found the familiar hand- and footholds, but the rocks were slippery with lack of use and I needed both hands free. I pulled the wet cap hard over my head, locking it in place, and began again the climb up the rocks.

Perhaps it was the way the wind was blowing, for I was certain that I heard something other than the pines. I stopped, head just over the high rocks, wet cap yanked down around my ears, and found myself staring at an older woman and a younger woman, both with hiking clothes on, just working their way through the spruce. I could hear them talking. German. Late-summer visitors who couldn't resist trying to make their way out to the entrancing point they must have seen from the nearby picnic grounds.

I slipped down and back into the water without a splash. Ann would have been impressed. I swam quickly away, in tight to the high rocks and out of their sightlines. I treaded water, worried they would look over the cliff and see a naked man in a baseball cap and wondering if the tea-coloured water would keep my secret if they happened to look. But soon I could hear no more talk, and when I swam out deeper and could look back onto the point, I saw nothing. They had vanished into the spruce cover as suddenly as they had appeared.

The Eganville Senior Hockey Team, 1927–28. Duncan is third
from the right, hair split straight down centre.

Christmas at Airy, 1947. Chief Ranger Tom McCormick and Bea at the head
of the table, Helen (holding Jim) and Dunc (holding Ann) stand behind.

Eganville Public School, circa 1915–1916. Dunc MacGregor,
back row, fourth from left, third to teacher's right.

Lumber baron
J.S.L. McRae
with Whitney
stationmaster, 1940s.

Helen, the cross-country skier, circa 1933.

Jim, Dunc, Ann and Roy ice fishing, Lake of Two Rivers, 1950.

Helen MacGregor returns to the point at Lake of Two Rivers.
The log home is long gone; a public beach is in the background.

Dunc's last fish,
August 21, 1990:
the indignity of a lawn
chair, the triumph of
a two-pound lake trout
on the very first pass.

*Bea McCormick and her
deer at Lake of Two Rivers.
Jim and Ann stand in front.*

*The old gang in Eganville: Front row—Irvine McCormick, Gertie Heintzman,
Roy McCormick, Betty Mills, Helen McCormick, Dunc MacGregor.*

The Brûlé Lake station, Algonquin Park, 1920s.
Brûlé Lake is now a ghost town.

Roy McCormick with
polio, Hospital for
Sick Children, Toronto,
1925. In some ways,
he never recovered.

Brûlé Lake had a year-round train, canoes in summer, and Ranger Tom McCormick's cutter in winter. The only other option was to walk.

Annie MacGregor, the resourceful one, with Jim in Airy, 1945.

Joe Lavally, or Lavalley, the poetic and eccentric guide of Algonquin Park.

Lake of Two Rivers Mill, circa 1938.

I scrambled up, hurried into my clothes and, now wet and shivering, worked my way back another direction to the road, where I found the car, fired up the heater and set out again for Ottawa, shirt clinging to my back. A week later, back to see Ann again, she laughed and laughed as I told her about the cap and the skinny dip and the two German women who nearly encountered some unexpected Algonquin Park wildlife. We talked on late into the night, Tom and Ann and I, Ann drifting in and out of the conversation as the morphine took effect, but she was lucid and funny and never once felt the slightest bit sorry for herself. We talked at length about the park and about dozens of other things, from her time at the University of Toronto to her years at *Maclean's* magazine, where she had found her glory and her calling as fact-checker and researcher extraordinaire—*Maclean's* renowned back-page columnist, Allan Fotheringham, called her "my guardian angel"—and at one point, in a lull of memories, I asked her what, in all her fifty years, had meant the most. There was no point in pretending at this stage.

"Oh," she said, as if it was a foolish question even to consider. "Lake of Two Rivers, of course."

Duncan MacGregor was already at Lake of Two Rivers when Tom McCormick began building his cabins and log home on the point of the shore opposite J.S.L. McRae's new mill. The 1930s were a time of far more activity in Algonquin Park than is found today. The Booth line was still running through daily, carrying grain from the West, timber from the mills, American tourists for the lodges and supplies for the lumber camps and work brigades. The road the old ranger had blazed was now open to traffic, and a new visitor was beginning to reach the park: less well-off but more adventurous tourists, anxious for cheap camping and disdainful of the fancy china and teas served at places like Highland Inn a few miles up the tracks at Cache Lake. Two Rivers along the west side had the perfect beach shoreline for campers, and the first large campsite went in there. The little airstrip was finished, meaning any small planes heading for Algonquin Park had only the one location to land. Lake of Two Rivers was almost a community unto itself. A lodge, Killarney, was up on a point across the bay from the long point the old ranger was building on. A half-dozen others, mostly American, had leases on towards the east shore, where the Madawaska River once again began to flow. And the McRae mill on the south shore was in full production, with more than two hundred men living and working there, the far shore of the lake often covered with log booms and the mill burner filling the air with thick white smoke from the bark and wood chips and sawdust that was then the detritus of timber production.

Tom and Bea McCormick were returning to the park after nearly seven years in Eganville, where they had gone so their five children could attend school. The children had all been born in the deep bush of Algonquin and had received their early education in the park at Brûlé Lake, north and west along the Booth line beyond Canoe Lake, but their need to attend higher grades had forced the family to leave for Eganville, the farthest from the park boundaries a chief ranger dared venture to live. There was a school in Eganville, and the final year of high-school was available in nearby Renfrew, reachable by morning train, with another train home at night. The McCormicks had left the park with mixed feelings. Tom McCormick had spent twenty-five straight years in the bush, first clerking and taking care of the horses for the McLaughlin Lumber Company, then as a fire ranger and now as chief ranger. For the children, it had been an idyllic existence—skating and hockey on the lake in winter, canoeing and fishing all summer. They kept horses and milk cows, chickens, a goat and often pigs. There were always big, long-haired dogs able to pull sleighs over the winter trails or, in a pinch, chase pucks on the lake when a shot from the rink area the old ranger would mark out and flood careered off across the bay towards the thinner ice where a small creek came in. Once, the three boys went through the ice together but somehow managed to scramble out before the cold numbed them to the point where they could not help themselves.

Their Irish luck, however, had not always held. After a fishing trip on a cold, wet September day in 1922, five-year-old Roy— called Boyo by the family—came down with a terrible cold that worsened to the point where it seemed they might lose him. Dr. Wilfrid Pocock had come in from Kearney on the train when Roy's legs stiffened, and soon it was known that Roy, the handsomest, liveliest one of the lot, had polio.

Roy spent more than five years at Sick Children's Hospital in Toronto. He had so many operations on his legs that the family eventually lost count. A volunteer, a Mr. Smedley, took over Roy's life and, in summer, would bring him back for a month at the lake, where the sickly boy would lie suspended in a hammock while Helen read to him and changed his bandages. Every week the family had to come up with $10.30, which they sent by train to Sick Kids for his care. On a ranger's salary, Tom McCormick could barely afford the weekly cost. Fortunately, the family's needs at Brûlé Lake were minimal. Housing was supplied, Bea kept gardens, the chickens produced eggs every day, the pigs fattened, the cows gave good milk and the rangers always had fresh game and fish.

The real cost, however, was to Roy. He lost his childhood. And even though he would largely regain his physical health, he would never really recover from the trauma of being ripped from his family and taken to a faraway place where a much-older weekly visitor, Mr. Smedley, sought to be father, brother and best friend all at once. Much like Native children who were sent off to residential schools and saw their families, with luck, once a year, Roy was essentially on his own, forced to live by his wits and luck. He became, for life, an extraordinary charmer, able to get the Sick Kids' staff to do anything he wished and even able to make contact with the street kids who lived in the area and frequented busy University Avenue. He would get a few coins in the mail from Brûlé Lake, wrap them in an envelope and tie the envelope to a long string, then let the string out his third-floor window. A kid below would catch it and read the written message—"Get me some candy!"—and a few minutes later a tug would signal that he could pull up the string and his sweets would be wrapped in the envelope. If only everything else in his life, including himself, had proved so dependable.

It was only natural that when Roy did come home to visit, Helen was the one who would nurse him. As sometimes happened in rural families, particularly among the Irish, there was often a designated daughter whose lot in life was to stay on and help out. Mary, three years older than Helen, was pretty and pampered and as good a canoeist as any of the guides in the park. Much was expected of the gregarious eldest daughter and everything was done to accommodate her ambitions to become a schoolteacher. Helen was tall and shy, heavier than Mary but a good-hearted, friendly young woman who stoically accepted what appeared to be her future. She was not to have any higher ambition or, for that matter, want marriage, and was expected to be perfectly content to help out in the kitchen, aid with the raising of the younger ones, eventually take over the running of the house and, in the end, nurse her parents through their old age. This was what they saw for her; this what she saw for herself.

Had the McCormicks never left Algonquin Park for the children's schooling, she might never have known anything different, and might therefore not have wished for anything more. But for someone who had known nothing but the bush, Eganville was as different from the park as Oz was from Kansas. Helen had just turned seventeen when the family caught the last train running from Parry Sound to Ottawa. It was Labour Day, 1932, and the trestles near Cache Lake had just been condemned. Soon there would be no more regular runs through the park on the Booth line. They got off in Whitney, where Mary, who had already been boarding in Renfrew so she could attend school, struck out for the village of Madawaska and her first teaching job. Meanwhile the old ranger took the family by car to Eganville, where they would live, summers excluded, for the next several years.

The McCormicks rented a red-brick house just down from where Annie MacGregor was still living. The house had belonged to another long-time park ranger, a French-Canadian Catholic, and the McCormick's arrived with no idea of the ecclesiastical social structure of the little town. They were, like Annie MacGregor, Protestants on the Catholic side—though Bea McCormick, unknown to even her closest Eganville friends, had once been of the Church of Rome. The two families were friendly, but Annie MacGregor's children were all now out of the house and gone. The youngsters on the street were now the McCormicks—shy Helen, with her ready smile, and the three boys, Roy, Irvine and Tom, all keen on sports. Roy was fifteen now, out of Sick Kids for more than four years, and though he walked with a slight limp, he was so determined in hockey and baseball that few knew he had spent five years of his young life staring out the third-floor window of a Toronto hospital. Dark and handsome, with thick black hair and notorious charm, he was instantly the talk of the young women at the little Eganville school. Irvine was a skinny fourteen and also talked about, but because he seemed so scholarly. Tom was just twelve, but already said to be the spitting image of the big ranger after whom he was named.

Helen was so amenable, so helpful, so reluctant to press her moods on others, that the young women of Eganville quickly befriended her and she soon became an easy, unnoticed part of a large circle of friends. Helen was the ever-dependable friend, the one they could talk to about their own concerns without her trying to twist the conversation back to herself. She was loyal and likable, and those who sparkled in the little town—Betty Mills, daughter of the largest merchant, Mary Reeves, daughter of the revered town doctor—took her on as a faithful, happy best friend. Betty, beautiful and high-spirited, had her eye on a prize that connected through Helen as well: Roy. "I knew the second I saw him that I wanted him," she would say more than a half-century later. All the heartbreak that would come—her well-off father, a merchant, setting Roy up in the lumber business; Roy losing the businesses; the drinking; the gambling; the spectacular charm that, in the end, could not turn back the endless spiral down to his early death—was never able to erase the haunting dream of the Roy who could have been, indeed who sometimes was, but never for long enough. They had one child, Robert, who would grow into a fine man and a good father, but he barely knew his own father. The divorce had come decades earlier, and Roy had drifted away, eventually ending up a cab driver in Sault Ste. Marie and too soon dead from hard living. Betty, who found happiness in a second marriage, often said she never stopped loving him. Everyone else felt the same way.

The old photograph books are filled with the happy times in Eganville. The boys are handsome, with their high-necked sweaters, wide pleated pants, dark wavy hair and cocky cigarettes; the girls beautiful in summer dresses, calf-long pedal-pushers and tightly curled hair. They appear, in the photographs, to be endlessly clowning. In the winter, they ski and skate and toboggan. Dances every Saturday night. Dr. Reeves's cutter taking them off to hockey games in Douglas and Renfrew and Golden Lake; old Model T's heading out for summer ball games at Lake Clear and Killaloe. That first winter, with the Depression bringing a virtual halt to home-building and furniture production, the McRae mill closed down for several weeks and the men were all laid off. Duncan returned to his mother's home in Eganville that winter and again during a couple of other brief mill shutdowns that followed in those years.

Duncan's initial link with the McCormick family was not Helen, but Roy. They both loved sports, particularly hockey. Roy, who could barely skate with his bad leg, was an exceptional stick-handler and managed to play on the town team despite his disability. He was also good at baseball, and knew almost as much about the majors as Dunc himself. Roy was a quick study at virtually anything he tried. Following his return from Sick Kids, he had quickly made up for the lost years and soon was renowned for his bush skills. Even without a compass and topographical maps, he seemed to have a sixth sense of direction and location. In his later years, when the drinking had taken its obvious toll, Roy could still astonish with his ability to find his way through the bush. Our cousin, known as Jon Pigeon—Jake—learned to fly and bought a small bush plane in which he and Roy would sometimes seek out potential trout lakes that had never been visited. After one low flight over the terrain, they found they could land on a larger nearby lake, set up camp, and Roy, using only a compass, could lead them, even in the dead of night, into the little lake they had spied, so that they would be there by dawn, when the fishing is often best. None of us ever understood how he could do this. Perhaps he didn't either.

Duncan was older than Roy, but their love of the bush, sports, cards and drink soon made them fast friends, and with so many hanging around the big, warm McCormick house, with Helen busy in the kitchen feeding everyone who dropped in, he soon found himself part of the gang whenever he came back to see his mother. He and Helen got on well, but there was a difference of eight years in their ages. Neither thought for a moment that their friendship was anything other than that between two close neighbours.

Besides, there were a few months in the mid-1930s when it seemed that Duncan MacGregor had a diferent romantic interest in Whitney. He visited often with a young woman whose name was Marie, last name forgotten by all but him, and they were either engaged or close to engaged at one point, but the plans fell apart when her strict Catholic family stood in the way. He would not switch—he had, by that point, nothing to switch from and a barely hidden contempt for organized religion. The relationship fell apart soon after. Yet more than a half-century later, long after Marie had been widowed, she tracked him down from a senior-citizens' residence in Perth and, at one point, even showed up to see a play Tom had produced at the Perth Summer Theatre. But she never introduced herself, and Dunc and Marie never actually met again. There were, however, unexplained telephone bills, and at one point Helen unwittingly went to war with Bell Canada over a twenty-five-dollar charge to Perth that she said neither she nor anyone else in the house had certainly ever made. Bell eventually gave up arguing that it couldn't possibly be a mistake and dropped the charge from her phone bill. Though Dunc often said he wished he'd become a Westerner when he had the chance, he never once said the same thing about the Catholic Church.

The photographs that remain from those few years when the McCormicks lived in Eganville are almost always of gangs of young men and women together, Helen McCormick large and shy and always standing back. In a couple of the little black-and-white pictures, there is Duncan MacGregor, his face dark with the wind burn from outside work, standing off to the side. Neither of them ever at the centre, but neither excluded from the posed pictures of

Eganville in the 1930s. Summers on the Bonnechere; picnics up at the large Mills cottage on Golden Lake; canoe trips; deer eating out of their hands, pictures of favourite dogs and horses and, far too soon, the skinny boys and pretty girls in uniform, cigarettes still at a haughty, invulnerable tilt, the laughter of the cutter rides fading somewhere over the hills. Some of them wouldn't be coming home from war.

The impending war had a different effect on those working far back in the bush than on those in the towns and cities. The moment war preparation began, the need for wood, particularly birch, which was used in the manufacture of aircraft, went up. The mills around the park were suddenly back to full force and being asked to extend themselves further. Although in his later life Duncan would be a pacifist and an early, if unheard, critic of the Vietnam War, he was no different from almost all other young men in 1939, when Canada declared war. He wanted to do his part to help. Any thoughts of joining up, however, were soon laid to rest by a series of incidents. First, Donald McRae beat him, and everyone else, to the punch. Donald had fought with his father, J.S.L., over a minor incident and had set off to join the air force without permission. He got Dunc to come with him to Toronto, where they got gloriously drunk in the old Ford Hotel the night before Donald went into the service, leaving Duncan to explain to his furious brother-in-law why he had let his son go. Bushworkers, of course, were considered vital services workers by the government, and even if there were to be conscription, unheard of at that point in the war, they would be exempt. It was made loudly clear to Dunc that the mill could not afford to lose a second top man, and that he was to get any thoughts of joining Donald, wherever he was, out of his mind.

Donald was soon shot down and spent the entire war in a prisoner-of-war camp, the McRaes uncertain for months whether he was even alive. Marjorie McRae was also overseas, a driver in the ambulance corps. Any romance that war might have held for the young men of the valley was soon lost to alarming headlines and dreaded telegrams. The issue of Duncan's ever joining up was finally rendered moot the night his appendix exploded deep in the Algonquin Park bush and he was rushed by train back to Renfrew for emergency surgery. Another few hours' delay, he was told, and he would have died. Once he recovered, he returned to the mill at Lake of Two Rivers and went to work handling the high-priority birch shipments that were tagged for England and the manufacture of Mosquito fighters. The birch had to be of the highest grade, and he was now in charge of grading. So he was, in a small way, a part of the effort, and was undoubtedly glad, in the long run, that he hadn't spent the war in a prison camp wondering if he'd ever get back to Algonquin Park alive.

Some might be tempted to call it fate, others coincidence. There would be months in which Helen would think of it as her singular bad luck. But no matter how described, the fall of 1940 found Helen McCormick back living in the park with her parents, only no longer at Brûlé Lake. The log house at Lake of Two Rivers was now finished, and the old ranger, happy to be back in the bush, was off patrolling, leaving Helen all alone with her mother on the north side of the lake. On the southwest corner was the McRae mill, where Duncan MacGregor was all alone with his books. Mary had finished school and was teaching in Madawaska, where she boarded on the farm of a French-Canadian Catholic family, the Pigeons, fifteen children strong, and fell for one of the blue-eyed sons, Lorne. They were married and soon also back in the park. Lorne found summer work as a fire ranger and winter work keeping the bunkhouses for the railway and cutting ice for the lodges. Mary opened a school for her own two boys, Tom and Jon (Jake), and several of the rangers' children in the sitting room of their little white cottage in the bay just to the west of Highland Inn. It must have seemed, to the old ranger and Bea, that everything was happening just a little too quickly for Mary. At least they still had Helen, and Helen, of course, would be with them forever.

Helen's other siblings were also marrying. Irvine had married Gertie Heintzman of Whitney, the daughter of another longtime park ranger, George Heintzman. Tom had been taken on by the lands and forests ministry, and he was going to marry a local girl, Agnes Etmanski. Roy and Betty Mills were looking as if they'd one day be married. The world, it seemed, was passing Helen by. She carried water. She cooked. She did the laundry, the cleaning. She beat the carpets so hard she sometimes vanished in a cloud of dust out behind the new log home. She dug through the sawdust in the ice house for ice blocks and broke them free with tongs, washed them off and heaved them across to the ice box. She canoed when the ice was off the lake, and became a beautiful paddler, the McCormick's long, red, canvas-covered canoe whispering over the water as she went off on her own to explore the Madawaska and the far shore by the mill, alone with whatever thoughts might visit a young woman in her mid-twenties with no friends close by and, seemingly, no prospects. When the long Algonquin winter was upon them, she skied the five miles or so up to Cache Lake for the mail and, sometimes, a short visit with Mary and her struggling young family before skiing home in the fading light. When Duncan MacGregor began dropping by, handsome with his wind-burned face and red hair, witty with his stories of camp life and welcome with the fresh trout he so often brought with him, it seemed as if there might be life beyond an eternity with her parents in the log home on the point, no matter how picturesque it might seem to tourists.

They married in Eganville on January 27, 1943. It was a cold winter's day with a fresh fall of snow on the ground. Irvine acted as best man, Marjorie McRae, Donald's younger sister, as maid of honour. Annie MacGregor came, delighted to see her youngest son married, and Tom and Bea McCormick came, rather less than delighted. They had always believed Helen would be with them, *wanted* to be with them. She had, after all, never complained. She had seemed, to them, perfectly happy with her lot in life. And while they considered Annie MacGregor a fine, upstanding person, and the MacGregors a good Eganville family, they were less amused by Duncan than it seemed everyone else at the party was. Duncan smoked constantly. The old ranger never smoked. Dunc was said to take a drink. Tom and Bea were temperance. Dunc apparently swore. The old ranger could barely bring himself to say Dang! in a vile moment. But Duncan did have some ameliorating qualities. He was a marvellous fisherman and a fine hunter, and the McCormicks loved fresh trout in the summer, venison and moose meat in winter. And he was as dedicated to a life in the Algonquin Park bush as the old ranger, meaning that Helen would at least never be far away.

It turned out to be closer than any of them could ever have imagined. The McCormicks had decided that, with no stay-at-home daughter around to help and with the winters so long and the old ranger off so often patrolling the park by snowshoe and dogsled, they would take temporary winter lodgings closer to Whitney. Bea wouldn't suffer such loneliness. Whitney had churches, a grocery store, weekly bingos to while away the long, dark winter. They found a five-dollar-a-month bargain in little Airy, the tiny little pocket of a half-dozen houses along the north shore of Galeairy Lake and less than a mile down the Booth tracks to the village. The McRaes were still in Airy, living in a large white-and-green clapboard house on a bare hill above the bay and the sun-bleached drying sheds that were all that remained of the mill that had burned down a decade earlier, and J.S.L. offered Tom McCormick the tiny two-bedroom house that stood empty on the western edge of the hill overlooking a pigsty and the barns that kept the horses that worked in the bush. The McCormicks were pleased. The little house had an attic with a bedroom, a large wood-burning stove in the sitting and dining area, a kitchen with a good woodstove, an ice box, a hand pump with a line to a water cistern that had to be filled by pail and hand every weekend, and an attached woodshed filled with dry slabs from the mill.

The little house hung off one shoulder of the hill, the McRae home stood on the other, and in between was another small house. It had variously held railway workers for the Booth line and mill workers for the old mill, but was empty now and available for the same price: five dollars a month, payable to the McRae Lumber Company. Duncan and Helen took it, though it meant having Duncan's oldest sister, Janet, to the right, and Helen's parents to the left. If Helen had ever felt she was escaping to her own world by marrying, she was badly mistaken. She had her own house to set up and run, and was expected to help out her mother next door. To Janet McRae's credit, she made no demands on her new sister-in-law, but Helen couldn't help feeling the pressure of being squeezed on one side by her mother, on her other by her sister-in-law and husband's employer.

Jim was born in the fall of 1943, Ann in the spring of 1945 and I came along in June 1948. Her sister-in-law, Gertie, Irvine's wife, gave birth to a second son, Andy, in 1947, and immediately fell ill, was sent away and then spent months convalescing at home. Today it might have been called a nervous breakdown, but back then there was no such language and no appropriate treatment, apart from waiting. The older boy, Donald, was looked after by her parents, but the baby was a problem. Gertie was incapable of caring for him, so Andy was immediately shipped off to the one woman everyone seemed to turn to in times of trouble. From 1947 through 1950, Helen was essentially raising three very young children and a rambunctious older youngster who was soon enough seven years old and had never been to school. There were few fond memories for her of those years. She had three babies at once in cloth diapers, and no running water, no electricity and no help.

She did, however, see a bit more of her husband. The McRae operation moved out of Lake of Two Rivers, where the timber rights had been all but spent, and closer to Whitney, building a big new mill at Hay Lake, right on the eastern border of Algonquin. So long as he was working at the mill, he could get a ride back into Whitney at the end of the day and walk up the tracks or road to Airy. Once he bought his first car, a used Ford, he could drive himself to and from work and was home every evening during the times he worked at the mill. Unfortunately, in the dead of winter, when she needed him most, he was often gone for weeks at a time, deep in the bush and moving, if at all, from one bush camp to another. When he was home, they got along well, visiting her brothers and their families in Whitney and spending time with the McRaes, especially his nephew Donald and his wife, also Helen, who were much closer in age than J.S.L. and Janet, Duncan's sister and Donald's mother. Donald and Duncan were doing essentially the same jobs in the bush: tallying up the logs, keeping track of the types of logs they were hauling and keeping an eye on operations for J.S.L.

Dunc served a useful role for his brother-in-law. These were times of great growth in the lumber industry. J.S.L. was buying up more timber rights, expanding operations, and the work itself was changing, with the use of power saws in the bush and bulldozers to put in the roads and huge logging trucks to haul the timber out. "The Boss" was used to having his way and could be difficult to deal with, but Duncan, it seemed, had special permission to take issue with him if he felt something needed to be done. They had one spectacular argument at Hay Lake over, of all things, whether the cookery should have butter or margarine, but Dunc won the day, and the thanks of the other workers, when The Boss declared that they could have butter if they insisted. J.S.L. was driven, a workaholic who had no ability whatsoever to relax. His family once talked him into coming with them to the Canadian National Exhibition in Toronto, but he was so miserable on the long ride down that they turned around and went straight back home. His rare breaks he took by drinking and he had a cardinal rule of refusing to do business whenever he was on a binge. "That was his holiday," Dunc often said. Donald and Duncan would then run the operation until The Boss was ready to go back to work. He might be gone a few days, or even a week, and only rarely, but he would come back sober, clear-headed and filled with new ambitions. They grew used to it. Once a year J.S.L. would head off to Montreal and the Canadian Lumberman's Convention, and he always took Dunc along to make sure he didn't get distracted. For Duncan, it usually meant a few days at the fancy Queen Elizabeth Hotel and, a couple of times, trips to the Montreal Forum to see the great Rocket Richard play. But there was also the time the Boss got away from both himself and Duncan, fell down and broke his arm, and Dunc ended up spending the better part of a week trying to pull shirts and jackets over a huge cast and fetching and tipping the whisky bottle whenever pain demanded.

As to how Duncan got along with Helen, it is important to note that children are often the worst evaluators of a relationship. We knew them best when they knew each other least, long after distance and money problems and time had set their cold stone wedges. But we know, from asking, that in those days there was genuine, infectious affection. They were fun together, and laughed and played and loved together. If we stick to our earliest memories—of the giggling in the sleeping cabin at Lake of Two Rivers and the long Sunday car rides when they would stop for ice cream and then let us play along the sides of creeks or minnow ponds while they sat together on a flat rock and licked their dripping cones and laughed and talked—then we see a small portion of why they found each other and why there were soon four of us. But children are poor witnesses; we turn, instead, to the evidence of others who were there and a part of those times, and who say they were a great couple to be around, just as, many years later, they were as individuals distinct from each other.

There were dances and cards, sleigh rides and skating in winter, the lake in summer. Like virtually everyone else in the post-war years, Helen smoked, but briefly and did not stick with it. She rarely had a drink and soon was, like her parents, an abstainer. Duncan, on the other hand, was sociable and a constant smoker and, like virtually every other man who worked all week in the bush, anxious to pack as much into his thirty hours of free time as possible. He came back from the mill bursting with energy; she met him sagging with the exhaustion of six straight days, often alone, with four young children—both feelings ironically called bushed. There were sometimes tensions and often words, always about money.

He wasn't making much at the mill. Labour was cheap with men coming back from Europe and willing to take whatever was available. Post-war construction was booming, however, and it was good news for the mill, with no shortage of orders and no shortage of men willing to go into the park and fell the trees and draw the logs to the Lake of Two Rivers and Hay Lake mills. A lot of wartime habits arrived at the same time. There was more drinking, more gambling. Dunc had always liked cards. But while he was a superb bridge player, he was a fool at gambling, convinced for the rest of his life that his ship was about to come in with the next poker draw, Irish Sweepstakes ticket, penny mining stock. I take that back: not *his* ship, but *her* ship, *our* ship. He had interest in money not for himself, but for his family, so there would be no more arguments, no more tension, and so he could head off into the bush and fishing without words or guilt or repercussions. He understood perfectly the writer's value system. Money buys time. Money buys peace. Money buys back that portion of the brain that would much rather be doing something other than worrying.

Fortunately, the slick stock promoters, the bootleggers and the all-night poker parties were as rare as winter tourists in Algonquin Park in those years. He could stumble but never fall. He might throw away a few dollars of his limited pay, but he was never so foolhardy, then, to blow it all on mad schemes. He gave her money for food. He always paid the five-dollar rent. He made sure she had enough spare change that she was sometimes able to hire one of the older Airy girls, at five cents a pail, to lug water up the hill from the community well that was nearly a quarter-mile away. When the babies napped she cut kindling and sawed the slabwood and fed the stove. She heated water and bathed the babies in a washtub, then washed out the clothes and diapers in the same tub with a washboard. Half her time, she once said, seemed to be taken up with washing and bringing in the laundry, the diapers smelling of pine in summer, stiff as boards in winter. No wonder she was so unimpressed to see, once again, a reminder of that old gasoline-fired washing machine from Lake of Two Rivers.

It sounds like poverty, but only in looking back from a time when poverty is a concept understood. No one thought of it then as the shame of the state or a trap or a vicious circle. It was merely the way things were, for everyone. There was little chance for comparison. Few ever went out front, as they called a trip to Ottawa. If there were exceptions, and the McRaes were certainly the one exception in Airy and Whitney, then it was the reward for providing work, and those who had less were not resentful but grateful. J.S.L. McRae gave them work. If there was no McRae, there would be no work. It was that simple. He was tough, in that he demanded a great deal from his workers, but he was also held to be fair. They got few holidays, but if they were hurt or sick, he took care of them. Most of all, he gave them the jobs that allowed Whitney to carry on. It was this bush gratitude that meant even a brother-in-law would never ask for a raise. Nor did Dunc ever mention the percentage of the profits that he had been promised. He was, like all the other men he knew in Whitney and the park, content just to be there.

Helen made her ends meet. She never complained to anyone except Duncan, and then only when he was throwing away their money on foolish chance and what she considered unnecessary items such as tobacco and alcohol. And she complained only about money, never her burden. She had accepted years earlier that her role was to serve, first the older sister and younger brothers—especially Roy, with his polio—then the parents, then her own family. Big-hearted, remarkably generous and blessed with a wonderful laugh, she took pleasure from her role as the one who could always be counted on. If she once held resentment towards her parents for trying to keep her with them as a virtual servant, it passed. She made no attempt to distance herself from them when the opportunity, however slim, arrived through marriage to Duncan and their first home. Family to her was everything—daily evidence that she was needed, proof that she had value—and she simply preferred the chance of her own small family to life with her parents, but not by all that much. She never avoided her mother's house. She just seemed grateful that she could hurry down the path to her own home in Airy and, for a few hours anyway, run her own little world as she, not someone else, saw fit. Like everyone else in the family, she worshipped the old ranger, ever dependable, always doing and saying the right thing, always impeccably turned out in a crisp uniform that, as often as not, she had washed and ironed on days when she still found time to help her mother. Tom and Bea McCormick always tried to involve her, inviting her along whenever others would be over for an evening of bridge or cribbage or euchre, but she rarely had time to spare, and when she did, automatically drifted into the role of tea maker and food server and dishwasher, more comfortable in the kitchen than in the sitting room. Once she left Airy, she never again played cards, with the telling exception of solitaire.

Those early years in Airy went quickly for her. She was so busy with her own three children and with her nephew Andy that there was no time for boredom or reflection or even self-pity. No one else, after all, had much more, so there was little to envy and no reason for self-pity. Pity was for the likes of the little fawn that the men found on the tracks one morning, the doe dead beside her. They carried the shaking little deer up to the Airy houses, and Janet McRae had them put it in her back shed, where the women fed it with a baby bottle and where it stayed for months, crying like a baby when they forced it to return to the bush and its own devices.

Helen's one overriding concern was what to do about the children's schooling. Jimmy was precocious, extremely bright, but still hadn't been to school. There was a tiny school in Whitney, but it would have meant him walking down the tracks, leaving in the dark and coming home in the dark in winter, and she could not break away from the babies to see him there safely, so she kept him back while other children his age went happily off. She was beginning to think about moving, perhaps to Huntsville, the first community on the other side of the park, where Mary was now living and teaching.

She was also worried about Jimmy's eyesight. He read early, vir-tually self-taught and with books always available next door at the McRaes, where Janet had resurrected Annie MacGregor's belief that every house should have a good library. He squinted when he read, and soon drew the pages closer and closer to his eyes. Ann was showing similar signs. The lighting was weak in the house, coal-oil lamps Helen wouldn't turn up too high for fear of fire, and the children insisted on reading and looking at comic books until bedtime. The closest eye doctor was in Orillia, far on the other side of the park and halfway to Toronto down Highway 11.

They set off on what, in later years, would become Duncan's favourite story of family travel. Ann was carsick on the way down. They arrived, unfamiliar with such traffic, unused to towns the size of Orillia, and had no appointment to see Dr. Woodward, the eye doctor. They decided to find somewhere to stay first and then go down to see about the eye appointments. They took a room at a motel, decided they couldn't show up with the children and left us there, Jimmy in charge, with instructions not to open the door to any stranger. Duncan locked the door from the outside and pock-eted the key.

Too young then to remember what happened next, I must rely on the Old Man, who never tired of telling the story. We children knew nothing about running water, and Jim and Ann were fasci-nated by the toilet and the taps. They plugged the toilet with paper and kept flushing to clear it. I, apparently, twisted on both taps and left them running with a towel in the sink. The water from the running toilet and blocked sink rolled out over the floor and out under the door, and the manager came and pounded on the door, but we refused to open it, terrified by the screaming stranger who was outside. The angry manager was off getting the pass-key when Dunc and Helen returned, and there was very nearly a fist fight in the parking lot before Dunc somehow settled the man down and, even more oddly, talked him out of giving us all the boot.

Perhaps he told him we were blind.

In 1950 they left Airy for Huntsville, driving a borrowed three-ton truck filled to the tree branches with mattresses and kitchen chairs and old dressers and tables and boxes of dishes and utensils and cooking pots. Not quite Steinbeck's Joads headed for California, but not far from it. They drove through the park, from the first village beyond the East Gate to the first town beyond the West Gate. Dunc, in fact, was fairly familiar with the road, having often come out with other loggers to visit a bootlegger known as Old Strawberries who had set up shop between the West Gate and Huntsville; sometimes a logging truck from McRae's would pull in in the early hours of the morning, the cab filled with bushworkers who hadn't had a drink in a month or more.

Huntsville, at the northern tip of Muskoka cottage country, was then a town of a little more than three thousand, with the economy split between lumbering and tourism. It was, and still is, a picturesque town, with the sun rising over a massive thrust of granite called the Lookout and setting over the reservoir hill, and the town proper lying in a steep bowl between the two landmarks. The original town layout was split by a gentle twist of the Muskoka River, and if things had gone according to plan, Huntsville would have spread along the flatter ground on the east side of the river heading towards the park. It did not, however, with both Main Street and the vast majority of houses clinging to the hill that rose from the banks of the other side of the river all the way to the high reservoir. The reason for this was delightfully Ontario, with its long history of prudery smashing headfirst into practicality. Two main original settlers, Capt. George Hunt and Allan Shay, had been first to divide up lots for sale, Hunt's down on the better land running east of the river, Shay's on impossible land on the side of the hill. Hunt, however, was temperance, and insisted on a clause in each deed that promised no spirits would ever be allowed on the property. Shay had no such clause and quickly sold out his lots. This quirk of small-town history made for generations of agile walkers and strong legs. Those who may have wondered how it is that such a small community could produce such marvellous lacrosse teams and players need look no further than the very thing that destroys so many other small-town heroes: alcohol.

Dunc and Helen bought high on the reservoir hill, a two-storey brick home with a fine view of the mountain and the Muskoka River as it empties out into Fairy Lake. The home was rough and in need of work. It had a dirt basement and a wood furnace, but three bedrooms for the growing family and, for the first time, running water and indoor plumbing. There was an ice box in the rundown kitchen. The iceman came by each week with a new block hanging from his tongs. Milk came by horse-drawn wagon. Bread and even wood by another. She had to feed the furnace, rising twice each night in winter to build the fire so we would be warm to dress in the morning, but she didn't mind at all. Helen was delighted with her new home. She could walk to shopping and to church, and Jimmy, now seven years old, could walk down Lorne Street and cross at Main and Centre and be at the public school in less than five minutes. Duncan was less excited: he had to borrow the down payment for the $5,000 house from his sister Janet, and he was just starting out on the long spiral of debt that would strain his marriage and lead to more and more borrowing over the next thirty years. Besides, possessions meant nothing to him. You kept a good trout, and anything else of lasting value you could always borrow from the library.

Huntsville was far more expensive than Airy. They had a mortgage now, and it was considerably more than the mere five dollars a month they had been paying previously. They had electricity and water, but there were bills for both. There was no longer free wood to burn, and slabwood had to be purchased from the local mill, Hay and Company. Even water and ice, which used to be free, now cost. There were school costs and eyeglasses costs and dentist costs and large doctors' costs. Tommy was born at the Huntsville Hospital in 1954, meaning there was not only another mouth to feed but soon need of more room. The dilapidated, breezy summer kitchen Helen was using year-round was torn down and replaced by an extension that gave Ann her own bedroom and the family a living room below. But it all cost money. Helen was furious and outraged when, one June morning, a police car pulled up and a uniformed Mountie presented a summons at the front door. Duncan Fisher MacGregor of 15 Lorne Street, Huntsville, Ontario, Canada, had not paid his income tax for three years.

If Lake of Two Rivers had been pivotal to their lives before, it became even more so after the move to Huntsville. The old ranger and his wife moved back to the log home the moment they could get in from the highway each spring. Helen tried to bring her growing family there on weekends and from the day school let out each summer until the day before it was to go back in again in the fall. She came fully aware that she and Duncan were granted the privilege of the cabins for the summer only in exchange for her helping at what was called the Big House, but her love of the lake and insistence that her children have the same park childhood that she'd had overrode any personal misgivings. Duncan also preferred having the family in the park. He could fish at the lake and spend time with the children. And once the McRae operation left Hay Lake to again establish itself in the park proper—this time where the Madawaska joined Whitefish Lake with Rock Lake—he was able to be with his family every evening and leave before dawn in time for a full day at the new mill.

We came in winter as well. Duncan left the car—when he had one—with Helen in Huntsville so we could drive the fifty miles into the park on winter weekends when weather permitted, and we would fish through the ice for trout. It was on a March weekend that Duncan left the children watching their rods off the end of the point while he and the old ranger sawed ice blocks closer to the bay. All at once, the hole we were standing over gave way and took Ann down under the ice.

She came back so quick it seemed she would leap straight out to safety, but the ice gave way again and she slid back in. Jimmy went down on his stomach to reach for her, but Duncan was already running and calling for us to stand away and back from the opening hole. He ran and slid on his belly, reaching as far as he could until Ann, now screaming frantically, was able to catch his big hand and hang on. With one movement, he wrenched her free of the hole and out, and pulled her along the ice to shore and safety. He took her into the log home, where they dried her off in front of the fireplace, but she could not stop shivering and by morning she had a sore throat and a severe cold coming on. It was some weeks, however, before the doctor knew that her condition was far more serious than a bad cold. Ann had rheumatic fever.

Little is heard of rheumatic fever now, but it is only in the past generation, and with the widespread availability of antibiotics, that it has ceased to be a widespread worry for parents. It is a most curious affliction, one where the natural antibodies the body produces to fight infection somehow turn on the body itself, attacking the joints. Worse, it is a disease that can return with no warning. I have little memory of Ann's two major bouts, the first when she was six, the second when she was ten. Both times, but particularly the second, she believed she was going to die. She said, when she was later so much sicker with a far more ruthless disease, that she'd already made her peace with death when she was just a child, so there was nothing to fear now. She'd been convinced she would die at ten years of age and, it seems, the doctors thought much the same. She lay in bed for months at a time, Helen spending hours rubbing her painful limbs and remembering, no doubt, how little time had passed since she had been nurse to her younger brother Roy and his polio. I would often crawl up onto Ann's bed and play with her, though I suspect now that it was me at play and Ann, if anything, watching as she dozed off and on. Duncan and Helen tried whatever remedies were available, often taking her to Ottawa, where a renowned specialist in rheumatic fever had developed a technique of wrapping the swollen, painful limbs of the child first in hot, then in cold blankets, on and off for days at a time. It did little good. The doctors in Ottawa told Duncan and Helen not to hope for too much. If Ann recovered, she would never play like other children, never ride a bicycle, never take part in any sports. Her heart, they told them, was like a balloon that had been blown up full and then released; it had entirely lost its elasticity. One doctor, even after Ann had recovered enough to return to school, predicted that she would never see forty. If only the doctor who found the cancer when she was fifty had been so wrong.

Summers at the cottage were marvellous, even those two summers when Ann was still ill with the fever. We stayed at Lake of Two Rivers with rare breaks. There were trips to Whitney for groceries, but those were few and far between: the old ranger ran the place much like a work camp, with supplies brought in in bulk and meals planned weeks in advance. He and Duncan would walk in from the highway with hundred-pound sacks of beans or flour over their shoulders, with pails of lard and bags of potatoes. Helen and her mother baked on the woodstove, Bea always making a downward curved fist into the open oven as the hairs on the back of her hand told her the exact moment to put in the pies or bread. We picked raspberries and blueberries, chokecherries and wild strawberries. Cabbage and lettuce came from gardens that were surrounded by chicken wire to keep the deer out. The lake provided bass and trout. Meat they bought in Whitney and could keep for a few days in the ice box, but beef and pork from the butcher were rare. In season, there would often be someone dropping by with venison or moose steaks and even, once, bear meat that had to be boiled for hours before anyone could get their teeth through it. Milk they were able to buy off the refrigerated truck that Brooks Transport sent through the park once a week to deliver perishables to the summer camps. And as a last resort, there was always the little store up at Canoe Lake, where supplies were sold, at inflated prices, to campers heading into the interior and cottagers who had run out of necessities.

We swam and fished and canoed. Jim and cousin Don built a raft and then rigged a sail and were able to take it up and down the lake with enough skill that they rarely needed to paddle. Jim built a baseball diamond that required running halfway up the trunk of a large red pine that had half fallen over and then touching the first branch for first base. He declared the woodpile out of bounds and strung rope like Christmas lights through the far pines to signal where a home run had to be hit. There were days when Jim and I and, when we were lucky, Dunc would play for hours in the fading light of the point, each batter for himself, two pitches only, and climb the tree to first base and back again to the flat rock or else you were out. When Jim and I finally did get to play organized ball, we could hit anything they threw at us; unfortunately, there is a crucial difference between a long ball heading straight for a roped-off pine and one landing in a casually tilted fielder's mitt.

There were more animals around than people. Cousins—Tom and Agnes's five children, Irvine and Gertie's boys, Mary and Lorne's two boys and once in a while, Roy and Betty's son Robert—came and went all summer, but the constant was our family, the old ranger and Bea, the deer who came to feed in the morning, the ravens and squirrels who argued all day, the whisky-jacks who flew from the branches to pluck bread right out of our hands, the loons and wolves at night, the mink who lay in wait for trout innards, the bears at the dump at the east end of Lake of Two Rivers, and the water bugs, crayfish, minnows and bloodsuckers that kept little children spellbound for hours in the small harbours that dotted the long rocky point. The old ranger spent his spare time walking and reblazing the old bush trails and collecting insect specimens for the ministry laboratories in Toronto. Every week he had his long, brown cardboard tubes—spruce budworm, canker-worm, sawfly larva, tent caterpillars—screwed tight and taped up and clearly addressed to give to the mail truck on its weekly run through. He also took it upon himself to keep the Algonquin Park Museum supplied with massive seventy-year-old snapping turtles. If one happened to crawl up onto the point to bask and sleep in the sun, he was soon organizing an attack force to move in from behind. First the old ranger would tip the huge beast onto its back with a garden rake—once failing when a particularly large turtle merely snapped the rake in half with its vice-like jaws—and then Duncan and the rest of us would move in with ropes to lasso about its limbs. The old ranger would gather the rope ends in his big hands, hoist the upside-down turtle up into the air, and Duncan would slip a burlap sack under it. The old ranger would then add a couple more burlap sacks for protection, throw the main sack over his back and head out for the museum, where the old turtle would amaze and terrify tourists all summer long before being released, well-fed, in the fall to hibernate in the mud of a nearby shoreline.

The deer were given a special place of honour. They had names—Sugar, Lady, Buck—and loyalty: Sugar, and later her offspring Lady, would greet us at each spring's opening with a new fawn, sometimes two. The fawns learned to fight in the clearing at the top of the hill, their tiny front hooves clicking against the other's as they boxed mercilessly while standing precariously on their thin back legs. We learned their calls, and could even recognize the does by the way they sighed. The deer would come for the salt licks and the handouts, and were friendly enough to feed from the hand. Bea, who paid particular attention to them, could even pet the regular visitors and stand with her arm draped over Sugar's shoulders.

Many years later, when he was well into his eighties, Dunc recorded some of this in the margins of *The Twenty-Four-Inch Home Run*. He titled his anecdote "The Rescue": "We had a pet deer at the cottage and every spring she produced twin fawns. For twelve years she would come every day for a handout from Grandma McCormick, who was very fond of her. One day she came and she wouldn't eat, only stared at the path to the woods. She did this three times and Grandma thought there was something wrong and followed her through the bush. Sure enough, one of the little fawns was hung up on the root of a tree and was stuck there and couldn't free itself. Grandma freed the fawn and they all went back to the cottage quite happy. That shows us how intelligent wild animals are at times. The deer did not die of old age, she was hit by a car and killed. She was at least fourteen years old."

One spring in the mid-fifties, this same deer, Sugar, showed up in terrible condition. Her fur was dry and dull and grey and falling out, much more so than normal moulting would suggest. She was thin, shaky on her feet. Bea managed to get close enough to her to see that a thick piece of wire had been looped around her neck and twisted tight enough to be choking her. When Bea tried to touch the wire, the deer bounded off, for once afraid of the touch of the one human closest to her.

No one could figure out what had happened. Speculation ranged from her getting caught in a fence—difficult, since there were no fences in the park—to someone trying to capture her when she approached, unwittingly, to take a handout. Why anyone would want to do this was beyond knowing, but one thing had already happened to the area deer that was beyond comprehension anyway. Killarney Lodge, just across a wide bay from the old ranger's point, had kept two pet deer for many years for their visitors to see and photograph, but one night two men had come in with knives and slaughtered them and raced off with their trunk filled with venison, only to be caught as they passed through the park gate. Perhaps the wire had been intended as a "leash," by which someone could lead Sugar off into the woods and similarly kill her. Who knows? The only certainty was that the wire would have to come off soon or Sugar would be dead.

The old ranger and Duncan went to work building the most extravagant "trap" ever seen in the park. They built it out of wood from the mill and made it large enough that a deer might walk inside if tempted to do so. There was thick fencing around the sides and tops to give a feeling of escape, and special little trap doors that could be opened along the side at just the right level to snip off the wire around Sugar's neck. The old ranger was such a perfectionist, measuring even the exact distance from floor of the cage to where the neck would be, that it is a wonder the deer didn't collapse and die in the span of time it took them to complete the trap. Duncan, of course, was convinced that the only possible solution was to grab the deer in a head lock and hang on until someone could cut the wire. But he humoured the old ranger, and they built the trap together and then stalked the poor, sickly animal for two weeks. The old ranger worked full time on his project. Duncan gave what time he could. The kids helped when we couldn't escape to the water and fishing and raft. Nothing, however—not salt lick, sweet bread, shortbread cookies, oats or sugar—would convince Sugar she should walk onto the boards that led to the cage. A few times she stepped part way in and the old ranger and Dunc moved too quickly, startling her out and away until she began to view their rescue machine as some alarming extension of the wire that was already pinching around her neck. Finally, one day she showed up, the neck rubbed bare where the wire had once been, the wire nowhere in sight. A cottager down the lake had walked up to the deer with a pair of wire snips, reached out and clipped it off, simple as that. The rescue cage, unused, remained at the end of the path for another ten years, a daily reminder that Dunc was right and the old ranger wrong. You can indeed plan too carefully.

There were, of course, visitors, and lots of them. The various cousins would come for one- and two-week stays—always sleeping up at the Big House while we stayed in the sleeping cabins—and other ranger families often came for an afternoon of sitting out on the point or an evening of cards. Uncle Bill MacGregor would come with his treasured war wounds; Uncle Ken MacGregor with his pockets spilling with spare change; and Janet McRae and her daughter, Marjorie, would always drop in once a summer. The most intimidating guest was always the eccentric Miss Winifred Trainor from Canoe Lake. Her sister, Marie, was married to the old ranger's brother, an older Roy McCormick, but she was much better known to us as Tom Thomson's fiancé. She had never married after the painter's death in 1917, and by the mid-1950s had become a large, dark, elderly woman with a booming voice and an opinion on everything that moved—including the McCormick grandchildren, who were definitely moving. She used to spin her glasses by the ear lug as she spoke, and once, in the middle of a particularly testy rant against "*tourists*" who had no right being in the park, she let go and the glasses flew high into the pine behind her summer seat and lodged tight. The old ranger had to get a ladder to climb up and retrieve them, and somehow did so, handing them back without breaking up. The laughter they saved until Winnie Trainor, her stockings falling down around the tops of her sensible shoes, had ambled out the long path to the highway and headed back down the road to Canoe Lake.

Our favourite visits were from George Phillips, the park super-intendent, who flew around in the Department of Lands and Forests' old Stinson Reliant and fancied himself a bit of a barn-stormer. Phillips seemed to get no greater enjoyment than calling ahead to the old ranger with word that he'd be by in the afternoon to pick him up for a patrol of the more isolated reaches of the park. The old ranger, who could stand face to face with an angry black bear, was petrified of flying. He'd be standing, chief ranger's uniform crisp, tie choking, at the end of the dock when the hum of the old Stinson would rise slowly out of the west. Phillips liked to sneak up, roaring in low over the trees and seeming to fly straight out of the woods back of the log home, rolling the plane over and over as if out of control. He'd turn, swoop back low over the lake, then take the plane into a steep climb before going into a deliberate stall, falling back in a helpless spin until, seemingly at the last moment, he would pull the plane out, loop out over the lake once and come back in for a sizzling, graceful landing in the calm waters of the bay. He would taxi up to the edge of the dock, throw the door open and grin at the ashen-faced old ranger. "Let's go, Tom! I'm low on gas!" His knees shaking, the old ranger would step out onto the pontoon, grab the strut and swing himself reluc-tantly into the passenger seat. Phillips, still grinning, would take off as smoothly as he'd landed, the old plane steady as it rose high and straight and remarkably careful over the trees.

We travelled rarely. Into Whitney for groceries and comics every few weeks, never to Huntsville, once a summer to a bingo up in Maynooth or Barry's Bay, where Jimmy had an uncanny knack for winning, and at least once a summer to Aunt Minnie's farm down along the Bonnechere River. She was an elderly aunt of Dunc's, a sweet and tiny woman whose attitude to children was very much the same as Duncan's own—let them do whatever they want, so long as they don't kill themselves—and who lived in an isolated, magical place with a deep, cold well, several barns, dozens of chickens, the odd cow, an adopted grandson who could swing from the barn rafters without disturbing his impressive ducktail and a sweet, berry-filled path that led to a small dam in the river and some of the best rock-bass fishing a few kids and a can of worms ever imagined.

Driving down to Aunt Minnie's place on the Tramore Road outside the village of Deacon was always an adventure, in part because the Old Man was a terrible driver. He actually believed he had invented something approaching automatic transmission by simply eliminating second gear from his repertoire. He started out in first, the car bucking with his quick clutching, roared it a while, then ground the shift up and straight through into third, the car sighing and coughing and sagging as third caught and hauled and the car continued on its way. Having lived his life along roads so rarely travelled, he had not the slightest concept of oncoming traffic. For him, the road was always clear, the next corner was always open. He delighted in passing logging trucks on the crests of steep hills, honking the horn in case he knew the driver and ducking down to read the owner's name on the driver's door. With Helen sitting in the passenger's seat, her arms rigid on her lap and her teeth grinding, he drove at half attention, whistling and singing and stopping whenever whim suggested.

He believed in shortcuts, whether in dress (longjohns steady from September through June), cooking (full heat and burn) or personal insurance (he didn't bother), and when he had discovered a back road that cut off near Wilno and worked its way along by Round Lake Centre to the Tramore Road and Aunt Minnie's, he insisted on taking it time and time again, though the road was gravel, rarely graded and had a bridge in poor repair over the Bonnechere. He tended to drive the same speed, pavement or dirt, with the car fishtailing and the dry gravel rising in a billowing yellow thundercloud behind. He didn't notice that the bridge had half split, and that the road had heaved on the one side creating a perfect launching pad for a car travelling in excess of forty miles an hour.

"*Dunc!*" she screamed.

"*What?*" he wondered, turning his attention back to the road.

And then we were airborne, the Chevrolet suddenly silent but for the whistle of wind through the windows, the sense of floating, flying, moving so silently, wonderfully, over the Bonnechere River that we had become like a great blue heron coming in for a landing.

Only we hit, and sprung, and bounced, and twisted, and turned, and caught, and skidded, and turned again, and shuddered and bucked and rattled and clunked to a long, spinning, cloudy stop.

"*For heaven's sake!*" she shouted.

"*Let's do it again!*" we screeched from the back seat.

He began turning the Chevrolet around, the back wheels spinning on loose gravel. The cloud of dust from our landing was wafting in through the open windows, choking us.

"*You're not!*" she said.

"*Why not?*" he asked.

And so we did it, again and again, mother outraged and father delighted, kids screaming as the old Chevy left earth and seemed to circle the world, floating silently, momentarily, eerily over the Bonnechere River and slapping, bouncing, crunching, chugging, sliding, spinning to a stop in a cloud of dust and shouts of *more*.

But there was no horseplay and no shouting the day of Aunt Minnie's funeral. She had died in her sleep well into her nineties, and the call had come for Dunc and Helen to head down to the Bonnechere for the wake. Jimmy and Ann they left with the old ranger and Bea; for reasons that were never clear, they took me along. We drove down quietly, Dunc in his only suit, Helen in a blue-print summer dress, me with a clean shirt and long pants. No fishtailing, no flying over the bridge, no laughter. I was terrified. I was five years old and had never before been to a funeral.

The laneway to the farmhouse was covered with cars when we arrived. Cousins I had never seen before. Old friends and relatives of Dunc's from all up and down the Ottawa Valley. Helen found immediate refuge in the kitchen, where there was tea and coffee to make, dishes to wash, small coloured sandwiches to roll and slice and set out. Dunc went off with the men to be in the woodshed. I would learn over the years that this was the way of the valley funeral: women in the kitchen with tea and sandwiches and cookies, men in the woodshed or the barn, or, in more prosperous times, the basement, with rye whisky straight from the bottle.

For years I could never make the link between water pumps and furnaces and generators breaking down every time there was a family gathering of any kind; but one day I came to understand perfectly the dance of the drinkers in deeply conservative, deeply religious rural communities. On the surface, all was temperance— spoons ringing on tea cups, happy chatter anywhere in the house proper—while somewhere on the fringe, out in the woodshed, barn or down in the basement, men who never did learn how to drink properly were pounding it back quickly, their throats catching and jowls shaking with the burn of neat liquor until they, too, were ready to go in and tinkle the tea cups and pretend that all was normal. No one ever seemed to get drunk, but some were, as they called it, tight enough to show. Never enough to create a scene, however. What is particularly baffling about all this is that the women were perfectly aware that there was no broken pump or dampened burner, that their men were drinking. But so long as no one fell down or got particularly obnoxious, and no fists started flying, it was accepted as part of the family ritual. If a priest was involved—a funeral, a wedding, a large visit—he, too, would be off to the woodshed for a few quick shots. So just who they were fooling I never quite understood. It may have been me, for it certainly worked for a very long time.

Aunt Minnie lay in the drawing room of the rickety old farmhouse. I could smell the flowers—sickening, cloying, gagging—as I picked through the plates of shortbread, date squares and brownies. There was also a strange sound coming from the next room, a sound not unlike that made by a tomcat on a warm summer's night. It was a wail and a cry and a moan, and something very near to screeching. I peeked in. There were three women, all in grey shrouds, and they were sitting on kitchen chairs closest to the largest display of blue and white and pink and yellow flowers. "What are they doing?" I whispered to my mother, who was rolling more sandwiches. "Keening," she said. She was much too busy to explain.

I felt a hand on my arm, pulling. There was the strong odour of perfume. I turned and recognized a distant cousin of Dunc's, an older woman we saw rarely but who always seemed to know everything imaginable about what we were up to in our lives.

"You need to pay your respects, young man," she said.

I had no idea what she was talking about. She pulled me, not hard, but firmly, out of the dining area and towards the alarming sitting room where the women were keening and the flowers were so rich in smell my nose could not hold it all. She ushered me in, a few faces I recognized turning and smiling sadly my way. I must have looked terrified.

The keening women paid me no heed. We moved past them, past the gagging flowers and came to a strange wooden chest that was too high for me to see into. There were handles on it, and I knew why without asking.

"Your aunt Minnie's sleeping," my escort said. I didn't think so. She pushed me close to the casket. Now behind me, she reached and, with strong arms, lifted me by my armpits so I rose high over the edge and peered in at the strangest sight I had ever seen. Aunt Minnie was lying there, her eyes closed, her hands folded gently over a black dress. The cushions about her head were white and looked very soft. But Aunt Minnie did not look like Aunt Minnie. Her skin was white and waxen, and yanked back, it seemed, so that her nose looked impossibly large.

Even with the oppressive flowers and my own fear of breathing at this moment, I could sense the perfume drawing closer to my ear.

"If you touch the dead," a straining voice whispered, "you'll never ever be afraid of them."

Touch the dead? I instinctively recoiled, my arms stiffening by my side. My armpits hurt where she had hold of me. She released one side and pressed my chest up against the casket. I felt like I was going to fall in.

With one hand now free, she grabbed my right wrist and forced my arm over the edge of the casket. She pushed, I pulled, but she won out, forcing my hand down onto Aunt Minnie's hand. My eyes and throat were burning.

She left my hand there and then forced it to rub along Aunt Minnie's. It was a feeling that made no sense. I could see that they were Aunt Minnie's hands, but I knew they were not hands at all. There was no sense of skin, no sense of warmth, no sense of response.

"There," she said, pulling my hand back and dipping quickly back under my armpit again. "You'll never be afraid of the dead again. Never."

She set me down, and I spun out from between her and the casket and away. Out through the dining area, where the teacups were still clicking; out through the summer kitchen, where Helen was at the hand pump with a huge pile of dirty plates and cups in front of her; out through the shed and into the bright sunlight of the yard.

I went over to the well and, fighting back tears, hauled on the rope until the wooden pail came slopping and splashing into sight. I cinched the rope and hurried to the pail, tipping the cool water over onto my hands and rubbing, rubbing, rubbing, tried to wash off the smell and feel of Aunt Minnie's death. I rubbed my hands in the grass and washed them again. I walked about the yard shaking my hands dry, surprised that out there, where Aunt Minnie had her own garden of irises and lilies and impatiens, the flowers had no sense of gagging sickness.

I took some of the stones around the garden border and dropped them down the well, listening for that deliciously cold and hollow echo, but I soon wandered off towards the machine and woodshed, where I could see the backs of men who'd gathered, suit jackets, for those who had them, held loosely in their hands, sleeves rolled high. They took no notice of me as I worked my way in the open side door. The air inside was dry and sharp with the smell of sawdust, though no one was sawing anything. There were bluebottles stepping slowly on the workbench—their movement almost paralyzed by the hot sun coming in through the window—and I stood staring at the flies but listening to the men.

"Should ship more'n double the board feet we did last year . . ."

"*Won't see much partridge this fall. Summer's been too wet, eh?*"

"*No goddam use even thinkin' trout in August. They're down too deep . . .*"

"*Oh I don't know, Dunc—you should see the size of the laker the young Lavalley lad took outta Opeongo last week . . .*"

The men were passing around a bottle, the brassy liquid sloshing as they tipped it high, bubbled a couple of swallows, then yanked it away, gasping and wincing in appreciation. It seemed to me to hurt, and I wondered why they would do this to themselves. The drink was having the same effect on the men that the hot sun was having on the bluebottles: they were slowing down, almost dozing as they leaned against woodpiles and sawhorses and the edge of the cluttered workbench. I slipped out and away, watching the chickens strut and scratch up by the barn and then turning my attention to the rotting boards lying to the side of the milk shed. There were salamanders and dew worms—both the colour of whisky—under the damp ones, sometimes a garter snake under the dry and always red ants you could drive crazy by poking a sharp stick down the little holes and flicking free their eggs.

"*Royyyy-eeee!*" It was my mother calling. Same call to come in from road hockey, swimming and, in this case, for the funeral. It was time for the service and burial, and the men, well fortified by now for the task at hand, were also making their way back into the farmhouse, their voices louder, those who owned jackets forcing them over sweat-drenched shirts, everyone fixing their ties and trying so hard to speak carefully that their sincerity and determination was a dead giveaway for what all the wives and spinster aunts knew had been going on in the woodshed anyway.

How they had taken Aunt Minnie's casket into the little farmhouse I had never thought to wonder, but they were taking it out, closed, straight through a front window, the sill and frame and jambs crowbarred off to allow space for the box and the big, callused hands that passed it through. I cringed at the sight of the casket, my right hand instinctively rubbing itself against the prickly trousers I was beginning to hate.

I looked for my father and mother. Dunc was standing just off the front porch, his shoulder against a little wind ornament with the wheels of a wooden train moving towards him. He was smiling at me but was helpless to come. He was to be a pallbearer and the casket was moving, through a sluice of big hands, towards him and five other men who were squaring their shoulders to the task to come. Helen was out of the kitchen now and looking for me. I took her hand, grateful for skin that was soft and warm and alive.

With Dunc and the other pallbearers leading and the priest directly behind the bobbing, sliding coffin, we made our way down the path, birds singing, flies buzzing, and out onto the dusty gravel road, where the solemn, slow procession turned and headed for the little church down on the first turn. I walked with my mother, thinking only of how hideous it must be to be trapped in that casket. *What if Aunt Minnie came back alive? Would any of us hear her shouts, her pounding?*

It was hot inside the little country church. The windows were open, but so little breeze blew there was no relief. I was next to a window and could hear bees in the honeysuckle and lilac bushes along the side of the building. The priest, too, was droning on, and I may have fallen asleep during the service, for I remember very little of what was said or what happened until they moved outside and Dunc and the other men carried the casket over to the grave, where the priest spoke and prayed again, women dabbed with Kleenex and the men stood staring at the ground, the sweat staining black under their arms. They had set the casket down on thick ropes, and then used the ropes to lift the box again and drop it slowly into the grave, a man calling out orders—"*Steady now, lower on the right, left, Dunc, steady, steady, steady*"—as if they were setting a dock crib instead of poor Aunt Minnie. The priest said a few more words and then the circle around the grave broke up, the women and several of the men moving off while the rest of the men, Dunc included, turned to the huge mound of earth back of it, reached for the spades that were sticking out and began filling in the hole. I can still hear perfectly the hiss of the shovels being stabbed into the mound and the rattle and heavy sliding sound the earth and stones made as they struck the casket. If she was calling now, no one would ever hear.

I was back at the well again, staring down into the pitch black and the small coin of bright sky and hoist and small boy's silhouette that was our reflection, when I felt a hand on my shoulder. I shuddered, thinking I was about to be taken off again by the perfumed woman to touch the dead. But it was Duncan, his jacket off, his tie missing, his other hand in his pocket.

"They want us to get some eggs," he said.

I nodded. I knew my mother had gone in to help with the sandwiches. They'd probably run out. I was glad, for gathering eggs was one of the highlights of a visit to Aunt Minnie's, though we were rarely trusted to do so.

We walked in silence up the sloping hill to the old barn. He lifted the wooden bar in the gate, opened it and, once we were through, closed it again, though there was not anything to keep in or out. The laying hens were scratching for feed in the dry earth at the side of the barn. Inside, with the sun baking down through holes and cracks in the roof, the air was sparkling with the dust raised by hysterical hens. I loved the smell of Aunt Minnie's barn: ancient, dried cow manure; wet straw; the acidic smell of chicken manure, old oil, machinery and boxes; coal-oil drums and old cracked leather harnesses and leads. I moved about behind him as he felt through the straw of nests, sometimes coming up with a brown egg, sometimes not. Someone else had collected earlier. The pickings were slim, but enough to fill his hands and mine. I could feel the warmth of the eggs in mine.

I realize now that this would have been the perfect time for a Polonius-Laertes talk between father and son about the meaning of life, but he said nothing at all. Nothing about eggs or old laying hens or the cycle of life or even about poor Aunt Minnie, trapped back there in the graveyard under all those shovelfuls of gravel and earth. He picked each egg as if it were unsuspected, a gift he had come to by accident as he felt his way along the various nests and rails. He made Leo Gorcey faces and kept pretending he was dropping eggs, bobbling and grunting and shouting—"*Ak-ak-ak-ak!*"—before, at the last possible moment, catching the falling egg a few inches from the ground. I laughed and giggled and began making faces with him.

We were headed back to the farmhouse, our hands and arms tight to our stomachs with fresh eggs, when he stopped and turned. I stopped, too, and stared up at him.

"She lived a good life, you know," he said. "She was a hell of a good woman."

That was it. He turned and continued on. No philosophy. No asking how I felt. No talking it out. It was gone.

It was to me, in an instant, as if Aunt Minnie had lived her long life and decided herself that she was entirely satisfied with it. She was probably perfectly content with where she was, not banging to get out.

I stared down at my right hand, where I had half expected to see the touch of the dead branded on me forever.

But there was nothing. Only the smudge of rich earth and the sense of the still-warm egg in the palm of my hand.

★   ★   ★

Here on this rocky point, on a hot August day in 1996 when the three pilgrims have come to sit with their own thoughts, they remember the way rain falls at Lake of Two Rivers, as it falls no other place on earth. We can hear it always: thunder rumbling in the distance, then suddenly shattering overhead with the sizzle lightning will make when it is much too close. We can see Bea, the mother and grandmother who could race headfirst at a bear, running for the closet farthest from the old crank phone, convinced the telephone lines will bring the lightning straight into the kitchen of her log house. We can see a hard rain sweeping in curtains across the lake; a light rain ringing on a still lake surface as we sit in the kitchen cabin, the windows open, and stare into dimpled water virtually within reach; and the soft overnight rain that falls on a cabin roof when there is neither ceiling nor leaks, the sweetest sound of all.

The three of us—mother, cousin, myself—sit on the rocks and eat the lunch we have carried in. It reminds us of, though it has no real connection to, the trout and venison and steaming blueberry pies that once came out of the woodstove that should still be standing virtually where we sit eating. But it is gone now, the magnificent log home from the late 1930s to the early 1970s remembered only by those who were here, the point once again much as it was when David Thompson realized the current was in his favour. Just as it once was with us.

The flag pole is gone. The mill on the far shore long gone. The log home and cabins gone. There is only a light breeze sweeping down the lake from the airport—which is how we cannot help describing it, though it has been many years since any plane bounced over the soft sand and blueberry bushes to reach Lake of Two Rivers. For us, when we stare down the lake past the island, we still see the airport.

It strikes me as strange that there are those who believe themselves of great taste and who will still disdain landscape, for it is the only art form into which we can actually step. "One looks from outside at works of art and architecture, listens from outside to music or poetry," Bob Marshall, the founder of the Wilderness Society, once wrote. "But when one looks at and listens to the wilderness he is encompassed by his experiences of beauty, lives in the middle of his aesthetic universe." Marshall would have liked this spot, for he, too, was afraid of the dark as a child and used to force himself to walk alone in the woods at night, both with and without a light.

But there was another aspect of the bush that Marshall treasured, and it is here on this rocky point just as it remains in the mountains he hiked. This, he argued, is the only art form that can gratify every one of the senses. Here on this point, an old woman and two middle-aged men, all three essentially silent, can taste fresh blueberry from the bush, smell the pine, feel the breeze off the water, see an airport that no one else can see and hear the slam of the screen door—even if we have not heard it for forty years or so.

I sit and am filled with such senses. I can hear again the creaking sound of the hand pump as the old ranger, khaki shirt drenched black under the armpits, pushes enough water up the hill for a bath. I can hear the sound tongs make when they catch on a big square of ice. I can hear the squeak of the old roller as the fishing boat is hauled up onto the dock and out of the pounding wind. The flag snaps; the washing machine burps; a match scratches across the gunwales of the fishing boat, the air fills with sulphur, with the crack of pine in the fireplace, with the sounds of children—our own children, myself as a child, my mother as a child—leaping out from the rocks, and again, for a moment, I see and feel and, yes, pray for Ann's beautifully arcing dive down, down, down to where she slits the water and disappears like a letter into an envelope.

She will not surface. Nor can I run to the Big House for a sheet and then back to the low rocks at the foot of the point, where I can unfurl the sheet and wave and snap it in the wind until Dunc sees and hauls in his steel line, Williams Wabler flashing in the sun, and turns the boat for shore, the old three-horsepower Evinrude roaring and the red wooden boat bucking over the waves as we call him for lunch.

No, we eat alone, knowing we are alone. Knowing, too, that there is something to be said for people who live good lives. We sit in silence listening to the wind in the high pines because we know, or at least we believe, that the wind makes a different sound on this point than it does anywhere else in the world.

It is the sound of coming home. Some to visit, some to stay forever.

CHAPTER FIVE

Tom and Jake Pigeon, the Algonquin Park cousins from nearby Cache Lake.

T HEY SAY THAT DAWN breaks, but not in Algonquin Park. Here morning seeps slowly in through the trees, soft and yellow on a good day, pink on a day that will often not work out. Heading east along Highway 60 in an old Chevrolet wearing a light blue canoe like a cocked air force cap, Jim and I crested Spring Hill into the first yellow hint of the splendid spring day to come, morning fog on the rise and the new grass along the shoulders silver with a heavy dew. We left the pavement at the Rock Lake turnoff, the dirt road rising behind us, a welcome sun in front.

We hadn't called ahead. There was no telephone anyway. We had simply agreed weeks ago to meet the Old Man for the opening weekend of trout season. He'd be there, waiting. He was never anywhere else.

It was going to be a fine day for it, the air warming and the bush on both sides of the rutted dirt road lightly dappled white with the first flowering pin cherry. The dogwood would soon follow. The poplar leaves were beginning to blossom, hinting at the weeks to come, but the bush was still far more purple than green. The only leaves fully out belonged to the ironwood high on slopes, but these were the rusted, stubborn leaves from last year— the old leaves refusing to fall until they were actually pushed out by the new. Ironwood, the perfect tree for the Old Man.

He was then still hanging on at the mill. He had passed sixty-five. He had reached seventy. And he was still there, still putting in his fifty-hour week, fifty-two weeks of the year. If he ever took a holiday, he liked to say, it would be in the park, so what was the point? There was no one to tell him to go away. The mill had been started up by his brother-in-law John Stanley Lothian McRae, then passed on to J.S.L.'s son, Donald, and was now being very capably run by Donald's sons, Bob and John. A nephew doesn't tell an uncle where to get off. A grand-nephew doesn't either. Besides, the two boys had adored the Old Man since they were toddlers; he was the always entertaining, endlessly kidding uncle who never failed to show interest in them and what they were doing. He had been as much a part of their lives as the mill itself. He worked; they paid. The subject of retirement never came up.

Some thought he'd just keel over dead on the job one day, but he seemed indestructible at work. Trees had fallen on younger men and killed them—he long kept one smashed hardhat around as a reminder—and heart attacks and car accidents and hard drinking and cancer and emphysema had taken a lot of others, including most of his immediate peers, but he kept showing up for work every morning, every day. Several years earlier, a young worker had picked up a fresh-sawn spruce board, swung to stack it and the end had smashed into the Old Man's head so hard it severed half his right ear. He couldn't find the ear part before he went down to the

Red Cross station in Whitney for stitches, but he was right back at work the following morning, a huge bandage giving his ear the folded look of a worried terrier.

A better bet would have been that he would die fishing. Fall and break a leg on a tough portage. Swamp the little boat in high water. Step over a log right onto a bear cub, as he once did walking into L'Amable Creek, and this time not be able to get away from the angry mother.

One spring earlier, it had very nearly happened. Shortly after the ice had gone out in the Madawaska River, he had headed downstream to fish along the narrows where the river flows into Rock Lake, and where he knew from experience the lake trout gather in shallow water to feed in the runoff. The old three-horsepower Evinrude sputtered and quit on his second pass. He had reeled in his steel line, set the trolling rod down on the floor of the twelve-footer and stood to start the engine again. It had sputtered and flooded. He waited, still standing, and then gave the cord one more mighty yank. The cord snapped, and he flew straight out of the boat, headfirst into the cold flush of the Madawaska waters.

In theory, that should have been the end of him. It was, after all, his third strike on drowning. He had escaped the nail under the Eganville dock when he was a child. He had escaped the car that flipped off the road into Hay Lake when he was in the prime of life. But he was now more than seventy. He was wearing high-laced, steel-toed workboots, insulated long underwear, heavy woollen pants, a thick deerskin cotton shirt, a sweater, a heavy winter jacket and, of course, his hardhat. The water was barely above freezing, ice still clinging to the south shore of the lake where the sun could not hit. And this time there was no one to dive in and pull him off the nail. Nor was there time to wait while the water slowly rose about him.

The experts say you have about five minutes in spring breakup water, if you're lucky. If the shock doesn't stop the heart, panic might burst it. Freezing waters and heavy clothes make movement difficult, if not impossible. Irrationality sets in quickly; hypothermia can kill even if the body is rescued still breathing, even if shore is reached and a fire struck.

"What did you think?" I had once asked him.

"Think about what?"

"About what was happening to you."

He drew hard on his cigarette, the uneven burn of a poorly rolled smoke darting up the paper. "Well, I figured that was that."

"*That was that?*"

"If this was how I was going to go, that was fine with me. I had no complaints. What the hell could I do about it?"

What he did was what he had always done: kick against convention. He kicked his way up to the surface, grabbed his hardhat, tossed it into the drifting boat, reached up and curled both hands over the transom, and began to kick.

The boat barely moved. His feet were in steel-toed boots that would not bend, the soles also with a length of steel under the arches to protect them from unexpected nails and spikes. He had no idea which would give out first: his feet or his cold hands, now losing all feeling in the frigid wind and against the ice cold aluminium.

There was a moment, he said, when it struck him how simple it would be just to give up. In a couple of days someone would notice he was missing. They would find the boat. They would drag the opening lake and find him eventually, even if it took a week or so, and everyone would say that the Old Man had gone out just the way he hoped to—with his boots on, trolling for lake trout.

He even found it oddly funny out there in the freezing waters. He held on with one hand, pounding the other to bring back feeling, and checked to see how far away the shore was.

And then he noticed the smoke.

It made no sense, but it was also no hallucination. Between the opening of the river and the widening of the lake, there was a small white cabin along the south shore. It was used rarely—in fact, entire summers would go by without a visitor—and yet here on a day when there was still ice along the shoreline and pockets of snow along the south banks, there was smoke rising, thick, white smoke curling and then vanishing into the wind. He began to kick harder.

I have sometimes tried to imagine what the man inside thought when he heard that first knock at the door. Whoever he was, he had come up from the city for some of Algonquin Park's treasured solitude. A fire was going in the woodstove. The lamps were lighted. Perhaps a good book was open. Certainly a bottle of brandy was either open or else about to be opened.

The Old Man stood there, dripping wet and shaking, his hard-hat back on his head. The boat was pulled up neatly on shore, tucked into the final banks of snow.

"Would you mind if I warmed up a bit?" the old bush man asked the city man. "I fell out of my boat."

He stayed long enough for a couple of bowls of soup and a few brandies, and for his clothes to dry over the fire. The two of them found a replacement cord for the old outboard, fired it up, and the Old Man headed back upstream towards the mill, half tempted to let out one more line before calling it a day, three hours after he had all but called it a life.

But the question now was when he would call it a career. The spring Jim and I came skipping over the washboard of Rock Lake Road was a time of transition for the logging operations. We were thinking opening day for trout—"the Sweet of the Year," the American fishing writer R. Palmer Baker had once so perfectly termed it—but there was a sour tinge to the soon-blossoming spring as we neared the final turn up a recently graded road and headed towards the old wooden bridge over the Madawaska. The old mill—south side of the river as it flows between Whitefish Lake and Rock Lake in Algonquin Park—was about to be shut down after more than twenty years of operation. It had been a grand run, but the timber limits were thinning. The company cut on a fifty-year cycle, and it was time to move back into timber territory that had not been worked since the 1920s and 1930s. If they kept this mill in operation, the distance between felling and finishing was going to be too great to be cost-effective. A new mill with new saws and new technology was going up at Whitney, on the eastern shores of Galeairy Lake. There were whispers in the mill that perhaps, when the actual move came, the old man would realize that it was time for him to close down as well, and that perhaps finally they could pry him loose from what was already becoming an awkward situation.

But as the boat transom found a spring earlier, when the Old Man got a good grip on, he wasn't quick to let go. He was still working. And even though the bunkhouses were already either torn down or being dismantled for shipping to the new mill site, he had staked out a room in the last of the buildings. No electricity. No water. But there was still one worker staying over: Dunc.

He was still sleeping when we arrived. The door to the rundown bunkhouse was unlocked and he was in a middle section. He had an iron bed, a mattress, one sheet and two moth- and mouse-eaten grey army blankets. There was a small table on one side of the bed, with a full ashtray and a coal-oil lamp on it. On the other side of the bed, nearest the window, he had a twenty-two rifle, fully loaded. His massive copy of Plutarch's *Parallel Lives* was across his chest, rising and falling with his deep, rattling snores.

He looked like a grizzled baby, his face untroubled, his head pink and stubbled above the ears and along the cheeks and over the chin. He awoke easily to a single touch, blue eyes clear and dancing with delight as they focused on two of his children. He was pleased to see us, but no more surprised by our appearance in his room than if two mosquitoes had breached the screen door. He had no questions for us: he knew why we had come. One of the perks of the bush is that there are no day planners. The sun rises, the sun sets. If you have arranged to meet with someone, you meet when they appear. Weekends are when the mill workers vanish and the tourists arrive. Fishing season is when the ice goes out. Winter is too obvious for comment.

We, however, did have questions. "Why the loaded gun?" He didn't know. Some punks from one of the villages farther down Highway 60 had driven in a few days earlier, perhaps thinking the mill had been shut down and was now open to scavenging and vandalism. They had thrown stones through windows before he had chased them away, a grizzled old hermit shaking his fist at a raked Plymouth as it fishtailed around the corner and away in a cloud of red-yellow dust. There were also wolves about, and ever since he had stood by helplessly while they ripped his little black dog to pieces not fifty feet from where we now stood, he had been rather less sympathetic to the laws of nature.

It was not his only rifle in the gun-free park. He also had, with the rangers' wink-and-a-nod blessing, a larger, Winchester model 30-30 hunting rifle, big enough to kill a grown bear with a single shot—which is exactly what it was intended to do, if necessary.

As Algonquin Park had phased out its numerous dumps—even *flying out* garbage from campers in the park interior at a cost that would make Federal Expressing garbage to another country seem a bargain—a few of the black bears had found their way to the Rock Lake mill yard, where the camp cooks still threw out the grease and slop that once would have gone to the pigs, even though it had been a full generation since the McRae camps raised their own pork. The bears gathered in the soft sand hills back of the drying lumber stacks, waiting for twilight, when they would make their way down through the piles to the back of the cookery to root for rotting vegetables and bacon-grease spills.

Twilight was also when the tourists began coming into the mill yard from the other direction. The desire to see a real bear while camping in Algonquin Park is stronger even than the desire to see a moose, but while the moose are far more accommodating—coming to the edge of the highway in spring to drink from the salt pools of the road runoff, coming in summer to escape the flies—the much less gregarious bears shunned the dangerous roads and the traffic that came to an instant halt at the first suggestion of a dark shadow emerging from the woods. They stuck instead to deeper woods, where only the logging operations could produce the berry crops that, decades earlier, used to follow fire. With satellite surveillance, air patrols and water bombers having severely reduced the incidence of fire in the park, new growth and berries were no longer what they once were. Nor were the deer that had once crowded the Highway 60 corridor like spare-change panhandlers along Toronto's Yonge Street. The deer had literally gone to greener pastures. The bear, never so forward as the deer, had simply retreated deeper, so deep that a sighting now was remarkable rather than the norm.

The last great tourist gathering for bear had been farther up the road at Lake of Two Rivers, where a huge dump had been bulldozed in off the road and the various camps and campsites would simply toss the day's waste into an ever-expanding pit. Throughout the fifties it had become a main attraction, tourists desperately trying to sight a bear through the camera lens in a manner which would ensure that neither the surrounding trash nor the chain-link fence that separated bear from human would show up in the frame. Tourists pressed tight to the fence for the best shots, and discovered that few things attract the wild black bear of North America better than the sickly sweet smell of an open bottle of cream soda.

In those years our grandfather, Tom McCormick, was still chief ranger of the park, and though I was only a child, I will never shake the chilling feeling of that August morning when he put me into the passenger seat of his old blue Dodge and we set out from his log home on Lake of Two Rivers for the nearby dump. It was closed off when we got there, several green Department of Lands and Forests trucks blocking the entrance and rangers in full uniform shooing away the curious. They backed up one of the trucks to let us through, and when we got in one of the young rangers told us what had happened.

One of the bear cubs had apparently not understood the strict protocol of scavenging at the park dump and had ventured outside the fenced-in pit. A young girl, her parents readying the camera for this unexpected but golden opportunity, had gone to the cub with a bottle of cream soda and the cub's mother, in a panic, had rumbled over and swatted the child away, cutting her on one arm. Technically, a bear attack.

It was hardly the first bear attack the park had known. In 1881, Capt. John Dennison, who had fruitlessly set out with his two sons to establish a farm on cleared bush near the edge of Opeongo Lake, was killed by a bear caught in one of his son's traps. He was eighty-two years old at the time, and apparently was able to hold off the angry bear long enough to command his eight-year-old grandson to paddle for the farm and help, which arrived too late for the old man. This attack paled in comparison, but Dennison was an old farmer, not a tourist, and the future of the park was certainly going to revolve around outside visitors, not potato harvests. This attack had been taken very seriously indeed.

By the time the old ranger and I arrived, the unfortunate scene had played itself out in a series of sharp rifle shots that had been heard as far away as the chief rangers' home on the point. The tourists had panicked, an ambulance had been called for the little girl and her scratch, and the park rangers had been summoned. Up at the park headquarters on Cache Lake, an official decision had been taken quickly by the park superintendent, a political appointee well aware of the need for visitors to feel absolutely safe. And now seven bears, two of them cubs, lay dead in the garbage pit, their stiff bodies swelling in the rising heat. We walked around like two detectives at a murder scene, the old ranger's silence a clear signal of his anger. He nodded to the rangers coming in with the heavy truck to cart away the bodies, and we drove home in silence. He spent the rest of the day splitting wood, the back and underarms and chest of his khaki ranger's shirt turning black with sweat as the axe tore into the blocks of wood with a ferocity that made helping him out of the question.

Bears could become a nuisance. Old or lazy or hurt, they would sometimes shun the hard work of the bush and the berry patches and the rotted logs and even the red suckers that would get trapped in shallow pools as spring creeks trickled into summer, and they would turn, instead, to the cookhouses or the mill yards in the hope of easy handouts and little effort. Competition from other bears could make them ill-tempered and desperate, and there were times when they would have to be controlled. The ministry had suggested Dunc keep his 30-30 at the mill for just this purpose, but in all the years he was designated to be the one in charge of the bears that would come around the McRae mill yards, he never once used it.

Bears had a way of amusing him. He liked, in particular, to watch an old sow deal with her cubs if they ventured too close to the cookhouse, growling at them and gently swatting their behinds until they did as she wished. And he loved the story of the little bear that had broken into the cookery in the years when Tom Cannon was the cook. Tom had been busy in the pantry when the bear came in through the screen, and he thought it was Donald McRae coming in to raid the freezer. Tom had stormed out, thinking he was catching Donald, and ran face first into the startled bear. Running out the door and down to the bunkhouse, Tom got Duncan and Donald to go back with him, and when they walked in the little bear was sitting in the sink, a pail of grease tipped up to his muzzle. The bear seemed even more surprised to see humans in his kitchen than Tom Cannon had been to see the bear, and he jumped so fast he broke through the window and away.

Duncan also took great delight in the futility of getting rid of them in any humane manner. The rangers would come in, trap a bear that had been coming too close to the campers or cookery, and then truck the beast forty miles or more before releasing it. "Four or five days later," Duncan said, "they'd be right back here."

Bears, to him, were company. In an evening, he could go up to the cookery, put out a pan of beans to soak for his molasses-sweet, and oddly renowned, pork and beans, and then go out back to sit on a stump, smoke a badly rolled cigarette and watch the bears work their way down from the sand hills, the little ones sometimes sliding on their haunches in the soft sand. He had names for most of them—Blackie and Three-Leg, Mother and the Boss—and he would sometimes even talk to them, as if they were all colleagues in the park simply gathering after work to share their day.

"It's dangerous to leave a loaded gun around, you know," Jim said.

"In what way?"

"What if somebody picks it up?"

"There's only me here."

"Well, what if you have an accident in here all by yourself?"

I do not know how to describe his look at such moments, but it is the facial equivalent of saying, "*Tch-tch-tch-tch-tch-tch-tch.*" The eyebrows knot, the forehead wrinkles, the mouth winces and the blue eyes widen as if Neville Chamberlain has just stepped off a logging truck and walked into the cookery to declare, "Peace in our time."

"How soon can you get ready?" I asked.

Again the look. It had taken us weeks to prepare. New line for the rods. In my case a new rod and reel. New lures to try out. A new rain suit for Jim in case it poured. Bait to buy. Gas for the outboard. Oil to mix with it. Telephone calls back and forth in the city. A division of duties. Two cars to co-ordinate. Alarm clocks to get us up. Coffee at the doughnut shop to get us going.

He stood up and was instantly ready. His trolling rod—a short, simple wheel-reel Murphy that was older than any of his other children—stood against the wall, the scratched and faded silver William's Wabler lure already dangling from the copper leader at the end of the steel line. Boots on, jacket on, hardhat on, and we were out the door and into the endless promise of opening day.

Over more coffee and some stiff, overcooked bacon at the cookery, we talked fishing, which is almost as good as fishing itself. The Old Man was still wondering about the Mystery Pond back of the mill where—five? ten? *fifteen* years ago—he had watched the "young lad" come walking out of the bush with a string of five magnificent speckled trout, the smallest about three pounds and the largest close to five. He had asked the young worker— always referred to as "the young lad" around the mill, no matter how many young men there were, how often they changed or, in the case of Mickey, who served as the mill's "young lad" through most of the 1960s and 1970s, how very old they grew—where he had caught such spectacular fish, and the young lad had simply pointed "back there" and headed off to the cookery to clean his catch and pack them in the ice house.

"It's got to be that creek that runs in spring," Dunc said.

"Then we should try it tomorrow," said Jim.

"Or maybe it's that little lake on top of the hill."

"We'll go tomorrow."

"Maybe it's where we used to keep the logs."

Every year it was the same story: this would be the year when we would find out where the young lad had made his historic catch. We'd tried the creek. We'd walked into different lakes. We'd fished the lake to which, in winter, they used to draw the logs and pile them out on the ice, letting them soak all summer until it was time to peel the bark and run them through the big band saws at the mill. But no one had ever found the sweet spot from which the young lad came walking back that long-ago day. The "young lad" was now probably fifty and had himself forgotten, if he wasn't already dead.

"We'll go tomorrow."

The young lad's Mystery Pond had become such an obsession with the Old Man that we had long since given up thinking it might be made up. You had to be careful, though, for fish stories were an art in the park. One of Tom McCormick's fellow rangers, Jack Gervais, had always claimed he knew a spring-fed creek where the water bubbled up so ice cold that all he had to do was walk upstream waving his hands and the speckles would race ahead to the source, where, in the snap of a finger, they would freeze solid. Jack claimed he could then reach in with his hands, yank the frozen fish out and stack them along the shore like cord wood. Robert, a sometime drinking buddy of Duncan's when he went into town, made the preposterous claim to Jim and me that he had once found himself up North without any fishing gear and came across a river so thick with Arctic char that he managed to catch thirty of them on a roll of toilet paper before the paper became too soggy to hold any more.

The Old Man had his own treasure-trove of fishing tales. He would tell the story of the time he and some other park loggers had portaged into a lake so thick with trout that he'd simply tied a line to his paddle while the others hurried off to cut poplar and alder poles to use as rods. The first trout bit on a bare hook, and when he lofted it up onto the banks, a fresh feed of shiner minnows had spilled from its gullet. Using the minnows as bait, he had his full limit before the first friend came back with his fresh-cut poplar pole. Some of his stories were hilarious, like the time he took Mickey fishing and Mickey yanked a lure out so hard it flew up into his face and stuck. He fished the rest of the day with a hook dangling out of his lip.

I have never known exactly how to take such stories. I think, because he told it so many times, there was truth, or at least some truth, to the story of the paddle and the trout, yet Jack Gervais's story was told so many times it was clearly made up, and everyone knew and enjoyed it for that. Good "fish stories," after all, have been around since Cleopatra pulled one on Antony back in the first century and the Old Man's beloved Plutarch wrote it down for everyone to enjoy. After the Roman conqueror had bragged about his fishing skills, Cleopatra ordered one of her men to dive under the boat and attach a salted fish to Anthony's line, giving it a mighty tug first. When Antony proudly hauled up his catch, already cleaned and salted, "They all fell a laughing."

I remember laughing, but probably should not have, at a story told in one of the books the Old Man left behind, Richard Llewellyn's post–Second World War classic *How Green Was My Valley.* There is a part in this lovely book where young Huw's father teaches him to "tickle trout"—something I could not, and still cannot, believe possible. But Llewellyn wrote that the Morgans would sit out on a flat rock on the village stream, drop pebbles to scare off the minnows, and then, when a fat trout came along, roll up their sleeves and plunge an arm, hand open, into the cold mountain water until the curious trout would begin rubbing up against their fingers. They would then rub the trout's stomach and "tickle his ribs. Sometimes he would flash away and you would lose him, but oftener he would stay on. Then you would work your fingers along him until your little finger was inside his gill. That was enough. Give him a jerk and pull out your arm, and there he would be, flapping on the rock."

However the young lad had caught those marvellous speckles, I knew for certain it had not been by tickling. Algonquin Park trout are not the same as Welsh trout. Nor, for that matter, do you find many flat rocks to lie on in the middle of shallow streams.

"He caught them on his lunch break," the Old Man said, as if it happened only this past week. "So it can't be far from here."

"We'll look tomorrow."

First, though, we would head down the Madawaska to Rock Lake, where he had fallen in that other opening day, and then farther down Rock to where we would portage into Pen Lake, an out-of-the-way and superior location for lake trout. We would use the little boat and three-horse Evinrude for the trip, both light enough for the portage. There were new rules in the park about bait—no bringing live minnows into the park—so we would also cart along a minnow trap to set once we got down to Pen.

"Did you bring worms?" the Old Man wanted to know.

"I did." I said proudly. "And trout worms, too. Smaller than dew worms. Cost a little more—but better."

He turned, skeptical.

"Coming up Highway 400," I continued. "At Epp's."

Eyebrows down, mouth wincing. "They must have thought you were an American."

He didn't have to explain. He figured I'd been taken. Since worms aren't found naturally in lakes or streams, by what criterion does one worm become a "trout" worm? And why pay more for smaller?

"Let's go."

We set out after washing the dishes, the sun now over the sand hills and taking the chill out of the day. He kept his little aluminium boat—the romance of the wooden boat lost long ago to leaks and yearly tarring—down by the Whitefish Lake pumphouse, which kept the mill's hot pond supplied with water. Our pant legs were wet and cold with dew from the catchy raspberry bushes as we pushed through with Jim's canoe to the pumphouse, but the sun on the sand shore was warm and eager to dry us out. We filled the Evinrude with gas, pulled the oars and a couple of life preservers out of the pump house, tied the canoe painter to the back of the outboard and set out, an early arrival blue heron flushing with the first pull of the starter cord.

Jim worked the motor, I sat in the bow watching for rocks and the Old Man took the middle seat, where he immediately began fumbling with papers and tobacco. Soon enough the cigarette was in his mouth, dripping tobacco and bent like a missed nail, and he was snapping a wooden Eddy's match—"The same kind Winston Churchill used"—across the bottom of the seat, lifting it to this ridiculous cigarette and dragging deep, white smoking trailing behind us. Under the stern seat, where he would have been sitting if he had been heading off alone to fish, ran a thousand red-and-blue lines where he had fought to get similar matches going out of the wind; to his left, a hundred or more knife marks where minnows had been reduced to tails for bait.

Sitting in front, I could not get the full benefit of the smell. In an inexplicable way, I abhor smoking just as much as I adore the first waft of a lighted cigarette in the outdoors. If I associate the first with death and stale smells, another part of my brain clearly identifies the latter with the Old Man, a boat and the open water of an Algonquin lake.

We cut into the river, mist running in loose snakes from the point of our bow, the water so still it sizzled as the boat sliced through the slow twists of the Madawaska that join Whitefish Lake to Rock Lake. Jim pointed off to the right, where circles were spreading. "Speckle," Dunc said through his cigarette. "Lake trout won't jump—they roll." Jim and I nodded as if we already knew.

Apart from the drone of the little motor, it was magnificently silent as we benefited from the same current that had so delighted the explorer David Thompson a century and a half earlier. Not all that much—aluminum boat and outboard aside—had changed in the years since. The Madawaska River still twisted quietly, running deep and dark through the cedars and alders and spruce. There were signs of otter sliding, beaver chews, heavy tracking on the banks where the moose had come down to drink.

We passed out of the river mouth, the mist now fully lifted, and chugged down past the white cottage where, a year earlier, the Old Man's life had been saved by a fluke and a fire. On table-still waters we headed down Rock Lake a good three miles before we hit the first portage of the day, the boat slipping softly and silently into the mud and cedar roots and rusted pine needles of the landing site.

The portage was long and decidedly uphill. "Go on ahead and take your time, Dad," Jim said. "We'll do it all." One disgusted flash of blue eyes and the extra paddle, the life preservers and the fishing equipment were all in his arms, leaving the two of us to take turns stumbling up the pine-needled path with the canoe on our shoulders. When we caught up to him, moving quickly, he was already at the far end of the portage and sitting on a rock near the small rapids. He was fashioning a new cigarette, enjoying the sound of spring rush trying to break a small log-jam.

Here was where we had intended to catch the necessary minnows. Pen Lake, however, was at an even higher altitude than
Whitefish or Rock, the ice so recently gone out that winter debris
still floated around the bays and small crusts of ice still clung like
broken window panes to the rocks along the shore.

"Too cold for minnows," the Old Man announced. "They won't
be around yet."

"Maybe I can catch a couple on worms," I suggested, fitting
together my rod and reaching for the expensive "trout" worms.

"They won't bite," Dunc said. And they didn't. I cast several
times into the still water to the far side of the log-jam, but nothing.

"Forget it," Jim finally called from the landing area, where he
had the canoe laid out and ready. "We'll just have to catch our
trout on lures."

Jim was already rigging his trolling rod with the latest secret for
success: a twenty-dollar assembly of leader, spoon, harness and plastic minnow that it looked like he had been building most of the
winter.

"*Tch-tch-tch-tch-tch-tch-tch.*"

"If we can just catch one," Jim protested. "We can cut it up for
bait."

"You'll have to catch the one first," said Dunc. He didn't sound
convinced.

The Old Man took over the role of pilot for this lake. Jim and
I took turns paddling at trolling speed, but the decisions as to
where to go were all his. He knew this isolated lake in the same
way that we like to think we know our own shortcomings. He
had never seen a fish finder in his life. He had never owned—and,
for all I knew, could not read—a topographical map. What he had
done here, as he had done with Whitefish and Rock and Lake of
Two Rivers and Opeongo and a dozen smaller lakes we were
never to mention to others, was to map out the bottom with the

click of his steel line and his hands. He knew where the shoals were and on which side the trout were likely to be feeding and when. He knew where the holes were and what weeks in the dead of summer the trout would be there. He had no thermometer to find out where the appropriate thermal level for trout would be. He just knew from feel, the way the blind learn the layout of a house. And he knew from faith, as convinced that he would be able to find trout in a certain lake as an evangelist is that there are answers in a certain book.

"What is it you like about fishing?" I once asked him.

It was a question I had heard myself a hundred times. To non-fishers, fishing is monumentally boring, but as the marvellous Canadian writer Roderick Haig-Brown pointed out, "Fishing is a very flexible sport. You make of it almost anything you will, from a considerable athletic effort to a quiet mood of observation and reflection." Personally, I had come rather to like the boring part of fishing. While I was out in a canoe or standing by the shores of a lake or wading about the banks of a creek, there were no meetings, no telephones, no deadlines but the setting sun and the distance back. Of course, he had no telephone anyway, and had never been to a meeting in his life. And as for deadlines, mill management already knew what he thought about matters like retirement.

It couldn't be conversation he sought. While he enjoyed company, he almost always fished alone and, like Haig-Brown, preferred being alone. Besides, the conversation of fishing is never about fishing, as television has never understood with those embarrassing shows that seem to parody the activity far more than praise it. No park fishers ever sat in a boat and discussed what they were using. They never dressed like they were Vietnam helicopter pilots headed behind the lines. They did not use the word "structure" or suddenly find they had developed Alabama accents just because they happened to be fishing for bass.

"I like the suspense," he said. "The anticipation. You're up here. They're down there. Maybe they'll hit today. Maybe they won't.

"I can sit here and imagine what's happening down there. Maybe there's this huge twelve-pounder just following along, watching. When I work the line, he sees the flash. Maybe he even knocks it with his nose. I like to think about what the bottom looks like and how the line is going over it and what the trout think when they see it. Will he strike now? Will he wait? He knows when he'll hit. I don't. So I have to be ready for him."

It took him no time to get his equipment ready once we reached the deeper water. The silver William's Wabler was already attached to the steel line, the steel line already threaded through the rod eyes and onto the simple reel of the old Murphy. He was not into the affectations of fishing. He had an old dog-eared copy of Izaak Walton's *Compleat Angler*, and, like Walton, the fish he loved "to angle for above any fish" was trout. But he wasn't much into intellectualizing the sport in either direction. Had he heard Byron's attack on Walton as a defender of "the stupidest of pretended sports," he would have laughed at the poet's misunderstanding of what fishing was. If Pound had come by to tell him that trout have souls, as he once argued, Dunc would also have laughed, but probably agreed. If man had a soul, which was not necessarily a point he was willing to accept, then certainly trout would have one, as well. More pure and more valiant to boot.

No philosophy, no pretending, no mannerisms. He simply lifted up his old rod, spit once on the Williams and dropped it over the edge.

"Why do you spit on your lure?" I once asked him.

"I don't know," he said. "I just did it once years ago and caught a nice fish. I've done it ever since."

Jim, on the other hand, had a tackle box like a condominium complex. He had the latest Finnish lures, the latest American inventions, the latest Canadian trick. He had fresh line. He had sharpened his hooks over winter. He had greased his reel and tested his rod and even had a little pink contraption that forced the line deeper and another contraption that could slide down that line, if necessary, and pluck the expensive lure off a rock or a log. The total original retail value of all that the tackle box held was likely as much as, or more than, the Old Man had in his single bank account.

We began to troll, Jim paddling while I, sitting in the bow, fished with monofilament line and the Old Man, sitting in the middle seat, let out his steel line on the other side. He pulled the old Murphy rod back and forth in his slow, methodical draw that snapped the spoon every few seconds. With each slow yank, he grimaced, a tightening and spreading of the mouth that seemed to have as much to do with prayer as effort. We worked the southeast shore in narrow figure eights, thinking the trout to be shallow.

But if they were, they weren't biting. After more than an hour, Jim and I were moving beyond suspense and anticipation into boredom. We were eating sandwiches, ham and cheese, that we'd brought from the cookery. To break the monotony, I hauled in, wrapped some of my ham over the hook and let out the line again.

My mind must have drifted. I could not do as the Old Man had advised and think of the lure and the line and what trout might be following, waiting. Instead, I was thinking of cold beer and scanning the far shore for something of interest. Perhaps a moose or a deer.

I felt a tug. Sharp but not too strong, then sharp again.

"I think I've got something."

"Bottom," Duncan suggested.

I reeled some line in. "I think it's still on."

"*Think?*" Jim questioned. "Can't you tell?"

"No. Not really."

But a minute later we could: a small white belly came twisting and skipping off the light wake of the boat and arrived at the side. The Old Man put the small net we were carrying under it, lifted, and the fish, still well hooked by a lure that all but dwarfed it, fell through the webbing and back into the water, where it turned lamely onto its side.

"For God's sake," he growled back over his shoulder. "It's smaller than your goddamn worms."

"Throw it back before somebody sees us with it," Jim said.

"I can't. It's dead."

"Never mind," snapped the Old Man. "We can use it for bait."

And so we kept it, a nine-inch, malnourished lake trout that looked as if it had spent the winter locked in the ice. "I really didn't think they came that small," Jim snickered. Yet it was still some encouragement to us all, and for another long period we trolled in earnest, until in the end we had to conclude that the one strike had been more an immature, or starving, trout's foolishness than our own skill or good fortune.

"Trout are like people," Duncan said as the first shadows began sneaking out from the western shoreline. "Some days they feel like doing something. Some days, nothing. And this is one of those days."

But Jim was hardly so acquiescent. "I've never been skunked before on opening weekend," he grumbled. "And I've no intention of starting now."

"You forget," I protested, "my trout."

But he saw neither truth nor humour in that. Saying nothing, Jim began assembling his equipment for what was to become an obsessive pursuit for evidence that we were smarter than trout. Duncan wisely elected to stay put. We landed at the far portage and he went and sat on a large rock that was already warm from the sun and began rolling a fresh smoke. Jim and I would trudge up the difficult portage with our gear. We climbed over fallen logs, through close pines that scratched our arms and wet our thighs, past new trillium shoots and fern curls just beginning to show, past tiny crystallized pockets of stubborn snow, and eventually we came to a perfectly still little lake. We worked entirely around the north side, stepping unsteadily on the rocks and catching nothing but a good view of a hawk circling. It hardly mattered, though: apart from the occasional sound of wind through ducks' wings and the irregular click of a cast on still water, there was nothing to listen to but the grinding of Jim's teeth.

Fishing, for Duncan and Jim, had taken on a dynamic different from that felt by any of the other children and their father. There was a competitive edge there, as there always seems to be with first-borns, and their relationship, oddly enough, had warmed considerably in the years since Jim had set out, even if a bit unconsciously, to prove himself as good or better a fisherman than the Old Man. Jim had left high school for a banking career, and he had often criticized Duncan for his terrible money-managing skills. There had long been a chill between them—Jim speaking up for his mother when there would be bills unpaid and cheques needed—whereas the rest of us had conveniently avoided this continuing family debate over finances. Years passed, the monthly money crisis faded and Jim, who had shown little interest in the bush since his youth, found himself returning to it with increasing fervour as a successful banking career became increasingly harried. He now belonged to a hunt camp and went on fly-in fishing trips and had all the latest gear and read all the right magazines and books. Technically, he knew many times more than the Old Man. And yet the Old Man still caught as many, or more, fish. They came at it from different directions, Jim pouring his energy into fishing, the Old Man seeming to use the drone of the motor, the warmth of the sun and the endless rhythm of working a trolling line to let him all but sleep sitting up. And yet, in result and in appreciation of each other's abilities, they had found more common ground here than they had ever known elsewhere. Jim took countless photographs of Dunc with his day's catch. Dunc didn't even know how to work a camera, but when he told others about Jim's catches—and word got back to Jim—it was as if Jim had been handed a full-glossy, framed portrait of the two of them, arm in arm, with a twelve-pound speckle in each of their spare hands.

Empty-handed, Jim and I came down from the lake, found the Old Man snoozing in the sun, roused him and again tried trolling from the canoe. Still nothing. Returning to the base of the lake, we set out on foot and tried the top and bottom of the long rapids, and again failed. We decided to give up and head back to camp, the portage longer, the canoe heavier, the Old Man still shouldering his share and setting the pace. He seemed not in the least bothered by this bust of an opening day. We had not yet reached the stage of acceptance that separates those who fish from those who seek fish. Roderick Haig-Brown claimed that he could get just as much pleasure from finding a dark, deep new pool as he would from a fine fight with a salmon. For him, the delight of catching a nice speckle was equal only to the delight of catching light at the perfect angle for seeing in under the skirt of a difficult bank.

"These things never grow stale," he wrote. "I may find them or I may not. It matters very little. In searching I shall certainly find other things, expected or unexpected, and from somewhere among them I shall take home at least one bright picture of excitement or beauty to make the day. After forty years, rivers remain places of enchantment and the fish that swim in them creatures of wonder. Some small share in this is the fisherman's real reward."

But Jim and I had many years to go before we could ever hope to reach that plane. The closer we drew back to the mill, the more Jim seemed closer to panic. Heading into Whitefish from the

Madawaska, he insisted we try several wide sweeps past the spot where he'd seen the speckle jump earlier in the day. But there were no longer circles and, it now seemed, no longer fish.

It was a costly delay. A quarter-mile from the boat's slip by the pumphouse, the motor kicked once and died, the boat coming to a quick halt in the current and soon enough heading backwards.

Perhaps we had run into the greatest fish story of them all—the Goby that Pliny the Elder, another of the Old Man's beloved ancient historians, had recorded as fact in his *Natural History*. The Goby was, according to Pliny, who didn't have a reputation for exaggeration, a two-inch-long fish more powerful than the heaviest anchors and the strongest gales. Writing with a straight face, Pliny recorded that when Gaius had been unable to make it back to Rome with his four hundred rowers, the baffled sailors had dived down to check the vessel and discovered a single Goby hanging on the rudder. And the truly amazing thing about this creature, Pliny claimed, was that when it was brought up out of the water, it appeared to have lost all power. "The Goby," wrote dear Pliny, "holds off their attacks and tames the fury of the universe with no effort or resistance of its own other than suction."

We, however, had just run out of gas. The little Evinrude was dry, and there was not a drop left in the single can of gas we had carried with us.

Another park old-timer was out on the lake and saw us rowing. He pulled up and turned his boat around, heading over. He would offer us a tow.

"Catch anything?" he called as he cut the engine and tossed a heavy rope over my outstretched arm.

He was clearly speaking to me.

"*Nothing!*" Jim and Duncan shouted at once.

*   *   *

That evening, there were no fishing stories told. Instead, we stood out on the back steps of the cookery in the fading twilight and watched the bears come down from the sand hills and work their way through the lumber piles. There were few, if any, campers in the park at this time of year, and none had come down to the mill this night, so the bears were less cautious. One huge one was bold enough to lumber directly up to where the grease was dumped and begin rooting around, oblivious to our presence not fifty feet away. He was large and older, the hair faded along his flanks so it almost gave him the look of an elegant touch of grey along the sides. As long as he stood by the slop pile, no other bear would dare advance closer. Only when he had finished did others come close, but by then there was nothing worthwhile left for them.

After dark fell, we sat in Jim's car and listened to the ball game fading in and out through the rock cuts surrounding the mill. The Toronto Blue Jays were playing the Baltimore Orioles. It wasn't the Yankees and the Dodgers, but it wasn't the 1950s either, and this time the beer came from the cooler, not the creek. After the game, we played a few rounds of cribbage, and went to bed early. Jim and I wanted to get a good start on the second day. We would use the canoe only for this leg of opening weekend. The Old Man had decided he would stay at the camp and read. It was too early for trout, he had concluded, a waste of time trolling for fish that weren't yet interested. Even when we announced that we would, once and for all, track down the young lad's Mystery Pond, he wouldn't budge from his decision.

"Good luck," he said. "I hope somebody finds it."

It rained lightly during the night. We rose early, the air chillier than it had been the day before, pulled on extra sweaters, packed lunches, gathered up our tackle and set out before the sun could rise over the sand hills. We set off walking in the direction from which the young lad had strolled with his speckled-trout catch a decade or two earlier, and we had some hope that, this time, we would finally find out where he had been. It wasn't as if there were a hidden lake back there no one knew about. We knew every creek and bog and lake for miles in every direction. But we also knew that there had to be a hidden spot in one of those creeks or lakes, a glory hole that, somehow, had been stumbled on by the young lad and no one since.

It was tough walking. The rain followed by a morning sun was calling up the first blackflies of the season, and the microscopic terrorists were finding their way under collars and up sleeves. We were loaded down with the canoe and paddles, a couple of life preservers, creels and rods, and the ground was loose where the snow had so recently melted and run. In the swampier areas, our feet made sucking sounds with every step, and our eyes had to be constantly down to ensure a boot always followed. Jim did most of the canoe-carrying, and so was unable to see more than a few feet in front at the best of times. But even I, relatively unencumbered, kept eyes down to the trail for fear of slipping or sticking. We could only listen to what was going on around us. In the lower, wet ground, the spring peepers were lightly ringing. A ruffed grouse pounded a wing. A raven was inventing sounds as he followed us, the gurgles and clunks and whirrs and poppings so bizarre that visitors to the park sometimes mistake the raven for a Rube Goldberg contraption that has been set up and left running in a hollowed-out elm.

We checked the creek we had always suspected of hiding the big speckles, but there was neither black hole nor action to be found there. We worked along it in a tangle of alders and cedar and black spruce, each flick of the wrist a reminder that fly rods, with their elaborate swings and loops and curling lines, were all but impossible in the Precambrian forest. Lures, too, were useless. We could only bait a small hook with one of my expensive little worms and try to loft the bait upstream, letting it bounce down along the gravel and among the rocks and hope against hope that it would bump into an open mouth. But nothing. We may as well have been trying to tickle them up out of the water.

Picking up the canoe again, we set off to higher ground, working ever closer to a small, round lake that had once been promising with speckles and then lost to bass, and that, some believed, was slowly coming back to trout. We broke out of the tangle and onto an old logging road, which made walking easier, but both of us were covered with sweat by the time we reached the first bay of the lake where, in younger years, we had learned to ride the log booms like river men of old. Difference was that our logs weren't moving. Another difference was that we kept falling in. And yet another was that we survived.

We put the canoe in, filled it with our fishing equipment and set out, Jim steering and me essentially free to ply the shoreline with gentle casts. Still nothing. I paddled and Jim fished. We drifted and both fished. We anchored and fished. We used the worms. We used small spinners. We tried small fly-like lures that might fool them into thinking a new hatch—black-and-orange hair, steel running through the middle, barbed hook curling up from the bottom—was in the air. But nothing.

By noon our legs were aching from kneeling. There are approximately a hundred different positions to take in a canoe on calm water, but none of them is comfortable after the third hour. We needed out, if only to go to the bathroom.

"Try the point," Jim suggested.

It wasn't really a point, any more than the so-called bay was really a bay, but in a round lake you still require some points of reference. There was the rock with the Indian painting on it, though it was rather more likely a rock that had been painted by a fisherman back when ice fishing was permitted so he would remember where he had had some luck. There was the deadhead. There was the swampy bay where the logs had once sat soaking. And the point, a small outcropping of flat, fractured stones that made it possible to stand and cast out into deep water. Also a great place to eat sandwiches and, when the sun was just high enough, lie down and sleep for an hour or two.

We pulled the canoe up onto the rocks and went about the task of groaning and small-stepping and heading into the chokecherry bushes and scratchy nettles for a leak. The spring violets were out. The moss was cool and soft, perfect for a snooze if only a breeze would down the blackflies.

"Look at this!" Jim called from back near the rocks.

I walked out of the bushes. He was pointing. A huge snapping turtle was moving over the rocks like some astronaut floating outside the capsule, his heavy legs bouncing him along sideways as he seemed to stare up, challenging. I hurried over to watch, still fascinated by what surely was one of the first monsters of my young imagination. Snapping turtles had terrified us as children at Lake of Two Rivers. They would often crawl up on the rocks to sit in the sun, and we would foolishly push at them with whatever was necessary to get them back in the water and out of the way so we could play and swim. We had seen them snap paddles and rakes in half with one flashing bite. We had seen massive snappers that required four men to flip them over and tie their legs and lift them into a burlap sack so the rangers could take them up to the park museum for display. But we had learned, eventually, that snapping turtles are absolutely harmless, particularly if you leave them alone, and always if you happen to encounter them in water. They have no interest whatsoever in being around anyone else, including their own kind. They are also the only creature in the park to live as long as the Old Man. Who knows, perhaps one day they will find out that shunning company is the real secret to long life.

"First sign of life we've seen," I said.

"I'm going to try it here for a while," said Jim. He was already rigging up a line.

We tried casting with lures, but nothing. We fished with bobbers, but there is something childlike and unskilled about bobbers, so we soon abandoned them as well. We then tried something of enormous skill: baitting a tiny dark hook, no leader, with a small worm, no weight, and tossing the damn thing as far as it would fly, letting it float to the bottom under its own weak gravity pull. We tossed out, set flat rocks over our rods and turned to our sandwiches.

I was just biting into a ham and cheese, the mill bread so big it had first to be sliced in quarters, when I noticed Jim's rod flicking slightly.

"You've got something!"

"What?"

He jumped so fast the sandwich fell and crumbled. Flicking the rock out of the way, he lifted his rod, felt the line lightly with finger and thumb, waited for a second, more convincing pull and then set the hook with one fine, deft and delicate yank.

"What is it?" I asked. "Bass?"

"I don't think so."

It is part of the fishing credo to believe that a fish can be positively identified—smallmouth or largemouth, speckled or rainbow, stocked or natural—by nothing more than the feel of the pull. Smallmouth bass yank and always break water; whitefish have such delicate mouths they need to be nursed to the surface; pickerel seem oblivious; Northern pike have nothing but contempt for anyone who would dare think they can out-muscle them.

"Speckle," Jim announced.

I immediately accepted this as truth. Jim has his father's fishing hands; I do not.

Quietly, as if deciding life and death in a library, Jim worked the fish in closer to the rocks, where it darted quickly into a crevice and out again.

"Speckle," he confirmed.

I had the net, and was prepared for the worst. I have lost so many fish for family and friends that it is a wonder I am even allowed to handle one any more. It may be wiser to have no net than one that is in the hands of someone who is apt to lunge out and catch the fish mid-belly at any time, knocking it free of the hook and back into the water.

Jim pulled it up on the rocks, the fish sliding on the slight slime of the granite and splashing a path farther up as it broke water. I set the net behind and under it, and when it flipped, I scooped.

"Got him!"

"Shhhhh! There'll be more there," Jim whispered.

It has always intrigued me that those who fish will spend thousands of dollars fooling a creature that has not the sense to move on when it sees one of its schoolmates suddenly wide-eyed and flying towards the surface with a vicious barbed hook through its mouth. But I have learned to accept that some fish—speckles and pickerel, in particular—hang out together, often too much so for their own good. If you catch one, chances are excellent you will catch others. It follows, of course, that if you catch none, chances are 100 per cent that you will not catch anything.

We fished frantically from that point on. I caught a small one-pounder. Jim caught two more, one small, one a good two pounds. He set a stringer and placed the trout down around the slight bend in the point, tying it to a small birch that was growing in a rock crevice and out over the water. They were in shade and deep enough to stay fresh, but far enough out of the way not to disturb or somehow signal the others that we were still chasing. I caught, but lost another. Jim caught one. I caught two. And then, as always happens, they quit hitting.

We cast and waited, bouncing the small hooks and worms back over the bottom and up the rocks. A few minnows would follow the bait in, but no more trout. We paused while Jim got his camera out and each of us, in turn, posed with the string of trout. I was just setting the stringer back on the birch branch when Jim cleared his throat.

"Do you smell what I smell?" he asked.

I sniffed the air. Not trout, which has its own smell. Not the moss or the blossoms. I sniffed again. There was something.

Something slightly skunky. Something foul, wild.

I looked at Jim. I could tell from his look that he was thinking the same thing.

Bear!

"I thought I heard some crashing a while ago," Jim said.

I had heard nothing. But now I could hear my own blood crashing.

I listened hard, straining. The breeze was slight, but it was coming from behind us rather than off the water. If it was bear we had smelled, he had to be in the woods back of us. He would be between us and the mill. It made sense. There were obviously bears around the mill. Perhaps it was the big silvertip we had seen the night before. The one with the poor disposition.

There were always sounds coming from the bush: the long whistles of the white-throated sparrow, the guttural grunts of the great blue heron, chickadees, ravens, squirrels scolding, crows gathering, sometimes the hiss of a deer. But none of them ever caused any alarm.

I kept listening. Wind in the pines. My own blood gushing

around my ears. And then a rumble and a crack—hard. Wood snapping. With force.

"There is something," I said.

We began talking louder. That, of course, is the smartest thing to do in the bush if you suspect bears, for they will always leave if they think someone is around them. Or at least that is the general belief.

We knew from experience that noise would frighten off a bear. We had seen our own one-hundred-pound grandmother chase a four-hundred-pound bear off by running right at him and pounding a pot with a wooden spoon. That had worked so well that the bear had somehow seemed to pull his butt ahead of his shoulders as he bolted for the safety of the woods. But neither of us had her nerve, and we knew it. We had both come across bears enough in the bush and in campgrounds to have a healthy respect for them. The two best bush people we knew, our cousins Tom and Jake Pigeon, were both extraordinarily respectful of bears, and refused to walk through the woods without an axe or, if possible, a gun in one hand.

I sometimes think that the only ones who believe there is a proper way to deal with bears are those who have just a modicum of bush experience—enough to consider themselves capable, but not enough to know the reality of fear. Those who know nothing about the bush and those who know too much about the bush are closer than they might imagine in how they regard bears—as unpredictable. Those who know too much about the bush, however, are honour-bound not to let their true fears show, and the art of bluff becomes as important to the handling of fellow travellers as it is to the bear itself.

"He'll go away," I said with supreme confidence, blood still rushing.

"Sure."

Talking a bit louder, dropping the odd rock, stepping heavily over the shoreline, we fished a little longer, but without success. Nothing was biting any more.

"Our noise may have scared away the fish," Jim suggested.

"Possibly," I agreed.

"What say we take the canoe back out for a bit and try by the marked rock again?"

"Good idea," I said. It was perfect. We would have the safety of the canoe and we would have rationalized our fight by convincing each other that it was only the pursuit of fish that drove us, not the pursuit of normal blood pressure.

"We'll come back here and pack up," Jim said. "Let's just go out and try our luck for fifteen minutes or so."

We got into the boat cockily, flaunting our disregard for whatever it might have been that we had smelled and heard. We were of the bush and the water, and we were chasing the speckled trout, and nobler than that one rarely feels.

The air was cool and fresh over by the rocks. I let out my line and sagged, happy for the comfort of the canoe. Jim cast towards the rocks, letting his line settle. I got caught on bottom and lost a hook, but that was all we caught.

"Look," Jim said softly.

I followed his stare. Over by the swampy bay there was a large black blur moving, then stopping. In the distance it seemed to have silver sides.

The bear.

"Big bugger," Jim said.

"That's the cranky one from the yard last night."

"I think so. But he's completely on the other side now. Let's gather up our stuff and head back."

I didn't have to answer. He was already putting down the rod and pulling out his paddle. He was just as eager as I to get going. We could pick up our gear on shore and leave from there, following a short trail back up onto the logging road and then back to the mill. The bear was in entirely the opposite direction, and heading even farther on.

I felt good and safe. It had been a glorious day. Perhaps this wasn't the young lad's Mystery Lake, but perhaps, too, it was. We had a fine feed of trout, seven in total, and a couple of them large enough to impress and perhaps even to suggest that this indeed had been the magical spot that had produced the finest speckle catch in Algonquin history.

The water was calm. The breeze was down, soon to change so it was coming in off the water. There was no smell of bear in the air. I had all but forgotten that he had even been around. Jim started gathering up our gear.

"You grab the stringer," he said.

I walked to the edge of the point, where the birch was overhanging. The stringer was still attached. I unclipped it and pulled up gently from the black, shadowed waters of the drop-off.

Our seven speckles were still there—in a way.

But only the heads were attached.

"Jim!" I called out. "You better come here."

Jim hurried over, his eyes questioning. I held up the stringer. Seven heads, followed by shreds of white, pulverized flesh and dripping blood.

"What the hell?"

I looked down, catching movement where the late-afternoon sun was still dancing on the rocks below the waterline. What looked like a dark branch stabbed down through the sunline—but there were long claws on the end of the branch! Then a head came into view. Then a shell the size of a car tire.

The snapping turtle.

"Jesus Christ!"

"Oh, no!"

"He ate them all," I pointed out the obvious.

"Goddamn it!"

"What're we going to do?"

Jim said nothing. He was red-faced and biting his lip. The snapper would have lain in wait until the speckles tired themselves or died, and then moved in for his meal. For all we knew, he had been working this point, and this trick, for decades.

"Should we take them back anyway?" I asked.

Jim seemed surprised. "Take *what* back?"

"The heads—at least we can prove we caught them."

Jim looked at me as if he'd never before seen me. "You *can't* be serious."

One by one, I opened the clips and removed the heads of our magnificent opening weekend catch. The heads were still fresh, glistening and sparkling in the falling sunlight. From the gills back, however, you could see even the cut lines where the hard, horned mouth of the turtle had chomped down and ripped away. I dropped each head back into the water, knowing they, too, would soon be eaten. There would be nothing to prove that we had ever even been here, let alone that we had found what may well be the Glory Hole.

"At least we have pictures," Jim said.

I agreed, slightly comforted by the memory that we had both posed for photographs with the trout, whole and wiggling, in our hands and the little round lake in the background.

We gathered up and left, the first mosquitoes of the new season rising from the bog as we pushed through the spruce and alders and headed, awkwardly, for higher ground and the logging road.

We walked back in silence, Jim with his head covered by the canoe, me with my cap pulled down as tight as I could manage and the arm that was carrying the rods brushing in front like a useless windshield wiper. We were tired, bitten and discouraged.

The walk back seemed longer than the walk in. The road was rough and overgrown, fat red pines reaching out to itch us as we pushed through. The sounds of evening were starting up: peepers and toads in full orgy, a loon calling as it flew low enough that we could hear the wind in its wings, ravens ridiculing and squirrels laughing.

The Old Man was waiting for us. There was beer in the cookery fridge and a feed of pork and beans warming in one of the big ovens. He hadn't, obviously, been expecting fish. He had read and slept most of the day, and looked as fresh as we must have appeared beaten.

I began the impossible task.

"That big old bear we saw last night was up there."

"Oh?"

"Came right up to shore."

"Did he?"

"I think we found out where the young lad was."

Now we had his attention. He turned back from the warming oven, blue eyes sparkling. "You found speckles?"

"Y-yeah. . ."

"Well—where are they?"

"Turtle ate them," Jim jumped in.

The Old Man stood up straight. "The turtle ate them?"

"Yeah," I said. "Huge snapper. We had them on a string."

"Seven of them," Jim added.

"You caught seven speckles and let a turtle eat them?"

What could we say? That we left the stringer hanging in the water while we moved off in the canoe? Right after the bear was there?

"We got pictures of them," I said lamely.

But he was already headed for the big cooler door, the handle cracking open and a cool blast heading back at us as he stepped inside for a beer.

A cool blast and a second, harsher, blast.

"Tch-tch-tch-tch-tch-tch-tch."

CHAPTER SIX

Helen, Roy, Tommy, Ann, and Duncan at Lake of Two Rivers, 1959.

T HERE IS, FORTUNATELY, a record of his final fishing trip. It lies inside a pale green accounting ledger that sits above the refrigerator in an unremarkable, rustic cottage on the south shore of Camp Lake. Camp is a small, cold lake that takes its water from Algonquin Park in the form of a small waterfall that slides and tumbles down a long, slippery rock along the park's western boundary and from there, eventually, into the Muskoka River via a small chain of lakes and the Big East River. It is water so clear and clean that we drink it, still, straight from the lake, and for those who know where to look, there are wonderful trout, both speck-led and lake, hiding in pockets between the final splash of the little waterfall and the first wash, many miles away through thick forest, into the darker, warmer North Muskoka.

The ledger began as an afterthought, almost an accident, as do most treasured rituals. The first entry is Saturday, July 23, 1983, and is essentially a weather report. It is little more than me copying the daily habits of the old park ranger, then long since dead. He had always kept a daily journal, carefully recording the date, the weather and, in point form, what he did and where he went as chief ranger of Algonquin Park. When he died in 1962, going on seventy-nine, his wife, Bea, asked Duncan to get rid of several boxes of these journals, and he took them back to the McRae mill at Whitefish Lake and threw them into the roaring burner. He was simply doing as she had asked. To him, they were merely the work logs a ranger was expected to keep, not the reflections we might today fantasize them having been before the flames made off with such precious thoughts. People who worked and lived in the bush, rather than visited it, had no time, and often no training, for journals as we think of them today. Still, we do wish they had been kept so we could imagine his movements, the weather, what happened each day, and so we might, because we cannot help ourselves, speculate on what he thought.

We are now into our second ledger at Camp Lake, the daily reports growing ever more detailed, the record of time spent at the cottage ever more significant even to those who, when that first entry was made, were yet to be born. They are entered by dozens of hands: my own, my wife's, her mother's, aunts and uncles who have visited, our own children and, most delightful of all, their friends who come here from the cities. There will be no burner this time. There are no plans for a final entry because there is no single recorder.

Duncan MacGregor's first appearance in the Camp Lake journal appears three days after that very first one. It is dated July 26, 1983: "Grampa and Grandma MacGregor, Alison and Karen out. Gorgeous weather. Alison caught a two-lb bass off the dock. Duncan caught a small lake trout (1 lb.) and lost another one he would have put on the wall. Gordon learned to wave." Alison and Karen are the two daughters of Jim and his wife, Stephanie. Gordon is the youngest of our four. Duncan is, at this moment, seventy-six years old. He has spent much of the last thirty months in hospital, recovering from the chip-truck accident that probably should have killed him.

That day marked the first time he had had come out to Camp Lake and actually fished. Up to then, he had disdained the idea. The lake wasn't a true park lake no matter where it got its water. The trout were small and far between. Most of them had been stocked in the 1970s and were identifiable because they had one fin, usually a pelvic fin, clipped off. The flesh wasn't quite as red as native park trout. The real problem, however, was that it wasn't his lake, wasn't his boat; he didn't like to intrude.

If the location seemed to him a poor comparison to what we had once had at Lake of Two Rivers, I could hardly blame him. The first time I saw this particular spot, at the end of the sixties, I thought it a terrible location for a cottage. A northern exposure. Too damp. Too steep. Overgrown. No rocks to dive off, no sand to walk on; the waterline beginning the instant the hemlock gave up. It was crown land, and the Ontario government had decided to auction off shoreline lots on this isolated lake with no road access in order to open up more land for cottagers and, of course, swell the provincial treasury. The auction had been held at the hockey rink in the nearest town, Huntsville. A chemistry teacher at the only high school had bid, with a friend, on the first two available lots on Camp Lake and won them for a pitiful amount of money: $1400 for a one-acre lot. It seemed to me that neither man had got his money's worth.

I had come along to check out the property because, back then, I would have done anything to be with a certain young woman. Even if anything meant mosquitoes and raspberry-cane scratches and tromping around on slippery moss behind a man, her father, who saw a dock where I could see only deadheads, a deck where I could see only poplar scrub and toadstools. The chemistry teacher had made the only offer on this sloping, pie-shaped lot, which should have told him something, but so desperate was he to have his own sacred spot on the water that he would have bid against himself, if necessary. He had been born on Manitoulin Island on Lake Huron and grown up, the son of a village blacksmith, in a world where fishing and hunting had often made the difference between the family eating or not. War, then school, then teaching had taken him away and kept him away, but now, in his fifties, there was enough money for a small dream of the outdoors, and he had enough sense to try to get as close to Algonquin Park as possible. If he pushed and scraped his way to the shoreline and held on to a cedar branch, he could look out and down the lake and see the green-purple hills of the park itself.

What he was looking for was a piece of land where he could build his own place. He and his wife could do it here, cheap and with their own hands. They could see it finished: a small cabin, the dock, a rough bush road in from where the township gravel road came to an abrupt end and turnaround. I could not share their vision, because I had become, without knowing it, a cottage snob. Nothing would ever be allowed to compare with the rocky point at Lake of Two Rivers. Between a prefabricated cabin and the old ranger's log home there was nothing in common, not even the wood. For me not only would the park never be replaced, it must also never be challenged.

Time, however, has a way of tempering the first impressions of the young. The sixties may have come late to Canada, but it made for a quick seventies, and in this little escape from the real world change came even more quickly. A bulldozer rammed a road into the lake that had no shore. The teacher retired, and he and his wife finished off their little prefab—more often than seems possible using material scrounged from the local dumps. The footings were solid, the framing strong, and with a large spruce deck around the front and side, it began to take on the appearance of a cottage. He dug a hole on the only space that wasn't rock and put up an outhouse. He built a crib on the ice, and when spring came, it collapsed exactly where he had predicted and, over the summer, he put up a dock that stretched far enough into the water to tie a little fishing boat on one side and a red fibreglass canoe on the other. Furniture came from older relatives who died off and, admittedly, from the back-road dumps in the years before the provincial government put up expensive chain-link fences, hired security guards and declared scavenging a crime. He put in electricity, but there would be no running water. If you wanted a bath, you had to go get the water first.

A hundred Teen Town dances later and the young woman and I were no longer teenagers but married. Too soon, it seemed, we had four children. Much too soon, the retired teacher died of a heart attack, and naturally we were expected to step in and help his wife, Rose, become to the cottage what he had been: handyman to euchre partner. The real question for me, of course, was whether this pitiful little attempt at a cottage could ever step in and become to me what the old ranger's rocky point had been. A selfish thought, but I did not understand then that a cottage is a state of mind, not a fixed address.

Slowly, the place crept up on me. It took years, but that, I suppose, is one of the great curiosities of ritual. When it first comes along—the daily ledger as a case in point—we seldom recognize the little act for what it will one day mean to us. But then one day, after a decade or more of working up to it, you find yourself breathing deeply when the door bursts open on a cold and musty cottage, and it is, the first time you suck it in each spring, the sweetest breath taken. The rituals roll so fast it is difficult to keep up to them. Someone always says the bugs are either better or worse than the year before, when they are always the same. The kids check in the bay for the sunken boat that has been there for thirty years. They look under the dock for the snapping turtle that collects a thousand missed heartbeats a year. The mice have chewed all the toilet paper in the outhouse. And for some odd reason, the news comforts.

By 1983, the summer we began this little journal, I had become a Camp Laker. It would never be as majestic as Lake of Two Rivers, but no one was going to live here year-round anyway. The water was the same water that drains out of the Algonquin Park watershed, the chances of seeing a moose on an early morning paddle were as good, perhaps better, and the trout were as red-fleshed and tasty, if smaller and fewer. The connection had been made, that stubborn thread that runs through Canadians and links them to the bush through cottages, camps, trailers and tents, and says, This is the way we homestead in summer. This is the way we build a better life away from the April muck and November sleet and January-February hopelessness. This is the way we shake off our cluttered city lives and are permitted to pioneer momentarily away from the madness and stress. This is where we would live, if only we could figure out how.

As the months and years move along in the little journal, the amount of description increases. A year later, on July 1, 1984, Duncan is back again, and at the end of a day in which everyone is swimming and paddling and even heading up the old logging roads to find wood, it is noted that "Duncan caught a beautiful two-lb *native*—pink, orange flesh—and all had it for supper." He began coming out more often, sometimes to fish with me, sometimes to fish with Ellen's uncle, Jim Griffith, who was about the same age, sometimes to fish with another uncle, Fred Whitlock, a Saskatchewan wheat farmer who liked cold beer and trout as much as Duncan himself. He always caught something, always. Others would get skunked, but never Duncan. Friday, August 5, 1985: "Duncan caught a 3-lb *native!!* trout, reddish orange." Others caught the stocked trout, when they were very lucky. Duncan seemed to catch only natives.

His last fish came on August 21, 1990, the week before his eighty-third birthday. "Sunny, nice," the book reads. "Winds died down. Roy and Gord spent a couple of hours over at Indian Point. Gord caught a salamander. . . . Duncan out for his annual fish—he caught one (2 lb) on *first* pass of the island. On second pass, nailed another—'Bigger!'—which took a long time to pull in and shook off 20' from the boat. Went well."

I remember why I wrote that—"Went well." It had taken some time to talk him into coming out. It always seemed there was a ball game on or a library book that had to go back or he was too tired for a full day in the boat or sun. But one warm day he suddenly announced that he was up for a fish. He was ready when I picked him up in town. He had everything he needed for a day's fishing: a pack of Player's tobacco, two packs of Vogue papers, a baseball hat for the sun. No silly Tilley hat that, the advertisements claim, is capable of passing through an elephant's ass (but whether this is before or after being worn by a city ass the ads do not say). No tackle box with a hundred plastic slots and windows. No fly dope, sunscreen, camera, film, sunglasses, bathing suit, change of clothes, bottle of wine for the host. Of course, if there had been a bottle, it would have been gone before I got there.

We drove out slowly, Duncan flagrantly defying the seatbelt laws, me shifting through every gear and signalling even for turns off one gravel road onto another. We talked about the news. There was election talk in the air, and he, of course, wanted to throw the bastards out. Trouble was, having thrown the bastards out every election for the previous thirty years or so, he no longer wanted anyone in. He had reached that ripe age where he hated them all equally. They were all idiots, all crooks, but he couldn't stop reading about them and he wouldn't stop talking about them.

"Tch-tch-tch-tch-tch-tch-tch."

We drove out the old Limberlost Road, past the summer camp and onto the gravel road heading towards Camp Lake. It was a beautiful day, dust hanging in the air from a truck that faded in and out of sight up ahead, a ruffed grouse—partridge, he insisted—panicking across the windshield and knifing into the dark woods on the passenger side. He talked about the timber along the hill and how he hadn't realized there was so much hardwood up this road. I looked for the first time: maple and beech and elm creating that perpetually damp and dark canopy up the sides of the hills, thin poplar, cedar and pine down low; spruce and tamarack where the damp became bog, sumac where the sun broke through. He seemed to be passing familiar faces; I felt like I was looking for the first time.

"Stop," he said.

I pulled over, thinking he was making one of his notorious washroom demands. Bush habit was simply that you went when your body told you to go, and he had in the past gone in the middle of Roy McCormick's funeral, as well as in the parking lot at Woodbine racetrack, where he had gone to see the Queen's Plate run and watch Queen Elizabeth herself present the trophy. He had twice, with brother Tom cringing in the seat beside, told the driver of a washroomless Grey Coach bus to pull over on the shoulder of Highway 400 while he, unfazed, unconcerned and unashamed, walked to the back of the bus and relieved himself on the side of the road as three lanes of traffic blasted past.

But this time was different.

"Go back," he ordered.

I put the car in reverse, the tires catching on stones and sending road dust up into my open window. "How far?"

"Just back," he said, craning his neck to see. "A little more. There."

I stopped and turned towards him. "What?" I said.

He was looking across the back of the seat and out the window behind me. I could see nothing, stumps, some dead tamarack, water that seemed to deepen as it turned out of view from the road.

"This is where I got that speckle," he said.

"What speckle?"

"That one with Jim. You know."

I did know. The previous summer he had gone fishing with Jim, just the two of them and a canoe and a morning to kill. They'd set out at dawn, and he'd never been exactly sure where it was that Jim had taken him to, but he'd been as impressed with the spot as Jim had been with the results. Dancing a light line with nothing but a thin worm on a simple hook, Dunc had caught, played and hauled in a gorgeous speckled trout. Anyone else would have mounted it. The Old Man ate it, fried up in butter with a half a shaker of pepper.

"Couldn't have been here," I said.

"You weren't there."

"No . . . but look at it. It's almost a swamp."

"You can't tell by looking," he said.

He was right. There were, within a short drive, two of the most perfect fishing spots I had ever seen, or fished. If they were shooting a movie on trout fishing, they would not have to look any further than these two spots. One was along the Oxtongue River, where the rapids gave way to a wide, rolling, dark pool, the shoreline solid rock. The other was a rocky point headed out onto Smoke Lake in the park. I had never, in good weather, driven by the Smoke Lake point without seeing a car or two or three pulled off and tourists, often Japanese, lined up to try their luck standing at the tip of the rock and casting out into the deep water. Same for the Oxtongue: always a fly fisherman out there, hip waders, flies sticking out of cap, the line snapping out onto the circling current and riding down through the wide pool by the rocks. And never, ever a bite. The perfect photograph, minus the fish.

We moved on, slowly heading for the cottage. He and Lloyd, the cottage builder, had shared a love of trout fishing, but had fished together only once. Duncan had shown Lloyd the good shoals to work along Lake of Two Rivers, and had even given him his secret spot on Rock Lake, and Lloyd had gone often with his little cartopper and always returned with his catch of lake trout. The favour had never been returned until after Lloyd's fatal heart attack in 1980, less than a week before the chip truck carried Dunc to his unwelcome retirement. He had come here grudgingly at first, but eventually had been forced to concede that there were good trout to be had outside the park. He always made it clear, however, that he was speaking of native trout, not stocked.

We arrived around noon, and while everyone else ate, he sat out on the deck in the shade of a tall hemlock, rolled a cigarette and smoked it, and sipped on a beer as he stared out over the water. It was calm, a light breeze periodically turning the glass of the water to cloth, but then vanishing as the water smoothed over. It was warm, and it was August—the worst month, he always claimed, for trout—and he wasn't convinced there was much point.

"We don't have to go out," he said.

"We have to go out."

He was torn between possibilities. Here, the seat was comfortable, the beer cold and the grandchildren catering to his every whim. The younger ones were rolling cigarettes for him, tobacco gathering around their laps as if it were a family trait. The older ones were offering to bring a fresh beer. He'd be just as happy to sit there and doze in the late-summer warmth, but he also wanted to go. Not so much because it was one more time, and one time would have to be the last time, but because he was eighty-two years old and still held bragging rights to something other than memory.

"They won't be biting," he said.

"Maybe." I said.

"They won't."

He was preparing his exit. If he caught nothing, it would be a triumph because he had known. If he caught something, it would be a triumph of skill over circumstance. There was still enough of the feisty young hockey player or the sharp little fielder in Duncan MacGregor that even if he could barely walk, he still liked to show off.

"Well, we'll give it a try, then."

How times had changed since the days when he first took me fishing with him. When he would haul up the lakers and, with the fish exhausted and trailing in the wake, hand me the trolling rod for the final two or three turns and then smile as I ran up the hill with the trout hooked in my finger and claimed I had caught it. When he would throw me on his shoulders when we walked deep into the bush to the far reaches of L'Amable or Mosquito Creek. Now I was doing the carrying.

I helped him back into the car and we drove together to the government dock, where there was a boat ramp and I could draw up tight, the rear wheels up to the hubs in the water. I could open the passenger door and help him step out onto the dock to wait while I hurried back down the road to the cottage, loaded the boat and motored over to pick him up. I had a cheap lawn chair with me and set it so it straddled the middle seat in the little aluminum cartopper. I then had him fall back into my arms and I laid him down on the dock so he was sitting on the edge, his feet in the boat. With one foot on the dock and the other stretched down into the boat, I lifted him and settled him into the lawn chair and handed him his old trolling rod. He was ready to fish.

"*Tch-tch-tch-tch-tch-tch-tch*," he said. "It's awful to get old, you know."

"No it isn't," I argued.

But neither of us was really listening to the other.

He never fit into Huntsville. The town was small and tight, lineages well known and society very delicately built around jobs, marriage, dwelling, sports history and standing in church. He worked six days in the bush and showed up Saturday afternoons, sometimes in his own car but just as often in a beat-up half-ton from the mill and once every so often merely dropped off by a logging truck headed south. He belonged to no clubs, no associations. He never went to church. He spoke with a heavy Ottawa Valley accent. He wore workclothes—worn plaid shirts with the sleeves rolled up over pink-grey long underwear, heavy woollen pants and steel-toed workboots, the toe of the right foot always shining through where it had been knocked and torn and rubbed by the turning over of several thousand board feet as he graded the lumber and tallied the shipments. He wore a snappy fedora for several years, before making a conscious fashion decision simply to wear his hardhat seven days a week. Perhaps because he liked to spend Saturday nights in the Empire Hotel beer parlour and down in the basement saloon that locals called the Snake Pit, a hardhat often made good sense.

We had moved in the late summer of 1950 so Jim could start school. By the time Tom was born four years later, Jim and Ann and

I were all attending Huntsville Public School and had become very much a part of the charming little town of Huntsville. Jim and, particularly, Ann thrived at school and soon accelerated a grade. Jim and I got involved, as all Huntsville kids seem to, in sports. Ann could not because of her continuing problems with rheumatic fever. We all, however, learned to skate on Munroe's outdoor rink next door, and we boys played football in the fall, hockey in winter, lacrosse in spring and baseball until school let out and it was time to head again for Lake of Two Rivers and the old ranger's log house. They were happy years, and Huntsville a marvellous, stable small town in which to be a child—so much so that a half-century later, the childhood friendships remain as strong as they were in the mid-fifties, and along the one block of Lansdowne Street heading up from Lorne Street to the edge of the bush that covered Reservoir Hill, the same three neighbours, now white-haired and elderly women, were raking the leaves last fall from the same sprawling maple trees they first cursed nearly fifty years earlier.

But there was a distancing between Duncan and Helen. They squabbled, as always, over money. The house was mortgaged and the family was growing. She wanted to put an addition on so Ann would have her own bedroom, and so there would be real kitchen, instead of a converted summer kitchen that was freezing in winter. He wouldn't commit. He made little and never seemed to care. He would never demand, or even ask for, a raise. He was, after all, making as much as any of the loggers and lumberjacks who lived in Whitney, although expenses were higher in Huntsville. He never missed a day's work, and he never entirely lost his money, but travelling penny-mining-stock salesmen preyed on mill workers and there was always a card game going and he wanted nothing more than to wind down Saturday night with a few cold beer.

We went to the movies. Often we went to the movies at two o'clock in the afternoon, when the double feature got underway and many times we would still be in the Capital Theatre at seven or eight or even nine o'clock at night, having sat through both features and all the cartoons two or three times straight, which was still possible then on a fifteen-cent child's admission. Sometimes Helen came along, and then there would be only the one sitting and we would be home in time for supper and, later, the hockey broadcast on the radio, but over the years she went less and less frequently and we stayed longer and longer.

The reason was simple. "I'm going out for a smoke," he would say to us. "You can smoke in the side aisles," one of us would tell him. "I want to get some air," he would say. And off he would go, perhaps for hours. It did not take us long to realize that while we were sitting in the Capital watching Gary Cooper and John Wayne and Audie Murphy and Randolph Scott and Johnny Weissmuller, he was down in the tap room of the Empire Hotel. Years later, when Ann was working for *Maclean's* magazine as a researcher, she became a bit of a legend in *Trivial Pursuit* circles for her knowledge of movies and was much in demand by teams that entered bar contests. How, her friends wondered, could someone so mild-mannered and quiet know so much about gunfights and war movies? Jim and I never wondered. While our father drank, we studied.

We never saw him drunk. We never thought of him as drunk. "Drunk" was a word for some of the men from the tannery down in the Hollow, who sometimes could be seen stumbling home from the beer parlours in those days when the Ontario government believed the only way working men would go home to eat was if they kicked them out for an hour around suppertime. Drunk was a classmate's father, who worked down at the Hay & Company hard-wood-flooring mill by the tannery and would get so blitzed that, on a winter's day, he would sometimes strip down to his long underwear and reel, workclothes in one hand, workboots in his other, up Lorne Street and high into the reservoir area, where he would fall through his front door. I can still remember my lifelong friends Brent Munroe and Eric Ruby leaving our hockey games to pull this man, mumbling and slobbering, out of snowdrifts when he would suddenly weave off the high sidewalks and plummet down the banks to the edge of the road where we played with our shaved sticks and frozen tennis ball. We would get him up, brush him off, set his clothes back in his arms, and he would head off up the hill, singing in French a song we never heard any other place but Lorne Street.

Duncan, at least, knew when to quit. He would come back into the dim, smoky light of the theatre and tap our shoulders and perhaps sit a while and then we'd go off home, the four of us—five of us when Tom was older—walking up Lorne Street towards the house where Helen, most assuredly, would not be wondering what had kept us. He smelled of smoke and beer and chainsaw oil and grease and, always, fresh-cut wood, and sometimes he sang as we walked up past the Pentecostal church and turned left at the stone wall, telling him about the great shootouts he had missed. Once one of us made the mistake of telling Helen that he'd been in the beer parlour while we'd been watching the movie, and there were sharp words. And once there was a bitter scene at the front door when she, justifiably, tore into him for wasting money she needed for groceries, and he answered her by reaching into his pocket, pulling out a fistful of small bills, throwing them in the door and slamming it so hard the glass shattered. I ran and caught up to him, and the two of us—a tipsy middle-aged man and his ten-year-old son—walked up and down Main Street in the dark until he thought we could go home, as if "we" were both involved. When we got back, the house was dark and the window had been taped over, but the door, thank God, was open.

Sometimes in winter we would go to the afternoon movies and

then, in the evening, down Mary Street to spend the evening with his cousin, Sandy McGregor, and Sandy's wife, Annie, who had one of the first television sets in town and, always, cold beer in the refrigerator. Sandy and Dunc would sit and drink beer and we would all watch the hockey game on the old Philco, Duncan usually staying for the strange end-of-game-to-11:00 p.m. "Juliette" show, during which the men would have a final beer and pretend they were interested in the songs the buxom blonde was offering. We would straggle up the road in the thin light of the streetlamp at the corner of Mary, then turn up Lorne and enter a house already darkened and quiet, everyone else asleep. I would take out my little box of Beehive Corn Syrup black-and-white hockey cards, lay out the stars who had played that night and try to remember what they had done and how their names had sounded as Foster Hewitt called them out from "the Gondola, high over the ice at Maple Leaf Gardens."

In those days, he came home almost every weekend, and those weekends when he did not often involved Helen packing up kids and clothes and groceries and driving—in those random stretches when we had a car—out to Lake of Two Rivers, where the old ranger and his wife lived from spring breakup to first heavy snowfall. We went sometimes in winter as well, the trail broken by snowshoes and the big log home barely warmed by the time we locked up and headed back to Huntsville.

We saw him often in those days. It seemed enough, for none of us has strong feelings of being abandoned. There was never any sense of friends regarding the relationship as strange because, in fact, there were other bushworkers in the town who lived the same weekend family lives. And parents were not as involved in their children's lives then as they are today. Mothers always handled the parent-teacher interviews, and activities, what there were, we got to ourselves: cubs and scouts and guides, choir and sports.

Looking back, it would seem that he himself felt inadequate as a father, endlessly, if a touch ironically, praising Helen for being such a good mother and for doing such a fine job running the house and raising us all. We never felt estranged from him. He was there for us, only "there" was in the bush, where he could always be counted on to be. If he wasn't in the bunkhouse reading or sleeping, he'd be in the cookery eating; and if he wasn't there, he'd be out fishing. You could always find him, always. I remember picking up Ralph Keyes's book *Sons on Fathers,* when I was myself working on a book on the strong relationship that exists between fathers and sons involved in professional hockey, and I was struck by one contributor's reference to a "stiffness" that always existed between father and child in his house, "as if we were both guests at a party and the host had gone off somewhere without introducing us." None of us ever felt so. Of course, one of the peculiarities of Dunc was that he went through life with no need of introductions.

Sport was the first great obstacle that interfered with the way we'd split our lives between the town and the park. Once Jim and I began playing hockey, weekend travel became difficult, if not impossible. Town-league hockey was held Saturday morning, the little arena packed solid with virtually every male child in town. Hockey and lacrosse were the town's face on the rest of the province, and nothing had higher priority. A local philanthropist, Don Lough, had even hired on a former senior hockey player from Sundridge, Mye Sedore, to work in his construction business. Only Mye never once actually reported to work: his job was to identify the young hockey stars and coach the all-star teams that played the other top teams from Bracebridge, Gravenhurst and Parry Sound. When I was eight, I began playing for Mye's teams and continued a rocky, cocked-eyebrow relationship with the old coach through peewee and into bantam, at which point he quite legitimately tired of a lazy fourteen-year-old who missed practice and told me to go back to the town league.

Duncan came two or three times to watch. He never yelled, never criticized, just watched and encouraged. Years later, when I coached minor hockey and the stands were filled with parents even during practice, with mothers sometimes keeping stopwatches on their child's ice time, I could hardly believe he had ever have been so non-involved, but in fact he was like every other parent in those days. None of them ever attended a practice. The town was so small that we walked, carrying our equipment, to every practice and game and would have been stunned to have been offered a ride, let alone have demanded one. His greatest memory of being a hockey parent had, in fact, nothing whatsoever to do with Jim's gift for scoring goals or mine for skating, but was of a game when he walked over to the arena and stood, face to the wire mesh, and watched a youngster from Parry Sound with a nearly white brushcut score against us at will. It was Bobby Orr.

"You could tell right away," he liked to say in later years.

But if he knew that Orr was destined, we did not. We argued for years about who was the better player, Parry Sound's Orr or our own Tim Kelly, a marvellous centre who busted up a knee when he went off to London for junior hockey. But then again, none of us will ever forget the game when poor Mye, at wit's end as to how to stop the little blond defencemen from Parry Sound, stood at the centre of the dressing room with the green card each team had to sign, held it high over his head and pointed to the careful signature by No. 4 for the Parry Sound Shamrocks. "He writes like a girl!" Mye shouted, his usually red face a blister of outrage. "How can you be afraid of someone who writes his name like a damn girl?" Good point, we all thought, until we slapped each other's shin pads and headed out onto the ice, where we discovered, to our great regret, that Bobby Orr intended to play the game with a hockey stick rather than a ballpoint pen.

Sports played an important role for us. For Jim and Dunc and I, who were most interested, it was the conversation point. If we had not seen him for a week or two, there was always a scoring race or a batting title to catch up on. We could talk hockey or baseball or football with him, and while he had known nothing about lacrosse growing up, apart from its historical significance in the 1763 slaughter at Fort Michilimackinac, he liked to watch us and the other neighbourhood kids throw the ball around and he made it to a couple of games when I was lucky enough to be a fringe player on the town team that won, as Huntsville teams often did, a provincial championship.

But our most powerful sports memories regarding Duncan have nothing to do with our playing and him watching. It came from those few occasions in the 1950s when he would end up with tickets to a real National Hockey League game at Maple Leaf Gardens from one of the lumber buyers out of Toronto. We would head for the big city, Duncan and Helen petrified of the widening lanes and impossible streetlights and testy city drivers. They would go to Port Credit, where Davis and Roberta Peever, old friends from Eganville, now lived, and in the evening Davis, as relaxed with city driving as Duncan was with trolling, would pack four or five of us in his big car and turn out onto the Queen Elizabeth Way and head east for the bright lights of the city and the even brighter Gardens. The first time Jim and I walked into Maple Leaf Gardens, we were speechless. We had never seen such brilliant lights and, in all probability, had not in our entire lives seen as many people as we saw in that one night. We went to the washroom together after the first period and were terrified of the seemingly endless line of stainless-steel urinals that ran down an entire side of a washroom that seemed as large as the rink itself. As we stood for hot dogs, a man in the crowd pointed out George Armstrong, an injured Toronto player, to Dunc and he took me over for an autograph, which I still have. The Leafs were playing Detroit, and later in the game he leaned over to me and said, "Don't ever forget that you saw Gordie Howe play." I didn't forget, but whether it was because of the sharp memory or because he wouldn't let me, I am no longer sure.

Sports took us away from the bush—weekends that were once for Algonquin Park now given over to practice and home games and road trips—but neither he nor Helen ever showed any resentment. Like other parents of the 1950s, they let their children dictate. Besides, his own great love of sport, as well as his extraordinary knowledge of it, meant that he enjoyed talking about the games we were playing and the games we were seeing. He could recite "Casey at the Bat" in its entirety, but also parts of Grantland Rice's legendary account of the 1924 Notre Dame victory over Army ("Outlined against a blue, grey October sky the Four Horsemen rode again. In dramatic lore they are known as famine, pestilence, destruction and death. These are only aliases. Their real names are: Stuhldreher, Miller, Crowley and Layden . . ."). He had read Jimmy Cannon and Damon Runyon and Ring and John Lardner. I have, in fact, just discovered an old book that lay in the closet of his room in Huntsville. It is entitled *101 Greatest Athletes of the Century,* and it was a gift from Jim. I see where, inside the front cover, he has listed his own personal top-ten sporting favourites, in order: 1. Ty Cobb; 2. Rogers Hornsby; 3. Babe Ruth; 4. Frank Frisch, the Fordham Flash (a National League ballplayer from the twenties and thirties who's not even in the book); 5. Ted Williams; 6. Leo "The Lip" Durocher; 7. "Gabby" Hartnett (a catcher who played in the same years as Frisch and is also not included in the book); 8. The Gas House Gang (the 1934 St. Louis Cardinals); 9. Dizzy Dean; and 10. Paul "Daffy" Dean, just because he was Dizzy's brother. Numbers 4, 6, 8, 9 and 10 are all connected by the year 1934, the year the Cardinals launched one of baseball's most impressive pennant drives to oust the New York Giants in the final days and then take the World Series against Detroit. Frankie Frisch managed and played, Leo the Lip was the shortstop, Dizzy and Daffy combined for forty-nine wins in the regular season and two wins each in the series, and the Cardinals lineup from that year he could recite perfectly more than sixty years after he had lingered over the *Ottawa Journal* reading about them: Ripper Collins at first; Leo at short; the Fordham Flash shifting between second and third, Spud Davis catching; Pepper Martin at third; Orsatti, Rothrock and Medwick in the outfield. I'm a bit surprised the hard-sliding, feisty Joe Medwick didn't make his top ten, for Dunc would have loved it when the wrath of the Detroit fans turned to so much tossing of oranges and apples and newspapers that in the bottom of the sixth inning of the final game, Medwick tried unsuccessfully three times to take his field position, only to have the umpires and, finally, the baseball commissioner, Judge Kenesaw Mountain Landis, intervene and send him to the showers "for his own protection."

He liked best the characters. At the bottom of his list he has written his all-time number-one quote—Dizzy's "It ain't braggin' if you done it"—and this he applied to himself in fishing and in reading and, towards the end, in just surviving. He loved Ruth and Satchel Paige, the press favourites, but he also had a soft spot for the nasties in baseball, Williams and Ty Cobb. He loved Hornsby, the arrogant, acerbic hero who took six batting titles in a row and managed the 1926 Cardinals to their first world championship, despite the fact that Hornsby proudly claimed he had no use whatsoever for books. Dunc's knowledge of several sports was encyclopedic. He knew the players and statistics of the Canadian Football League. He knew baseball from beyond the turn of the century to the previous night's box scores. He knew the National Hockey League to perfection in the days long before there were official record books for radio hosts to keep by their side as they pretend nimble fingers are a fair substitute for quick minds. He did not find basketball interesting, and he did not think car racing even remotely a sport. In later years, after he had moved to a place with television reception, he came to love soccer and would watch the early morning broadcasts from Europe with the same passion he normally reserved for baseball. Sports, he said, kept him going. Long after all his friends had died, there was still sports. First thing in the morning, he had to read the box scores. If sport, as George Orwell claimed, was nothing more than "an unfailing cause of ill-will," it was never so with us. It was, in our time and our family, the way awkward people could touch each other.

I counted myself lucky. He hit me only once, and I richly deserved it, having tried to put an axe through Jim while we fought out by the woodpile and, fortunately, only nicking his elbow as I swung the weapon I could barely lift. The Old Man spanked me, two blows, I yelped and then we all headed off for the movies, Jim's arm bandaged and Ann and I hurrying on ahead to wait for them by the ticket line. "Just going out for a smoke," he said after we had found our seats, and he was gone for the evening.

He was never violent. Perhaps even then he was reading Plutarch —"Children are to be won to follow liberal studies by exhortations and rational motives, and on no account to be forced thereto by whipping"—or perhaps it had to do with the fact that he himself had had no father in the difficult years, so that the father-son tensions, which seemed, at times, all around us, never intruded in our house. His contempt for authority and disdain of discipline courses now through the veins of his children and grandchildren; whether it got there by accident or intent I don't know, but I like it. We argued only sports and politics, and always in fun. Apart from the one justified spanking, he never hit, although getting slugged by fathers, and even male teachers, was common in small-town Canada in the 1950s. I know he scrapped as a youngster because he often talked about it, laughing at the tough little Runyonesque kid he thought himself to be, and I heard, much later, that he had been forced to lift his fists against more than one millworker who challenged him, apparently winning easily each time. But around us and our friends, he was always gentle and funny and kind and adventurous. Our friends adored him. He seemed, to them, so romantic, almost exotic as he came in from the bush, often wearing a fedora at a cocky level, always with a cigarette, sometimes with fresh trout or venison or even moose steaks. They liked to banter with him. They liked the fact that he talked to them, as he talked to everyone he ever met, as if they had known each other for years and were merely two friends stopping a moment to catch up. He had time for everyone. He cared about them, asked about them and became, in an odd way, almost an adjunct friend to some. By the time he died, in fact, he was probably closer to my closest childhood friend, Eric, than Eric and I were to each other. When he had a car, he liked to take kids for drives, waiting patiently by the side of a creek or a pond as they explored and played. When he later came by truck he showed contempt for the usual parental rules and contempt, I now realize, for the Highway Traffic Act. It wasn't his truck, there was no insurance—but he would toss the keys over as he headed out for a few beers, not even asking where we would go or what we would do.

He had a fascination with crime—in particular, with murder. He read detective magazines and true-crime books and mystery novels and followed trials in the daily press with fascination. The movies he stayed for, delaying his "smoke" as long as possible, were invariably set in Chicago and New York during the thirties and always seemed to star James Cagney or Edward G. Robinson. He took us for a drive out to Injun Joe's, a tourist stop along Highway 60 on the way to the park, and we stood in the grass by the tents as he tried to figure out how an American tourist could have asked "Joe" to pose in Indian headdress and holding shotgun for a home movie. At the inquest that followed in the Huntsville town hall, the movie had been the central piece of evidence: Joe smiling, the gun lifting, aiming straight at the camera, a puff of smoke—no sound—and the scenery around Injun Joe's suddenly spinning in circles as the American tourist fell dead. How, he wanted to know, *everyone* wanted to know—could someone not realize a gun was loaded? How had it happened?

In the summer of 1959, the little town of Huntsville itself was shattered by the murder of two taxi drivers. Violence had never seemed so close. The two drivers, Bruce and Fritz, were well-known men who would wave to us as they passed our road-hockey games and were always careful to straddle the fragile snow-chunk posts of our nets. The C&H Taxi stand, where they worked, was in a vacant lot across from Miss Winifred Trainor, the eccentric old fiancée of Tom Thomson, and she had long fought a futile battle to have the stand moved, claiming it attracted a bad lot. They never seemed bad to us.

The two drivers had been called to a gravel pit just outside Dwight, not far, in fact, from Injun Joe's roadside stop, and they had been robbed of twenty-seven dollars and a wristwatch, beaten and shot. One had lived for more than a day, only to be brutally attacked a second time when the thieves returned to the scene of the crime, found him struggling, and repeatedly dropped a boulder on his head until, finally, he died. It could hardly have hit closer to home. One of the two murderers was in Jim's class at school; the other, a nineteen-year-old who combed his hair like James Dean and rolled the sleeves of his black T-shirt so they held his cigarette packs, was known by us all. His sister was in my class.

Never had murder felt so near at hand. While the actual crime had taken place while we were still at Lake of Two Rivers, the murder was still the conversation from morning until night when we returned to town. The two murderers had escaped into Northern Ontario and had, at one point, picked up a seventeen-year-old girl, taken her father's speedboat and were apprehended, finally, speeding down the Ottawa River. Where did they think they were headed? Down the Ottawa and out the St. Lawrence to the Atlantic Ocean, turn right and head for South America? Their escape made no sense; but then, neither did their crime.

Police divers came to the Reservoir Hill, where they donned wetsuits and masks and tanks and slipped through the fence to the black waters of the town reservoir, and here they found the sawed-off twenty-two that the murderers had used. The town filled with reporters. I had a *Toronto Star* route that fall and winter and distinctly remember the strange, semi-proud feeling of delivering headlines and photographs that treated Huntsville as a place of great and sad importance.

The murder and the trial and the aftermath were to have a profound effect on all of us growing up there at this time. We had considered guns to be toys, only to learn that the same gun with which we headed off into the Reservoir Hill bush on weekends, a single shot twenty-two, had the ability to kill more than squirrels. We saw, in our classmate, what shame feels like, the poor girl afraid to return to class and those of us who were there, eleven years old going on twelve, not knowing how to treat her when she did. We said nothing, which was at least an improvement over grade four, when the father of one of our classmates fell into and died in an acid vat down in the tannery. We had been told by the teacher to welcome the boy back, because he had been through a terrible experience losing his father, but when he walked in we had applauded, not knowing what else to do, and he had burst into tears.

The trial was a sensation. Duncan came in from the mill on Saturday and had in his hand the latest *Police Gazette,* and there, on the cover, were our murderers. One of them now even had a nickname—Babyface—and it made us all feel just a little more worldly to know that little old Huntsville had found its way to the cover of the *Police Gazette.*

In later years, I went back and looked up the trial. The one called Babyface, the one in Jim's class, pleaded guilty and, in return for his gruesome testimony about the boulder, received a prison sentence for manslaughter. Marvin, the James Dean look-alike, pleaded not guilty. His trial was brief. The judge sent off the jury with a message that, today, would cause a sensation: "I remind the jury that hunting season opens first thing Monday morning and there are some of us with commitments." The jury, also wanting to head for the deer camps, took forty-eight minutes to find him guilty.

They hanged Marvin in the Parry Sound jail and buried him in the yard. He remained on the front pages of the papers I was delivering because there was some thought that he would be the last man Canada would ever execute. Capital punishment was the debate of the moment in Parliament, and the papers were predicting that the House of Commons would vote to bring an end to it. Marvin found God in the Parry Sound jail and decided to donate his eyes. He also requested that his pauper's grave be marked with a special plaque warning other boys not to do as he had done. His last words, reported in bold type on the front of the paper, were "God Bless You All."

There was something about this unexpected attention that made those of us who were young and impressionable feel different about ourselves and our little town. We felt connected, if only peripherally, to something that mattered far beyond our tiny world. The notion that suddenly Huntsville was *known*, perhaps even feared, tended to cloud our sense of what mattered. The murder had taken us to the front pages, but it had also taken two lives, and a third when they hanged Martin at the Parry Sound jail.

Death—like Aunt Minnie's—was alarming enough to the very young, but violent death was so very much more disturbing, and 1959 seemed, to us, filled with it.

Duncan's younger sister, Isobel, had married a banker, Alex Heron, who was fluently bilingual and was sent off by the bank to Timiskaming, on the Quebec side of the northern reaches of the Ottawa River. We had visited them there, baffled by the language and puzzled by their residence, which was an apartment above the bank branch, our first experience with a home that didn't stand alone and have at least a root cellar, if not a basement. Isobel and Alex had two children, Douglas and Elizabeth, who were both extraordinarily bright, sophisticated and, to us, intimidating. Douglas was slightly older than Jim and Ann; Beth was my age.

Helen got the call. I can still remember the way her voice broke when she asked the caller to repeat what had just been said, and I can still see her hand at her throat as she replaced the receiver and stood, for a long moment, staring at the phone as if she was, for some reason, still waiting for it to ring. We were sitting around the table, eating. "Uncle Alex has been shot," she said.

It was worse than she had told us. Alex Heron, a gregarious, happy man, always impeccably dressed, had risen in the morning, eaten and, as always, waited for Beth to be ready so the two of them could walk down the dark stairs together and out onto the main street of Timiskaming where he would see her off to school.

That Friday morning had been different, however. The bank's main teller had already been greeted by a gun in his back as he opened the doors to the bank, and the man with the gun—another was waiting outside with the getaway car running—ordering the teller to open the vault. Uncle Alex and Beth heard the commotion and Uncle Alex went ahead to check. He surprised the gunman and the would-be thief ran. Uncle Alex tackled him on the steps leading down to the street. The man twisted and fired twice, both shots hitting Uncle Alex in the head. He died on the sidewalk, his terrified daughter a witness to the murder.

Duncan came in from the mill to prepare for the funeral, which was to be held in Timiskaming. He brought with him the afternoon edition of the Ottawa paper. "Quebec Bank Manager Slain," the headline across the top of page one read. "Two Men Held; Dies Foiling Theft at Timiskaming." The story, complete with art showing the place where Uncle Alex had been shot and died, and the roadblock where police had stopped the getaway car, seemed so unreal, so made-up, but there was no doubt from the look on Duncan's face as he came hurrying in the door, or on Helen's as she read the paper, lips trembling, that this, for once, was no story about someone else somewhere else. This time it wasn't just close to me, it was home.

Duncan needed a suit and went down to Ruby's, where Murray Ruby, Eric's father, fixed him up and sent the jacket off to be let out a little around the shoulders. Murray, it turned out, had known of one of the suspects when he was growing up in North Bay. He wasn't surprised.

While Dunc waited for the jacket to come up from the little tailor's shop down in the Hollow, he went next door to Munroes', where Brent's father, Maurice, offered him a beer. They sat in the kitchen, talking about what had happened and about what might happen to the murderers. Capital punishment was still under debate, yet it was widely held that no one else would ever again hang in Canada. (As it turned out, the man who shot Uncle Alex did hang.)

Brent had passed through the kitchen on his way to pick up Eric and then me. He had paused for a drink of water and listened to our fathers talk. "I've never seen your dad so upset," Brent said when he got over. "He says he hopes they both hang."

We threw around the lacrosse ball a while but I lacked spirit. I was feeling sorry for myself, was in that odd way proud of myself. It seemed almost heroic to be part of a family that had suffered a great tragedy, and therefore deserved to be treated differently from those who had not.

Brent and Eric found me dull and decided to head off down the street to the outdoor lacrosse box at the back of the hockey rink. I knew I had to stay near home. My parents would be leaving for the funeral as soon as the suit was finished.

I played by myself, hammering the lacrosse ball into the brick of the house, the steady, solid *thump-thump-thump* comforting in its repetition and mindlessness. I whipped the ball forehand and backhand, the Indian rubber smacking into the wall—"You're wrecking the brick!" Helen would yell, with no effect—and barely acknowledged it as it flew back and whispered to a stop in the soft, leather cushion of the stick. *Whip . . . smack . . . hiss. Whip . . . smack . . . hiss. Whip . . . smack . . . hiss.*

I didn't see him come up behind me. I don't know how long he had been standing there. I think I smelled the smoke first, then realized he was there, watching.

I spun my stick, trapping the ball, and turned.

He indicated with his cigarette that I should turn back and keep going. "You're getting pretty good," he said.

"Thanks," I said.

"Show me that backhand again."

"Okay."

And I did—the ball whirring off the catgut and smacking into the brick; the ball coming back as fast as, or faster than, it had been thrown in the first place; the ball meeting stick pocket perfectly, the sound so satisfying, so comforting.

But I was showing him nothing. He was showing me: he was crying. The first, and only time I would ever see him weep. And I knew at that moment that death is something that happens not to you, but to someone else, and that it offers not glory, but horror. If it made him cry, I should cry too, and stop feeling sorry for myself but think of those who had real need of sympathy. Like Beth, who would never again walk down those stairs with her father.

We pulled away from the government dock. He was settled in his seat, even if a bit outraged to have to sit in a garden chair facing backwards when expertise and tradition should have had him in his old position, slightly off-centre in the stern seat, back to the outboard, wrist on the steering handle, rod across his lap, eyes checking shoreline for the markers that would tell him which shoal was coming up and when and where he should begin his turns. Now I was steering. I was deciding on the line we would take across the shoals. I would determine the turns.

He stared at me and laughed, no sound above the outboard, but a laugh all the same. And no wonder. He saw the absurdity of me being in charge. If imagination counted, the walls of my home would be filled with mounted stumps and rocks, each one a strike, each one a certain record. I had always loved to go out with him, was always lingering about the docks as he poured the gas and set the oars and checked the minnow traps. I loved nothing better than to fish, unless perhaps it was just to be with him and watch him do it. He had never been angered when I, dozing at the end of a short rod, would let the line slip against the propeller, the rod suddenly jerking half out of my hands as yet another modern lake-trout record was set and the motor abruptly chunked and coughed and quit altogether. I have sat, sullen and embarrassed, hour after hour as he leaned over the upturned motor and worked the crimped and tangled steel line free with sharp-nosed pliers and his jackknife. He never called me an idiot, though he certainly must have thought me one at such times.

My favourite fishing story of his would be the time he was supposed to be off fighting that forest fire in the park and ended up catching all those lovely speckles that the intense heat of the blaze had chased upstream into a large pool near where the firefighters were encamped. His about me would have to be my trip to James Bay, when, striking out to fish Lake Wawa one cool June day, I impatiently cast my line as we left the dock at the Cree camp and watched, horror-stricken, as the fluorescent Rapalla flew towards the shore, then spun thirteen times around the neck of a duck decoy that had been set at the end of the dock. I know it was thirteen because, as we idled waiting for one of the men to unwrap the multi-hooked lure, an elderly woman counted the circles off in Cree, so much to the delight of the dozen or so gathered on the dock that some of them lay down on their backs and held their stomachs as they howled. When I came back to Huntsville and told him that story and showed him the beautiful photographs of the wonderful trout we had caught, he barely acknowledged the pictures but asked twice to hear again the story of the duck decoy and the impatient white.

Duncan had the best hands for fishing I ever saw. Ellen's father, Lloyd, had good hands as well, always certain where the bait was, the line always tight, the pull-and-pause-and-reach-back-and-pull-again motion of trolling enacted as smooth and sure and sensitive as a physician feeling for a pulse. The hands did not come to me, and yet they—his hands or Lloyd's hands—showed up in our fourth child, Gordon, who at sixteen was tying his own flies and could fish as long and well and happily as the Old Man in the best years of his life. I remember once coming across an old poem by the American Robert P. Tristram Coffin and thinking immediately of Gordon and his grandfathers, and of the special hands of the fisherman.

A father is a strange thing, he will leap
Across a generation and will peep
Out of a grandson's eyes when unexpected
With all the secrets of him resurrected.

Dunc had the breast pocket of his shirt filled with roll-your-owns. He pulled one free, the loose tobacco tumbling down his shirt and onto his pants, where he brushed it onto the floor of the boat. Perhaps some of the cigarettes had been fashioned by the kids. It was impossible to tell the work of the eighty-three-year-old from that of the eight-year-old. He took out a wooden match that had been tucked in with the cigarettes, and leaned over to strike it. I inhaled the sulphur burst as if it were a welcome friend.

We had our rods ready, mine a long, whippy rod that ensured I would never again get caught in a propeller, and his the short, old Murphy, the only trolling rod any of us had ever seen him use. It was, for him, in surprisingly good shape. He had the same silver William's Wabler that it seemed he had been using since I was a child, and he had his jackknife out to pry open the small circle that held the triple hooks. His hands worked quickly, surely. He was eighty-three years old and had been run over by a truck, but his hands were as steady as a surgeon's. How often, right up until his final month, would he hold out those hands to show visitors that they never shook, that they were as steady at seventy, eighty, nearly ninety, as they had ever been at twenty or thirty or forty—or for that matter, forty-nine, his age of choice for the last half of his life?

We headed towards the island, the motor running at quarter-speed, the boat licking through the very light chop as the wind came out of the east. Another bad omen. He had already said that lake trout would not bite in August. Now there was the wind that old Joe Lavalley, the trapper and guide, had hated so much he worked it into a little ditty:

East Wind no good
South Wind worse
West Wind blows the bait right into their mouths
North Wind they bite best.

Perhaps it didn't matter. We weren't really after trout. We were after time together. I had stuffed four cans of beer in under his seat. We would fish and we would talk and we would not talk at all. For those who do not know what this means, it is all but impossible to explain. Byron's great mistake when he attacked fishing for its stupidity was that he failed to appreciate the appeal of stupidity for many of us who fish. Stephen Leacock, another of Dunc's lifelong loves, understood perfectly. "This article is intended to put the reader to sleep," Leacock began in his brilliant essay "Why Do We Fish?" "Let it be understood right away," he wrote, "that real fishermen don't go fishing for the sake of the fish. They pretend they do." He also said, elsewhere, "Several of the friends I like to go fishing with are only about half-witted, and some even more." Fishing is about talking and laughing and nothing at all.

He had the treble hook off and set by his side. I handed him a minnow.

"Too small," he said.

I picked another, only to have it squirt through my hand and into the air and down off my lap onto the floor of the boat, where it half-wiggled, half-swam, under the seat. Forced down on hands and knees, I groped for the escapee and finally came up with him backwards in my palm, tail flailing, and handed him towards a smiling, head-shaking Duncan.

"Tch-tch-tch-tch-tch-tch-tch."

He took it easily, long, tobacco-stained fingers folding over the minnow gently, the minnow quieting. He lay it down on the seat, calmed it and took his jackknife up, cutting off its head. He then tossed the minnow's body overboard.

"What did you do that for?" I asked. Perhaps someone could discard the head—but no tail? Was he beginning to lose it?

"I don't know this lake very well," he said. "I'll be bouncing off the bottom, and I don't want to lose my bait, do I?"

He took the treble hook and shoved the shank up through the back of the minnow's head and out its mouth, then he took the knife up again and pried the circle apart so he could loop the hook back on to the Wabler. He jangled it and let it sit. It didn't look pretty, but the minnow's head was on so solid I doubted a cat could get it off.

I was, as usual, looping a full-bodied minnow around a hook.

"Time to let out?" he asked.

I checked the island. We were coming up to the first shoal.

"I guess."

"Give me some speed," he said.

I twisted the handle, the outboard roaring slightly and the boat rising to a higher plane.

He pulled some line free, then cupped the William's Wabler in his hand and brought it to his lips.

He spit on the minnow's head, smiled at me and dropped his line over the side.

He was back in his world.

The sixties are difficult to catch. They began, for me, with a public school teacher, Bill Bolger, writing "1961" on the blackboard and telling our grade eight class, "This is the only time in your lives in which the date will read the same right side up or upside down." The next year this would happen would be 6009, and given the state of the world in 1961, most of us believed there wouldn't be anyone around to mark the occassion, let alone scribble it down on a blackboard. I was thirteen in 1961, a teenager on the cusp of the most bewildering, self-indulgent, exciting decade of any in our lives, and when it was over I was twenty-one—old enough, finally, to drink legally—and the world as I knew it was still upside down. Duncan was fifty-three when the decade began and sixty-three when it ended. I was young and had the world at my call. I had university and a girlfriend, I had motorcycled around Europe and planned to spend my life exploring the inner and outer dimensions of my self-obsessed universe. The Old Man was in the bush, where he had started the decade. He was, however, reading a different book.

There were no typical sixties experiences with him. While everyone I knew was battling with their fathers—one close friend even wrestled his father into the bathtub before he broke for the front door—there was never any sort of argument with Duncan. I never once had a falling out with him, and neither did any of the other children. When I failed grade twelve—the principal writing, "Going, Going, _____ (You fill in the blank, Roy)" on my spring report—neither parent said a word; they let me fail the year without retribution. Perhaps they knew, as I soon found out, that failure is often a necessary course.

He was different in a decade when difference was celebrated. He worked in the bush when simplicity and getting back to the land were worshipped. He read deep books when philosophical discourse was appreciated. When I showed a great passion for folk music early on in the decade, he stunned me and my long-haired friends by grabbing a harmonica off one of them and playing it beautifully, a sad old Irish song from the valley. It was the first I knew he could even play. When we fled for Europe and an easy, feckless life on the Spanish islands, he wanted to talk about the history of the Balearics and how Homer had written of them. He asked me once if I had ever tried marijuana and, when I fudged about sometimes being around it, said he wouldn't mind trying a bit of it himself.

Friends found him fascinating. He was against the Vietnam War. He believed that Communism was probably a better way for Vietnam and Cambodia to go, and he saw the American presence as bullying and wrong-headed. He was not, however, perfectly in tune with the times. At the dawn of the seventies, when the sixties were still very much hanging on in Canada, he came into town and on Saturday night went off to see what he thought might be a good western. *Midnight Cowboy* became the last movie he would ever see on his own.

He came home for fewer and fewer weekends. He and Helen were growing apart the way cedar shoots clinging to the same rock face will twist away from each other towards their own space and light, yet remain joined at the bared root. They grew apart as so many married couples seemed to do in that time and in that part of the world, where divorce was frowned upon and separation more often a factor of work than a choice. The distance hardens, the gap widens. It is no secret that the couple no longer gets along very well, but no one, and certainly not the two people involved, expects them to break apart.

For Duncan and Helen, the problems were obvious: money, above all, but also drinking and gambling. He never forgave himself for failing to put his money down on a horse called Royal Chocolate in the Queen's Plate race we had taken him to. He would remember so vividly how he had stood staring at the odds board, watching this horse move to more than 20-1 and had failed, for once, to go for the long shot. He had intended to show those who sat with him that he had restraint and sense, and when these failed him on Royal Chocolate it seemed only to confirm to him that his basest instincts were right.

He was careless with whatever money he made. He lost at least one car, we think to gambling. He lost several thousand dollars on a wild scheme to cut pulpwood and then sell it to the big cutters when one of his trusted "partners" took off with the money. His sister, Janet, J.S.L.'s wife, had to bail him out more than once. He was lucky, really, to be married to Helen, who had an extraordinary ability to make ends meet and who, once the four children were all off to school, began taking whatever odd jobs she could. She knit beautiful sweaters, and a shop downtown sold them to the tourists for a 50 per cent cut. She began working at the local lodges as a short-order cook and moved on, finally, to work full time in the kitchen of two of the better resorts. She took nothing for herself. And except for when she had to ask him for her weekly cheque, she kept up her good humour. They no longer laughed together. They no longer went on drives together and stopped for ice cream at the edge of the lake. They rarely talked except to discuss bills. They did not, however, shout at each other or tear each other down in front of the children. Neither made a case for himself or herself to anyone else. They seemed, instead, to accept their changed relationship with a sad resignation, as if they knew something had been lost, almost accidentally, along the way. The children could only wonder what sort of relationship they might have had if money had not been the third party.

We did not spend as much time together in the sixties and early seventies as we had earlier. He had retreated into bush life and books, and we, of course, had gone the opposite direction into sports and city life and distant schools. Sometimes one of us—Tom, in particular—would head off to stay with him at the mill for a weekend or a few days, and the visits were always pleasant. Tom began going when he was barely of school age and continued right into high school, and in those years he spent more time with Duncan than anyone else in the family. There was always plenty for a youngster to do at the mill, even if there was no television to watch (even radio reception was impossible during the day). There was the mill itself, fascinating in full operation. There were the trails and lakes around the mill. There was always fishing. And in the evening the bears would wander down from the sand hills to gather back of the cookery.

In the late fifties and early sixties we had often hunted with him, trekking the hills and bush roads around Whitney for partridge and the marshes for ducks. In the seventies, Jim and I, and sometimes Tom, returned to hunting with him again. We would drive up on a cold fall day, pick him up and head out into the bush that he knew so well. He had no interest in birds, and soon we had little either. He said there was no point in hunting the way people hunted these days, with all that expensive equipment and their four-by-fours and winches and special calls, not when meat was so cheap at the store and wild animals so valuable. He wouldn't hunt himself, but happily went along for the ride and walks. I soon quit hunting altogether as well, though we still would head off into the woods to look for animals, as excited by sight as perhaps we had once been by the kill.

He was drinking more, when he could get it. The children began to dread driving up with our mother to get the cheque for fear he'd be into a quart of whisky. She could tell immediately. They wouldn't fight, but the tension could be suffocating, particularly if he was short on money and she long on bills, as was often the case. More and more, one of us would volunteer to go up and see him and pick up the cheque for her. Ellen and I would make a full day of it: walk one of the park trails that the old ranger had blazed, visit the museum, have lunch with Dunc, spend some time with him, pick up a fresh trout from the mill freezer and, of course, the cheque. For the first time since we had all become aware of his love of a drink, it seemed there was always a case of beer or a bottle at the mill. The difference was access. Previously, there was little coming and going in the park, but now the roads were good and always cleared. You could even buy booze in Whitney finally, and it was a simple matter for him to have someone pick up some booze for him and bring it into the park.

He had never learned how to drink. He hurried his drinking. It sometimes seemed as if he were stocking up, laying in the booze for the coming long, dry winter. He raced to get "tight" and would get to a point where he slurred his words and perhaps even drifted slightly as he walked, but never to the point of falling down, and certainly never to the point of passing out. He never missed a day's work. He never even seemed to have a hangover. You would call him a drinker; you could never call him a drunk. "I've drank much less than you might think," he once told me. "You couldn't hardly get a drink in the thirties, you know. I've gone months in the bush without even thinking about it."

I wondered if age was bothering him. He was into his sixties. He still walked with a jaunt. He still liked to pick up a sharp-looking hat when he was in town and wear it everywhere, even out in the boat. For several summers he fancied a ridiculous straw golf cap with a sliced plastic ball glued to a silly plastic flag, even though he had never played the game and never would. He still smoked like Bogart and Cagney. We'd been expecting him to cough his life out since the fifties, but he was still strong as a horse and, supposedly, facing the prospect of a retirement in which he had no interest. The old ranger had been allowed by the Department of Lands and Forests to skip the usual retirement age of sixty-five and been given an extra five years as chief ranger of the park. After seventy, he spent two summers supervising the provincial government's archeological digs at Rice Lake near Lindsay. Finally, however, there had been no more work for him no matter how healthy he was and how badly he wanted to keep going. Duncan was in the same situation: more afraid of having to go home than of having to get up the next morning for the rest of his life and put in a hard, often bitterly cold, eight to ten-hour shift.

He leased a car one summer. I'd never even heard the term before, but he had somehow arranged to have a fairly new Ford at the mill one summer and was apparently paying some exorbitant price to a dealer in Renfrew or Bancroft. I went up to the mill one hot summer weekend and found him carrying jacks from the machine shop back to the far side of the mill. He'd put the car up on a stump and couldn't go forward or backward. He was stumbling this time.

The drink never seemed to leave its mark on them. He and other park bushmen could drink all night and work the next day as if nothing had passed through their systems but sweet dreams. Hard drink, to them, was something like that Algonquin Park brainworm that deer carry without the slightest harm but that kills other animals, particularly the moose, that come in contact with it. They drank until it was all gone, unless, for some reason, they had stashed it somewhere for later and happened to forget about it. The best story like this was when Jim joined with our cousins Tom and Jake for a long fishing trip into the park interior and Lornie came along with them. They were setting up a campsite when one of the men dislodged a rock and stared in disbelief at what he'd just found.

"There's a bottle here!"

"Brandy?" Lornie called over from the fire he was building.

"Y-yeah . . ."

"It's mine, God dammit—I hid it there three summers ago. Hand it over."

But they were all getting older. Roy was ill from drinking and would soon die in a Sault Ste. Marie hospital. Lornie was retired from the lands and forests department, now called the Ministry of Natural Resources. There were reminders of his age all around for Duncan. His old friend, Felix, who had fought with the Polish Brigade and who was the only other person at the mill who loved bridge, died of a heart attack. His brother Bill—Willie MacGregor, the magistrate—died and was given a full military funeral in Pembroke, a piper leading the casket and a uniformed medal-bearer carrying a handsome box with his war medals laid out on satin. When John Stanley Lothian McRae died, it was, for Whitney, much like a state funeral. The church was overflowing with mourners; both the Protestant and Catholic priests spoke; the pallbearers were all men from the mill, only three of whom owned jackets to put over their starched white shirts and ties; and the streets of the little village were lined with mill families, children turned out in their best clothes, as the funeral cortège wound through the streets and turned out onto Highway 60 for the long ride to Eganville and the McRae family plot at the side of the Bonnechere River. A couple of years later the plot would add his brother Ken and, not many years after, his kind and generous sister Janet.

Duncan was suddenly down to few friends and fewer relatives. Sandy McGregor, the cousin who had become perhaps his closest friend, was timber cruising near Kearney, on the western edge of the park, north of Huntsville. He had left the snow machine he was riding to walk onto higher ground when a timber wolf suddenly began stalking him. Sandy was well into his sixties at this point, tall and wiry, and normally a wolf will quickly bolt from such an encounter. But this time, he knew, there was something different about the animal, something wrong. He was moving back to the snow machine when the wolf attacked. The wolf broke through his hands and badly bit him about the chest and arms and neck. He fought back, eventually freeing himself, and made it to the machine with the wolf jumping onto his back. Sandy made it back to the camp, barely conscious, and they trucked him out to the hospital. The wolf was shot and tested and revealed to be rabid, meaning Sandy then had to endure weeks of painful rabies shots. He recovered slowly and never completely, soon dying following a severe heart attack that everyone connected to the trauma of the wolf attack.

A few years later, wolves would again attack close to Duncan. It came several months after a logger had showed up at the mill one morning with a little black mongrel puppy and handed it over to Duncan with the message that the dog was now his. The men at the mill thought it was the perfect gift. With most of them now heading home by car and bus at the end of the workday and arriving back each morning, they worried about him being there so often alone. The Old Man said he wanted nothing to do with a dog, but no one would listen to him. He asked and ordered, but no one would take the dog back to Whitney, and since no one else was stepping forward to care for and feed the little puppy, he took it on. Just as the men had expected, in a matter of days the Old Man and the dog were inseparable. He named the dog Blackie, and cared for it like a child. It slept on his bed. It ate with him, spent the days with him at work and the evenings sleeping at his feet while the Old Man sat at the office desk reading under the best light running off the mill generator. When spring came, Blackie sat at the edge of the little dock down by the pumphouse, waiting for the sound of the three-horsepower Evinrude that meant Duncan was coming back up the river from an evening of trolling.

He had Blackie for little more than a year. In the second winter the wolves began moving closer and closer to camp. He could not believe their boldness, and wondered if perhaps their own food supply was so low that they were looking towards the camp for garbage pickings and even a chance at the little dog who kept barking back at them as they slipped down from the sand hills and in along the stacks. He tried to keep Blackie in more, and rarely let him out of sight.

He was alone at the mill when the attack came. He had just eaten up at the cookery and had walked down the icy hill towards the mill office, where he planned to read some old newspapers one of the men had brought up from Whitney. It had snowed lightly. Blackie was trailing along behind, sniffing everywhere in the light, new snow. Duncan went inside, knowing the dog would soon bark to get in, and he closed the door behind him just as a hideous, unnerving screech went up from the side of the building. He turned to the window, ducking down to block the light as he stared out. He was just in time to see three wolves descend on the little dog.

There was no time to reach the 30-30 he had hidden in his room. He foolishly went outside, running at them and screaming and beating his arms, and fortunately the wolves broke for the lumber piles again and instantly slipped into the dark. Blackie, however, had been eviscerated in the few moments the attack had taken, his intestines ripped whole from his stomach. He died, whimpering pathetically, while the Old Man knelt in the spreading bloodstain and tried to do the impossible and put his dog back together again.

He cursed the fact that this had happened. He cursed himself for leaving the dog outside when he had previously seen the wolves moving in ever-closer circles around the empty mill. Yet, oddly enough, he never cursed wolves as a whole. Not for this. Not for Sandy. He put it all down to instinct, and instinct made it broadly understandable, if not individually acceptable. Wolves had their rights as well, even if they sometimes hideously infringe on others. He could not blame them for being wolves.

I went to Europe twice in those years, once in 1968 and again in 1970, and we exchanged several letters. I do wish I'd kept them, for his seemed to come from Europe and mine from nowhere. I told him where I had been, and he would write back and explain to me where I had been. His letters were filled with history, geographically perfect and more appreciative of the late-sixties Grand Tour than I was capable of being. He was in the middle of the bush envying me, seeing where John Cabot had set sail, seeing where Napoleon had fought, seeing where Arthur had ruled, while I was often sitting in smoke-filled bars and rooms in places like Helsingør and Ibiza talking about how noble it was to live close to the earth and water and to fish for your food and to feel and smell the grain of the wood you cut for heat.

This romantic notion lasted all of one day in the summer after first-year university. I headed off to Algonquin Park to work at the mill with him, stayed overnight and the next night, then spent eight long hours working with other men piling boards that had been graded by him. There were lovely walks in the evening, the warm spring air filled with earthy smells and the ring of spring peepers and the blackflies kept at reasonable bay with a dousing of 6-12, but I was very young and very foolish and very much missing a girl back in Huntsville, and when the opportunity arose to take another job back in town, I leapt at it to be closer to her. Regret is a waste, but of course I regret not sticking that summer out, something I would beg to do at fifty but had not the sense to do at twenty. But I might have regretted more, I suspect, not racing back to that girl, for a few years later we were married. Not everything is life is explainable.

He thought it was funny. He never expressed any disappointment, never ridiculed, never held it against me. In the fall, when Ellen went off to the University of Guelph, I went off to Europe, where Ralph Cox and Jack Andrews, two friends from Laurentian

University, and I purchased motorcycles in London and set out to see the continent. It was, as they say in later years, a learning experience. It was wet and cold, and, heading into Scotland, two of us thoughtlessly separated from the third over an absurd argument about whose turn it was to find the night's lodgings. We never saw each other again until we were all back home in Canada. Jack and I took a boat to Oslo and rode down through Sweden and Denmark, where we stayed some time, and from there into Germany and Holland, headed for warmer weather. In Holland my travelling companion pulled out to pass, was forced to swerve back in by a suddenly accelerating car, and smashed hard into the rear of the braking vehicle ahead, motorcycle and rider catapulting over the roof, across the road and onto a soft, grassy knoll, where he landed flat on his back, possibly uninjured. The motorcycle, unfortunately, was right behind him and, spinning, smashed into his side, badly cutting him and shattering his shoulder. Our trip was over.

It was early November and somehow I managed to talk myself into school, two months behind everyone else in the course. I was also broke. I was able to get a student loan and grant—the maximum of $1,200, largely because Duncan's annual income was barely over $4,000—but it was still not enough. I got part-time work but was still short, and was forced to resort to a lifestyle that meant I was showing up at the cafeteria, sitting with my friends and then taking one of their plates back for "seconds." I went home at Christmas, gums bleeding and in desperate straits.

We talked a lot that Christmas, him sitting upstairs with his presents, all books, his smokes and the beer one of us would carry up from downstairs. He asked me how I was making out, and I told him it was pretty tight. Before he left to go back to the mill, he came and shoved a folded blue Bank of Montreal cheque into my pocket. It was for $300 and it carried me through.

Three or four times in later years I tried to give it back to him.

I badly wanted to say I had put myself through school and I felt this $300 was preventing me from making a vainglorious claim about my own enterprise and resilience. He refused to take it. I misread him at first, thinking he still believed I needed his help, but the last time I tried to pay him back I knew I was trying to do the wrong thing. It was more important to him to have quietly helped than it could possibly have been be to me to claim loudly that I had done it without help.

We were alone on the lake. We had waited, as he had advised, until late afternoon, the wind stalling before it shifted and the sun beginning its long slide down towards the dam at the far western end of the lake. No one else was on the water. Perhaps later the troller from the island would be out, and perhaps even the elderly couple who liked to anchor over the largest shoal and jig for trout would settle down with their drinks, their forgotten lines and the pink-purple sunset, but for now there was only the one fishing boat, us, and no one else within sight. I would never go as far as Nick Adams's claim in *Big Two-Hearted River* that anyone else's being there "spoiled it," but I would also never disagree with those who say that there is something very special about being the only boat on a lake, with the only lines in the water. Unless, of course, there were also no fish in the lake, which fortunately wasn't the situation here. But it was August, and the Old Man had already said they would not bite.

I loved to watch him let out his line. He first worked the line out the tip of the rod, then flipped the bait, ran a little more line out from the big wheel of a reel and let the William's Wabler, minnow head and spit catch in the wake of the boat and begin pulling themselves out and down. He concentrated on the letting out, careful not to allow any dangerous kinks in the steel line, but seemed oblivious to how deep he was going. Unlike my father-in-law's equipment, which still had Band-Aids wrapped around the line every hundred feet, Dunc's had no marking, nor did he appear to be counting the turns of the reel so he could calculate when the line was out two or three hundred feet. Once I slowed the motor and we let the weight of the lines pull down on their own, he simply reeled in a few times to find the bottom, letting the bait bounce briefly and then pulling up until he felt, in his hands, that the wiggling, glittering Williams and the delectable minnow head were about six feet off the bottom. Not dragging in the silt. Not about to snag on a branch. Not about to snap on a rock. I tried to feel the same thing in my hands, praying with them that I was at least close, and if down too deep only bouncing through the silt well clear of the rocks.

We passed along the accepted line, island to rock face, wide turn and return, trying to hit the main shoal where the trout fed in several different spots. The air was cooling, shore-bound breezes seeming to shake the water surface before vanishing. The sun was lower and thickening yellow, the water close to shore dancing soft light in the green green branches of the cedars along the shoreline. The outboard missed periodically, a cough that I caught with the throttle and saved, the engine jumping slightly each time. It was a comforting, familiar sound, a thirty-year-old trolling motor that needed new gaskets and spark plugs, but that had needed them last year as well, and the year before that, and the summer before that. The equipment of the procrastinator, acceptable and understandable to all who believe summer in the bush is something more than checklists and quick trips to town.

Sometimes we talked; sometimes we did not. No one measured the silences, no one worried about them. In fact, we treasured them. "There are a great many books that talk about the poetry of fishing," David Adams Richards wrote in *Lines on the Water:*

A Fisherman's Life on the Miramichi, "and yet silence might be the best way to understand it." Absolutely. It is both the silence and the talk of true fishermen that make television fishing shows something so alien to fishing it is a shame they disgrace the activity with them. Perhaps Byron was thinking about television fishing shows when he sat down with his quill and rising bile. People who truly fish together usually say nothing, and when they do speak, it is never to talk about such silly, hopelessly obvious matters as what equipment is being used or who makes it. Most people who truly fish in the wild would last about five minutes with a fish-show host before lashing the anchor rope around the fool's leg and dropping a shoulder into his side. If only all these silly television hosts would read, and understand, Paul Quarrington's lovely *Fishing with My Old Guy,* where he captures the true value of fishing perfectly with a single line after having just spent a full page describing the tying of a certain fly: "If none of this makes any sense, don't worry about it, because it's not all that important."

When the Old Man spoke, it could be about any topic at all, fishing excepted. He could complain about married life—"She's awfully mad at me this week"—while at the same time praising Helen for running a fine home, managing her money well and raising the children, now all grown, virtually on her own. I see in an old letter I somehow stashed away back in the spring of 1977, when he was seventy, that he had come down with a bad cold at the mill and headed off to Huntsville for some rest. He ended up at the beer parlour with Wam Stringer, one of his old park cronies, and he had a bit of a run-in when he stumbled home several hours later. "I tell you now, Roy," he has scribbled in pencil, "I won't live with her at home. As long as I can look after myself I'll stay right here." He has signed it, "Your Old Man," and closed with a note that I, somehow, will understand. But of course I didn't. If I were ill or old or tired, there could be no more pleasant prospect than heading for Helen MacGregor's wonderful, warm kitchen in Huntsville, where everyone was always made welcome—with perhaps one significant exception. None of us ever bothered to discuss their marriage with them. Years earlier, all four of us had decided that we liked each of our parents just fine, got along with each of them and, if they couldn't get along with each other, then that was their problem. He complained about her; she complained about him. She would even complain about being lonely when he had finally gone.

He loved to tell stories about the characters of the park, and some of the best were about Wam Stringer and his brother Jimmy, both of whom had lived their entire lives at the far end of Canoe Lake. How they lived no one was ever quite sure. They did odd jobs in the summer. They guided a bit when both were younger. They cut wood and hauled supplies for better-off cottagers. They worked a bit around the big lodges in the days of the big lodges, now long since gone. And they struck agreements with numerous Algonquin cottagers who lived in distant cities that, for a designated fee, they would clear the roofs of the cottages of snow at least once during the winter to make sure nothing caved in. Wam and Jimmy, of course, did nothing to collect their cheques. The summer visitor would arrive and find his dwellings still standing and be grateful to Wam and Jimmy for keeping an eye on matters. If, by some chance, a roof sagged or a support beam snapped, the excuse was always the same: "Sudden blizzard—tried, but couldn't get to it in time."

Wam is remembered forever for pulling off the greatest tourist scam in the history of the park. He was hired by the Department of Lands and Forests in the summer of 1963 to check incoming tourists for appropriate life preservers. Wam was given a new ranger's uniform and assigned to the portage docks at Canoe Lake, where campers were lining up every morning to head out for the

Tom Thomson memorial cairn. All Wam had to do was check the canoes and rented boats, count the life preservers and the passengers and make sure everything evened out.

Wam was in his sixties then, but with his sparkling new uniform and ranger's cap, his bootblacked hair and a clean shave, he struck a fine, authoritative figure. Tourists asked to have their picture taken with him. They asked about Tom Thomson, and as luck would have it, Wam turned out to be an expert on the painter's life and mysterious death. Unlike Thomson, a fair-weather park visitor who arrived on the spring train and stayed at the lodge, the Stringers, more than a dozen of them, had lived year-round in a rambling home on the far shore. Wam told the enthralled visitors how his brother, Jimmy, had once painted with Tom Thomson. He told them how the Stringer brothers had once nailed Tom Thomson originals onto the wall of the old rundown house at the end of the lake. He did not add, that the paintings were lost the winter night Wam and Jimmy got in a fight over whose turn it was to go out to the woodpile. With neither trusting the other to be left alone with the last of the bottle, they decided to burn the oil paintings instead. But he did tell them that Jimmy claimed to have Thomson's shin bone stashed in the shed—proof that Thomson's body had never been dug up and taken back to the family plot in Leith, Ontario, as the family had always maintained, but was, in fact, still buried in the tiny graveyard on the hill overlooking the far shore of Canoe Lake. And he saved, to the end of this marvellous dissertation, the story of the time Wam and Jimmy were out guiding and this man who looked exactly as they remembered Tom Thomson looking had stepped to the edge of the shore and called out that there had been an accident downstream and someone was drowning. They paddled fast but were too late to save the young man who had turned over in the rapids, and they had never been able to find the man who had come to tell them.

The tourists hung on his every word. In a few short weeks, Wam Stringer, with the most insignificant job lands and forests could give out that summer, had become the most significant "ranger" in Algonquin Park. His stories gave him credibility. His new uniform game him authority. Why not, he soon asked himself, put himself to better use than checking canoes for life preservers when the lake was perfectly calm anyway?

Wam soon moved operations off the dock and down the narrow road towards the highway coming through the park. Hair slicked back, chest out like a rooster, resplendent in his ranger uniform, he set up at the end of a twist in the road and began randomly stopping cars to ask but one simple question.

"Excuse me, sir, but would you happen to be carrying any alcoholic beverages?"

He had such an air of authority, such a sense of understanding —not to mention the advantages of a lonely road and a uniform— that the answers were instant and, usually, affirmative. A car headed into the bush for two weeks usually carries more than food and fishing gear.

"I'm very sorry, sir, but alcohol is prohibited in the park interior. I'll have to confiscate it, I'm afraid, or else you'll be charged."

Wam's new assignment lasted less than a week. Tie askew, bootblacked hair hanging down under a cock-eyed ranger's cap, he eventually fell flat on his face holding up his hand to stop a van filled with American college students. Real rangers were called to the scene and investigated. Down the bank and under a spreading spruce tree, they found a cache large enough to last the heavy-drinking Stringer brothers through the coming winter.

In their later years, Dunc and Wam, now both well into their eighties, the two park "lifers," would sometimes sit in the Empire Hotel, each man with a cane and a rum and Coke, Wam's hair still curiously black, and they would quietly laugh about the characters and incidents they had known, and the family and friends they had lost, Wam's snow-white-haired brother, Jimmy, among them.

I had myself been a part of this sad tale. I had been asked to write about our family's Tom Thomson connection for *Maclean's* magazine shortly after leaving university, and had naturally turned to the Stringer brothers for first-hand accounts. I met Jimmy in the Snake Pit in February of 1973, and he had several beers before talking me into going to the liquor store with him, where he picked up two two cheap bottles of Bright's sherry before heading back to the eight-dollar room he was renting at the Empire. I asked him about the Tom Thomson ghost he and Wam believed they had once seen, and he became adamant that Thomson's body had never been removed from Canoe Lake. He swore that the shin bone in the shed did indeed exist. As soon as spring breakup came, he promised, the two of us would settle Canada's greatest mystery once and for all. He would take me and show me exactly where he and the other park old-timers had secreted Thomson's body before the family sent that drunken undertaker to dig him up and take him home. "There was nothing in that box but sand," he said. And together we would prove it. I left him sitting on the edge of a ratty bed, the second bottle between his knees, and the next day, an unusually warm one for February, he left to return to Canoe Lake. He got a ride into the park and began walking over the ice towards the old house where Wam was waiting for him to return with the groceries. When Jimmy failed to show, Wam went out looking and found Jimmy's pipe pouch floating where he'd broken through, Jimmy himself drowning at almost the precise point where, more than a half-century earlier, Tom Thomson's bloated body had surfaced.

We talked about the park characters and, of course, we talked sports. He talked not only about last night's game, but also about games that had been played fifty and sixty and seventy years ago. He could bounce from Roger Clemens to Christy Mathewson, from Wayne Gretzky to Newsy Lalonde, from Doug Flutie to Knute Rockne. He loved to compare eras and players, and he could argue for hours that this, more than anything else, was what proved his beloved baseball was superior to any other game. More than the other two sports he loved, football and hockey, baseball had remained largely intact with what once was. If you ignored the salary talk and bad behaviour—something the press conveniently ignored in Ruth's day—they still played the game essentially the same. There was the designated hitter (something he despised) and the more extravagant use of the bullpen (something he liked), but the players were pretty much the same size and in the same shape, the equipment wasn't all that much improved and the strategy remained very much the same. Hockey—with its growing players; its growing obsession with size and strength and fitness; its laminated, curved sticks, lightweight equipment, helmets, modern rinks and confused officiating—could not make that claim. And football wouldn't even begin to argue. For him, the only difference between Sammy Sosa and Babe Ruth was batting gloves.

He also liked to talk books. It would be wrong to say we discussed literature, for while he might talk about Mark Twain and Charles Dickens and Dr. Johnson and Plutarch, the treasured book Tom gave him one Christmas, it might just as likely be Mickey Spillaine and Al Capp. He might be reading Arrain's *The Campaigns of Alexander*—"You know why his men loved him? Because he refused to drink water when they had none. They worshipped him after that, you know"—or he might want to discuss something he'd found in the Toronto *Sun* and had ripped out and folded over and stashed in his wallet for quick reference. He could rail against the government, the justice system, the banks, the establishment—whatever happened to rub him the wrong way. But he was no ideologue. He could be so far right wing it would shock, so far left wing it would stun. I once gave him a book called *The Pessimist's Guide to History,* a compendium of all the horrible, hideous, incomprehensible things that had happened to mankind from the eruption of the volcano on Thera in 1628 B.C. to lightning striking a spectator at the 1991 U.S. Open. "A wonderful book!" he has written inside the front cover. As he said in that same 1977 letter, he considered himself "rather eccentric."

But it was more than that. He could be surprising, and always interesting. He had spent half a century in the bush working for a lumber company, and he had come to the conclusion that one of the great tragedies of Canada was that no one had ever bothered to pay much attention to those who were supposedly "harvesting" the trees. The clear-cutting along the West Coast appalled him. Much of the waste he had seen in the Ontario bush embarrassed him. One of the last times I had him out to Camp Lake, perhaps it was even this trip, he had stared up into the massive hemlocks that surrounded our little cabin—some of them more than two centuries old—and said it was "terrible that they'd once cut trees like that down just for the goddamned bark. Terrible."

I know he meant it. Ian Radforth, a University of Toronto historian with a strong interest in the lumbering industry, once taped a session with Dunc and Donald McRae in which the two lifelong loggers told a story of a spectacular white pine they had found not far from the Lake of Two Rivers mill in the late 1930s. It was one of last gigantic stands of white pine left in the park, and some of the trees were so large that they had to be dynamited rather than brought down by axes and saws. The tree the two men could never forget was five feet across when they measured the stump. "It was just so wonderful to look at," Dunc told the historian. "It should have been left for posterity. It's a damn disgrace, you know, that it was cut."

"Any fool can destroy trees," John Muir, the American environmentalist, had written years earlier. He spoke from first-hand experience, having been introduced to the forest as a pine cutter. "They cannot run away; and if they could, they would still be destroyed—chased and hunted down as long as fun or a dollar could be got out of their bark hides, branching horns, or magnificent bole backbones. Few that fell trees plant them; nor would planting avail much towards getting back anything like the noble primeval forest. During a man's life only saplings can be grown, in the place of the old trees—tens of centuries old—that have been destroyed. . . . God has cared for these trees, saved them from drought, disease, avalanches, and a thousand straining, levelling tempests and floods; but he cannot save them from fools."

But Duncan never felt quite this strongly about the issue. He thought the loggers of Algonquin Park different. They were watched carefully and had to harvest selectively. Besides, he often pointed out, it was logging that opened up the park, logging that created the access points and many of the hiking trails. And while some might wish the park had never been opened up and the trails never blazed and marked with signs explaining the difference between ironwood and ash, he was not one of them. If it had not been for logging, he would never have found the park, and if it had not been for logging again, he would never have been able to stay there and fish there and spend his entire life in the bush. How could he, or anyone else, have possibly stood up during the Depression and told the Polish loggers from Whitney and Wilno that they must not destroy natural beauty? It is also natural to eat. It is also natural for one to want to provide for a family.

He always recognized that there was a profound difference between those who lived in the bush and never travelled from it and those who did not live there but sometimes travelled to it.

Both tended to love it in different ways, but only the one side, those who actually lived there, loved it in a fashion that would permit the other side enjoyment. The reverse rarely held true, for those who visited and treasured the bush would remove those who lived there and used the bush. There was always something elitist and privileged about the attitude towards the bush presented by those who had the ability and the means to present their case. The men and women who worked at the mill and kept the camps and tried to make a bare living hauling pulp and cutting wood and signing on to the winter bush camps had no access to television or newspapers or books, but it did not mean they did not love the woods just as dearly in their own manner. When the weather turned bad, when the flies were at their worst, when the roads were impassable from muck or snow, they had nowhere else to go, and yet they loved it no less.

The one literature that the Old Man did not waste his time on was nature writing. He had read Thoreau, of course, but Thoreau had seemed terribly wimpish to him and interesting only as a philosopher, not an adventurer. Nature writing to Dunc was what he found in the old outdoors magazines *Argosy* and *True,* and even these, with their obsessive chase of record game, held him poorly. Ernest Thompson Seton, the great Canadian outdoors writer, would have seemed an English children's author to him. He would have agreed with John Burroughs's devastating review of Seton's work in the *Atlantic Monthly,* when Burroughs had spoken of "the danger that is always lurking near the essay naturalist, the danger of making too much of what we see and describe." As Burroughs put it, "Such dogs, wolves, foxes, rabbits, mustangs, crows, as he has known, it is safe to say, no other person in the world has ever known. Fact and fiction are so deftly blended in his work that only a real woodsman can separate them. . . . those who know the animals are just the ones Mr. Thompson Seton cannot fool." Dunc loved, instead, the Canadian outdoors satirist Gregory Clark, who wrote marvellous stories in the old *Star Weekly,* and revelled in making fun of the city slickers who had all the equipment and thought they had all the answers. Clark held in joyous contempt the prissy experts like Seton, who thought they—better educated, better connected—understood best a natural world already inhabited by those who understood it perfectly well, thank you very much.

But I do wish he had read Calvin Rutstrum. Of all the legendary North American nature writers, Rutstrum came closest in his Minnesota and Northern Ontario experience to Algonquin Park. He and the Old Man shared a lack of formal education, a love of books, a long life and a marvellous materialism. Dunc would have liked nothing more than to win a sweepstakes or a lottery, but not because he was interested in buying fancy things. Apart from his trolling rod, he owned nothing and cared about owning nothing else. Had he ever won the money he dreamed of winning, he would have used it to buy peace and time and to pass on to his children in the mistaken belief that good parenting is about making it too easy for those you bring into the world. "People have more interest in the dollar than anything else," Rutstrum told the American writer, Jim dale Vickery, when Vickery was researching his *Wilderness Visionaries,* "They fight for it until they become the richest man in the graveyard, and they die. No one remembers them. They're a lost entity."

The Old Man and Calvin Rutstrum could have talked long into an Algonquin Park night about the meaning of life as well. They could have looked into the stunning, three-dimensional night sky, stars with depth, stars with form, and laughed together over the utter vanity of man to think that there is something special up there reserved for him. "I'm convinced," Rutstrum told Vickery, "beyond any question or doubt that when this life is gone you are a forgotten entity. I don't think there is any afterlife. The same biological process that occurs when a cockroach dies is when you die. Exactly. . . . Man has no concern for the hundreds of billions of years that occurred before he got here; that doesn't bother him at all. He wants to be considered as living forever. The only promise you got of living forever is that you'll be taken up into the ether to a platform somewhere and you're going to be allowed to strum on a harp all day long. . . . I don't even like music that well."

It was rare to fish with the Old Man and not get into a discussion about religion. He did not begrudge anyone the church. Helen went faithfully every Sunday to early communion in Huntsville and he would even concede that the church was good for her and she for the little stone Anglican church down along the banks of the Muskoka River. He never went himself. Sunday, for him, was a day of thanks for the water and trees and pine-scented breeze coming down Lake of Two Rivers or Whitefish or Rock Lake, or a day for the spiritual renewal of a long, difficult walk into Mosquito Creek, where a man could lean over the tangle and, with luck, stare down at glittering speckles hanging in the current, fish that had never before seen a human shadow, never before tasted a baited hook. This was worship. Religion, on the other hand, was everything from the Inquisition to the conquest of North and South America, everything from the Hundred Years' War to Ireland, the Middle East, the Balkans—even, in his opinion, the political absurdity that Canada had become.

We had just passed by the island heading for the shoal when he suddenly clenched his mouth and caught the rod hard, the tip snapping hard, then springing, then bending back sharply.

"Got one?" I asked.

He nodded. Once. Curt.

There was nothing to say. For forty years we had been going through this ritual with small variations on the same theme. He had a fish on. No more talk. No more concentration on anything apart from getting that fish in. I straightened out the boat but kept the motor running at trolling speed. Unlike many trout fishermen, he believed the boat should continue on its course, partly to ensure the tension on the line, partly to avoid drifting off a shoal that had obviously produced results.

I had nothing to do but steer. I stared at him, so out of context in a lawn chair, so in context with his mouth clenched tight and his arms suddenly sprung to action, right hand gripping the rod just above the big wheel of a reel, thumb holding the brake off, left hand winding smoothly, surely, stopping only when the rod would jerk and bend.

He no longer seemed eighty-three years old. The skin on his face had tightened with the effort. His nostrils flared. His arms were working hard, muscle answering more out of instinct than recent practise. I was four again. I was ten again. I was twenty, thirty again, and he was as he always was: forty-nine forever.

I wished, for once, that the lake was filled with people fishing. I wished there were bass boats surrounding us, pot-bellied guys in satin sponsor jackets and aviator glasses stopping to stare at this Old Man who knew—better than any of them, better than any book they had ever read, better than any rod or reel or lure they had ever pushed, better than any television program or movie that had ever been produced about trout fishing—what it is to have one on and know exactly what to do with it without saying a single word. I wished his friends could see him, those who had died and those who couldn't even imagine being out here. I wished the schoolchildren who sometimes pointed at the Old Man with the cane hobbling up from his daily run to the library and the beer parlour could see him now: Duncan Fisher Mac-Gregor, with a fish on, a *trout*.

Fifty feet back of the boat, the trout broke water in a cauldron of foam, glistening dark back and flashing white belly as it turned.

It rolled and slid and danced on the wake and then dipped back down, the Old Man holding steady so the tension would break its one final gasp for freedom. He had probably lost more trout at this critical moment than most trout fishermen had taken, and he knew that the one matter most necessary at this moment was the one least considered: patience. But he had it; he always had it.

"The net," he said.

He said it as a quiet statement—not a question, not an order, not a worry. I reached beyond him, jiggling the old net to release it from the gas tank, and brought it back to the stern, keeping it well away from the rod and the jerking, glittering line.

He reeled again, slowly, surely, and I could see the trout, beaten, riding just below the glassy roll of the close wake. I dipped the net down, waiting, and he drew the fish perfectly into it. Even I could not have lost this one.

I raised the trout high out of the water. Perhaps someone on shore had been watching through binoculars. At Lake of Two Rivers someone would always shout, "He's up!" if they happened to look out onto the waters and see, in the distance, a single figure standing in the red wooden boat. If he was up, it meant he was playing a trout, and if he was up, it meant, almost certainly, there would be fresh trout for supper. He could no longer stand without help and a cane. He could not even get into the boat by himself. He was sitting in a lawn chair. But he was still *up*. The trout wrenched and flopped and twisted in the net, the William's Wabler in its mouth tangling badly in the frayed green netting. But still I held it up, the sun sparkling off its lovely, glistening back, the water spraying in golden raindrops onto our laps.

"Put it down," he said. "You want *everybody* to know?"

"Yes," I said. "I do want them to know."

"Tch-tch-tch-tch-tch-tch-tch."

CHAPTER SEVEN

Dunc at seventy. He believed bass lacked personality, and they interested him as little as people who react predictably to whatever passes them by.

THE CHIP TRUCK SOLVED a lot of problems for a lot of people. When that huge truck slid on the ice of the cookery hill and pinned Dunc with its locked rear wheel, it answered the question everyone was posing to each other, but never to him: *What are we going to do with the Old Man?* It was early December 1980. He was seventy-three years old, didn't take a single pill apart from Tums when he drank too much and was still putting in a full workday at the mill, five days a week, fifty-two weeks of the year; and yet everyone—with one obvious exception—knew it could not go on forever.

"I'm worried about him," Donald McRae had said to Jim and me when we had come on a rainy Thanksgiving Saturday to pick up the Old Man for a day of partridge hunting. Donald himself was winding down, passing the family operation on to his sons, Bob and John, and had even started to winter in Florida and take up golf. Duncan was Donald's uncle, older by eight years, yet he had shown not the slightest interest in retirement, and certainly none whatsoever in Florida or golf or, for that matter, even Huntsville, though Helen had just turned sixty-five and had herself retired from her last job as the dessert chef at Grandview, a resort on Fairy Lake.

"What if he starts a fire?"

The Old Man was now living by himself at the mill, alone at night and all alone on weekends. The McRae operation had moved again, this time returning to where it had been when John McRae had started up and when Duncan MacGregor, then just turned twenty-two, had started his first, and only, full-time job. He was again on Galeairy Lake at the edge of the village of Whitney. All the workers but one went home at the end of work each day. There was no bunkhouse. Instead, to accommodate one eccentric lumberman and great-uncle, the McRae boys had hauled a used camper trailer onto the mill yard, wired it up for light, put in a heater and turned it over to the Old Man. It was an incredible mess. Churchill might have spent the lonely hours of the Blitz organizing his books to keep his mind off the worst, but Duncan's library—those books he hadn't given away or thrown away—looked like the bombs had struck. The sink was full of books. The cupboards were full of books. The counter and table and bed were covered in books and magazines and week-old papers. Once a week or so a woman from the village came in and put down a fresh change of sheets. These were the best accommodations he had had in years.

He had held this same job for more than fifty-one years and was now an old man. Despite the constant smoking and the periodic drinking, he was in far better shape than most other seventy-three-year-olds, even if he could no longer hit a line drive through the open doors of the Catholic church. Still, he was aging. His blue eyes didn't pick up print as well and he was wearing glasses now to read. In recent years, he had shown a tendency to fall asleep with a book in his lap and a roll-your-own cigarette still burning in his mouth. The proof was all over his shirt and in his books. You could look it up.

"He's set himself on fire more than once," Donald said.

We knew. He was the reverse of spontaneous combustion, somehow escaping the smouldering sweaters and singeing pages, his reading table black-gullied and scarred with cigarette burns, his books marked with Player's tobacco and smudged with dark, spent match heads, many pages with small, circular, black-framed windows where a spark had landed and eaten through the words and margins. Teddy Roosevelt once became so engrossed in a book that his shoes caught fire from the fireplace, but compared with Duncan MacGregor, he was a light reader.

Donald wasn't trying to get rid of him. The two were still the best of friends. In September they had gone together to a lake in Quebec and caught several of the best lake trout of their lives, Duncan pulling in a magnificent twenty-four-pounder on his old rod. He had kept it on ice and given it to me "for a big meal" when I had last been up to see him, but I had taken the huge trout, instead, to a taxidermist outside Ottawa and was secretly having it mounted for him. He had never done this before himself, had no use for trophy fish, in fact, but his children had decided to split the cost of the mounting just in case this turned out to be his last great fish. We had, after all, been expecting him to die since the 1950s.

Still, he was becoming a problem at the mill. Years of screaming band saws and roaring chainsaws, pounding generators and double-clutching logging trucks had reduced his hearing, and they worried about him being around heavy equipment. He tired at the end of long days and at the end of the week. Because he was left on his own for the weekends, they worried about his diet, even though it was a bit late for that. Baked beans so dry the bacon tastes like pemmican, half a shaker of salt and pepper, butter an inch thick on burnt toast, and, it seemed, you might live forever.

We said we'd talk to him, and did, but he cut us off as if we might spook the ruffed grouse strutting around the next turn in the logging trails we hunted up and down that drizzly, cool October day. His business was none of ours.

As we always have, we let it go, let it drift. The leaves fell from all but the ironwood, the first snow came, and by early December he was the last thought in our minds. Ellen's father, Lloyd, had suffered his fatal heart attack and we had just buried him in Huntsville. On the drive back, we had stopped in at the mill to see how Dunc was doing. He took us to the cookery, where we ate a quick snack and talked about him coming over to Ottawa for a visit before Christmas. He liked the museums. He liked driving around, looking at the buildings where those he had only read about—Laurier, Mackenzie King, the governor-general—lived. He liked the refrigerator in the basement and the cold beer. He would have come then, but there was no room in the car. I said he could either come out on one of the logging trucks heading east from the park, or I'd drive back and get him on the weekend. We left it at that.

Two days later the truck lost its grip on the icy slope. We didn't hear about the accident until he'd already been sent by ambulance to Peterborough and was on his way to Toronto for surgery.

He was now, officially, retired.

He would not be coming back to the mill or the bush. He was, whether he liked it or not, headed for Huntsville. Frost may have said of hired hands, "Home is the place where, when you have to go there, they have to take you in," but in the world of those who work entire lives in the bush, it often applied to husbands as well.

*　　　*　　　*

It took months for him to get home. They did the surgery at Wellesley Hospital in Toronto where he charmed the staff and fascinated the doctors. They would parade in interns to thump his chest and stare down his lungs and wonder how it was that he had lived long enough to be hit by the truck. The passage to his lungs looked, the chief of surgery told him, "like a mine shaft" and he joked about sending "men down with pickaxes" to work on him. He was advised to quit smoking immediately. He responded by getting an orderly to wheel him down to the entrance, where he bummed a cigarette and thought about it, momentarily. They set and pinned his hip, sewed together the fragile pelvis, scraped his prostate gland since they were in the neighbourhood and put him to bed, they figured, forever. We were told, in those first days, that he would probably never walk again and would likely always require a wheelchair. Perhaps it was the lack of wheelchair access at the Empire Hotel beer parlour, but whatever had inspired him, he was soon hobbling down the hospital corridors for therapy, refusing to sit in a wheelchair even for rest. Following the minor prostate operation, he delighted in the realization that he could now easily last through a two- or three-hour bus ride without demanding that the driver pull off to the side of the road while he stepped out for a leak.

Just before Christmas they returned him by ambulance to the little Huntsville Hospital for further therapy. Step by step, he was coming ever closer to what he had dreaded: retired life in town. It was the first Christmas ever that he would not be at the house, and we took turns visiting in those weeks. He had only two demands for visitors: fresh books and, if you can, sneak in a bottle of beer. The nurses turned blind eyes to whatever he did, delighting, as all seemed to, in a devilish patient who never complained and seemed to have an endless supply of witticisms and fishing stories. "That's not a word of a lie," he finished off most of the tales. "Not a word of a lie." As Dizzy might have added, "It ain't braggin' if you done it."

The taxidermist had finished with the trout. It had been a difficult mount, as the fish had been gutted to be eaten, not displayed, but the job was superb, the huge laker turning on a large piece of driftwood. We drove over from Ottawa with it and decided to have a little fun with his "not a word of a lie" habit. My friend Eric, who had a particular knack for getting the Old Man going, got him talking about the fish, and the story began spilling out about Donald and him on that Quebec lake he wouldn't, or couldn't, name and how Donald had caught a huge pike and then, in deeper water, how this massive lake trout had all but ripped Dunc's arms out of their sockets.

"How big?" Eric asked.

"Twen-ty-four pounds," he answered, pounding out the consonants.

"But you said twenty-one when I was here last week."

"The hell I did!"

"You did. This stupid fish of yours grows every time you tell the story. How big's it going to be tomorrow?"

"It's twen-ty-four pounds. We weighed the goddamned thing right there."

"Prove it."

I was watching from the hallway, just barely peeking around the door frame. It looked, for a moment, like the Old Man was going to fly right out of the hospital bed. Others in the room were watching with alarm.

"I don't have to prove it! You can take my word for it or you can go to hell, for all I care."

"You said twenty-one."

"Twen-ty-four!"

"Twenty-one."

"TWENNN-TEEE-FFFOURR!"

"That's just your word. I never saw it."

"Well, goddamn it—if it was here, you'd say twen-ty-four!"

"It *is* here."

The Old Man didn't quite grasp it for a moment. He sputtered, tried to lean up on an elbow. He winced from the pain."What did you say?"

"It *is* here."

"What's here?"

"Your stupid fish."

"What are you talking about? I gave it to Roy's family. They've eaten the goddamned thing!"

"What's *that* then?"

Eric pointed behind the Old Man, who turned, straining to see as I walked in, holding the magnificent trout out with both hands. Dunc blinked, confused.

"What's that?"

"Your trout."

"How can that be?"

"We didn't eat it. We had it mounted for you."

I laid it on the edge of his bed. He ran his hands over it. I had never seen his hands so smooth and clean. The nails were still long and yellowed on his smoking hand, and there were strong liver spots darker than the freckles that had always been there, but the hands seemed to belong to anyone but him. He had always had outdoor hands: the creases lined with grit, bandages on a finger or healing scrapes on the knuckles, the nails black underneath and broken, the skin hard and rough. A month of hospital life had given him new hands.

He looked up, dubious. "This is it?"

"That's it."

"This is the one I caught with Donald?"

"Same one."

He turned, eyes triumphant, to Eric.

"Twen-ty-four pounds!"

He stayed in the hospital another two months or so. Helen fretted terribly about him coming home. Would he be able to use the stairs? Would he be able to get to the bathroom on his own? Would he stay upstairs once he got there? Would she have to carry up his meals? A lot of good, sensible questions, but never the one that mattered most: can we live together?

The sliding chip truck had carried him, helplessly trapped, all the way to Lorne Street on the side of the Reservoir Hill. There was no going back. In the early spring, I drove him up through the park so he could see the leaves and the ice coming out and so he could visit at the mill. The trailer was already gone. There were a few books stored for him, a bit of clothes, and his trolling rod—his worldly possessions in a couple of boxes. He knew from the way the men gathered around, all talking and laughing and smoking, that he was no longer one of them. He was a welcome visitor, but they knew, and he knew, he'd never be going back to work. We drove back largely in silence, Duncan crushed against the passenger door, seat belt lying undone, his eyes staring out into the hardwood hills until eventually, with the sun steaming in and the musty, fetid, joyous smell of spring dancing in through a crack in his window, he fell asleep, jumping violently several times as if reality was hitting home when he least expected it.

When the therapists thought they had done as much as could be done, they sent him home with a walker and a pair of canes. He used the walker only briefly and then ignored it until the home care eventually took it away. He cut down to one cane, but only when he began walking up and down the sidewalk outside the house, practising for his first walk down to the corner of Main and Centre, where the Empire Hotel was located. He made it down in spring, as soon as the sidewalks were clear. He had a couple of drafts of cold beer and then walked over to the town library, one block away. He joined immediately and would spend the next fifteen years ploughing through, shelf by shelf, until the librarian, at one point, wondered if she still had anything he hadn't read. Two or three books a day, two or three or four pints a day; every day, a good walk, a good drink and a good read—something for the hip, something for the throat, something for the mind. He had discovered a routine that suited him. Back home, he began watching television for the first time in his life, never before having had reception good enough to bother trying in the bush. He watched sports—baseball above all, but hockey and soccer if there was no baseball on—and he read, constantly.

He had his vision checked, and they discovered a cataract in his left eye. Had it been any other part of his body he probably would have let it go, but the words had been blurring and he quickly agreed to an operation. It was necessary for him to have it done in another small town closer to Toronto, and he came back with a huge bandage over the eye that wasn't removed for several days. When they took it off, the eye wouldn't open. The doctor who had done the operation explained that he had suffered a rare collapse of the muscles in the eyelid, and Dunc was furious that he'd ever agreed to the surgery. For six months he read with one eye and walked around like a man eternally winking. It was only on a routine visit to his own doctor that they discovered the problem: the inept eye doctor down the road had forgotten to remove one of the stitches. The stitch was cut out, the eye fluttered open, and he could see, he claimed, as well as he ever could.

He was, hip, pelvis, eye, pretty much mended now and gradually becoming resigned to life at home. So, too, was Helen. The distancing of the past thirty years in the bush while she had been raising the children in Huntsville largely as a struggling single parent precluded any complete *rapprochement,* but it was not nearly so awkward and difficult as we had anticipated. They no longer spoke to each other in the same frosty tones as before. She worried about him and he seemed grateful that she had taken him in without protest. He even bought her chocolates for Mother's Day. He moved into a bedroom that had once been mine, with a fine view far down the hill of the Muskoka River as it spread, sparkling in the morning sun, into Fairy Lake. Here he moved his extra pair of pants, and three or four shirts, took over an old tweed jacket of mine and dumped the rest of his wardrobe into a single drawer of the old black dresser against the wall. He leaned his rolling rod against a wall in the back downstairs room. He set up a card table at the edge of the bed, piled it high with books, dusted it with tobacco and sat down to read.

The room became his court. Here the visitors came to sit backwards on old vinyl kitchen chairs and listen to him. Eric became a regular, the two of them duelling with repartee the way spring-training ball players will sometimes play pepper with each other, each advancing on the other, throwing harder and harder, until, finally, one concedes the match. As soon as the grandchildren arrived, they had to dart up the narrow staircase to visit with the Old Man, and there would be many times when one of us would walk in on them with the Old Man trying to light a roll-your-own fashioned by the hands of a five- or six-year-old, sometimes grandfather and grandchildren sitting in a circle, all three or four of them with rolled cigarettes in their mouths, sometimes all three or four of them going. There was no point in saying anything. Neither eighty-year-old nor eight-year-old would listen anyway.

The relationship with the grandchildren was something to watch. To be forty and able to stand at his doorway, staring at him as he dealt with your own children as once he had dealt with you—the whisker burns, the singing, the feigned slights, the animal sounds, the poetry, the history lessons, the great, dramatic stories of stepping on bear cubs or minks stealing trout or wolves twisting around the lumber piles on a wintry night—was to see the magic in another light and to understand how it could work. He somehow came across more as accomplice than parent or grandparent; a Peter Pan who held adult ways in contempt; a funny, engaging, caring buddy who somehow knew exactly where to stand between common sense and foolish danger; a man who, somehow, could convey to a child a sense of perfect safety while dabbling in perfect insanity. You wouldn't want to be married to him, but you sure would want to be a child or a grandchild to him. A fervent non-smoker who can cringe at his own militancy when checking into a hotel and finding an ashtray where the reservation said there should be none, I sometimes felt like rolling my own and joining them. Heading for their grandfather's bedroom was like running away to sea, like joining the circus, like skipping school. If only we did not lose the joy of whim in our organized, stultified, get-ahead lives.

Our youngest, Gordie, took to him at once. The fish stories, the singing, the tobacco and smoke, the pockets filled with sharp jackknives and broken matches and change to be given away—it was all irresistible to the very young. Once, when Duncan had come to visit and was staying downtown with Tom, who was now also living and working in Ottawa, I arranged for Gordie to get together with his grandfather at a meaningless old-timers' hockey tournament I happened to be playing in that weekend. Tom would drop the Old Man off at the arena and I would have Gordie there with me. Duncan was keen to come. It flabbergasted him to think that grown men still played games like softball and hockey, but rather than ridicule it, he said he wished himself that he had never grown up in a time when Depression and war meant that he had to put away foolish things too soon.

The game had already started when Tom dropped the Old Man off at the front doors. Gordie, wearing a jean jacket and a baseball cap pulled down tight over his eyes, had been watching from beside the bench. When he saw his grandfather come in and sit in the empty bleachers at the far end of the rink, he moved to sit with him. I could see them talking, happy that grandfather and grandson had met up and were enjoying each other's company. I had presumed everything was fine and lost myself in the game.

They were standing by the boards waiting for me when the game was over and I had showered and changed. The Old Man looked a trifle worried.

"Do you know whose kid this is?" he asked me.

I looked at him. A joke? Had he had a stroke? "It's Gordie!" I said.

"Eh?" he said, clearly taken aback.

I yanked the kid's cap off, his smiling face revealed.

"My God!" he says. "I had no idea it was him."

He had been dropped off to see the game but had not been told that both Gordie and I were at the rink. He had been sitting quietly when this little four-year-old kid with the blue baseball cap struggled up the stands and plunked himself down beside him. The Old Man had talked to him because, well, in his world you talked to kids.

Between periods, he'd gone out for a smoke. The kid had come along with him. He'd lighted his cigarette and decided to hobble up the street on this fine spring day. The kid had come along. He'd begun to worry that someone might think he was making off with the kid.

He'd come back to the rink and found a woman coming out the door. He'd asked her if this was her child. She'd told him no and then watched him, suspiciously, until the Old Man had risen again to his seat and the little kid in the cap had struggled up and plunked himself down tight to the Old Man's thigh. They'd sat like that for the rest of the game, Dunc watching every turn of the door for an angry parent or, worse, a policeman. But he wouldn't abandon the kid either. The kid seemed to like just hanging around with him.

"I tried to give him away to a woman," the Old Man said, aghast at himself. "I didn't know who he was."

"Doesn't matter," I said. "He knew who you were."

He sometimes got angry with himself for growing old. If he felt forty-nine in the mornings, he certainly felt his age at other times during the day. In a way, he was like a car that had been driven too hard and neglected. The chip truck had forced him in for repairs—the pelvis, the hip, the prostate—and from that point on the regular checkups, something he would never have done himself, kept finding more reasons to tinker.

He complained to me once that he was having trouble moving his bowels. He was eating Ex-lax like chocolate but it was having little effect. Far more imaginative than him, I shuddered at the prospects and arranged immediately to take him over to see the doctor, who, like most people who met him casually, seemed end-lessly amused by the crusty old logger. Before moving on to the main complaint, he insisted on checking blood pressure and lungs, and clearly didn't believe what he was hearing as he held the stethoscope to the Old Man's back.

"When did you stop smoking, Dunc?" he asked.

"At the door."

It was true. He had butted out just beyond the entrance doors.

"You still smoke, then?" the young doctor asked.

"Yes."

"How long?"

The Old Man figured in his head a moment. "Seventy-three years."

"Then there's no point in trying to get you to stop, is there?"

"No."

I left the room while the full medical took place. When they called me back in, the Old Man was dressed but seemed somewhat indignant. The doctor quickly explained: it was nothing to worry about, a few polyps, a simple procedure and his blockage would be gone. He'd come in as a day patient, be sedated, and it would all be done in a matter of hours. He could then head home.

"Maybe you'd like to explain the procedure to your father," the doctor suggested. It was clear from his look that he had tried, and failed.

I tried. But words like "sedated" and "day patient" and certainly "polyp" were all foreign to him. Finally, in exasperation, I said, "They're going to put this thing up your butt that'll clean you out."

"*What?*" he said.

I presumed it was his hearing. I raised my voice. "It won't hurt a bit—they'll go up through your butt and clean out the blockage."

"You don't have to shout."

The simple procedure went as expected. The night before he took some liquid that acted like radiator flush, and I took him in first thing in the morning. They gave him a tranquilizer, he fell asleep and they wheeled him away. I was there when he woke up three hours later. He could hardly wait to get home.

They got along better than expected. Helen fell easily into her life-long habit of caring for whomever needed her. Better she did the cooking than him, she decided, for he'd invariably leave the element on. Like Donald, she was petrified that he would set fire to the place. We screwed in smoke detectors, bought fire extinguishers and set out wide, cavernous ashtrays wherever he might land, but still she worried. She worried when he went downtown, knowing full well that the library was but one of the stops, and she worried even when, at the end of the day, he finally fell asleep, the catch and choke and rattle of the lifelong smoker filling the house with night sounds that she hadn't heard in years.

They still argued over money—he reluctant to paint the house, dubious about replacing the roof—but in fact, they were better off than at any other time in their lives. He received no pension from the mill, nor did he think he was owed one. He had a small nest egg in the little Bank of Montreal branch in Barry's Bay. He had his government pension and Helen hers. Both qualified for the old-age supplement. Helen bought herself a car, a little Chevette, and they began, at times, taking rides into the country together to look at the changing leaves and water and the endless march of homes that seemed to go deeper and deeper into the North Muskoka bush. They went into the park, where there was no building and where, for ten months of the year, there were often no people apart from them, driving by the roads that once led to old mills and, at Lake of Two Rivers, to past lives. They may not have spoken much on these drives, but they did go, and often, which certainly caused the rest of us to talk.

Helen was busy with the church. She had returned to cross-country skiing, using the same skis she had when she had lived at Lake of Two Rivers and used to ski up to Cache Lake for the mail just to escape the constant demands of her parents. She spent time at the Camp Lake cottage in summer. She travelled, often with Ann, often with one of her old friends, and saw Europe and much of the United States and went out West for the first time. She was blossoming in retirement, busy and healthy and, it seemed, the happiest she had ever been. She even had someone to worry about—sixty years after she had nursed her brother Roy with his polio; decades after she had taken over the care of Andy, the baby nephew; years after she had cared for first the old ranger and then his wife, Bea, until they had died. Having always carried the burden of others, she seemed oddly content to have reason to hurry home.

He knew he got on her nerves. To give her a break, he too began travelling, always by train, always to see things he had long wanted to see. He went to New Brunswick by train to visit an old friend who had once worked at the mill but then moved back to the Maritimes. He went out West to stay with Tom, who was then working for the Edmonton *Sun,* and when the the train stopped briefly in the little Saskatchewan town of Biggar, he asked the porter for his suitcase and stepped off. He didn't know a soul in the town. Nearly eighty years old, hobbling on one leg, with a suitcase that had only half a carrying handle, he found one of the town's few taxis and handed the driver a fifty-dollar bill.

"Just drive me around the back roads for a while," he told the cabbie.

The man drove out past the sign that says, "New York May Be Big, But This Is Biggar" and into the rolling wheat fields of the surrounding countryside, the Old Man in the back seat with his head half out the window as he searched for that magical property his father had once owned back at the turn of the century. He had no idea where, exactly, his father's land had been, no idea if there had even been a farmhouse on it, but it didn't matter. He wanted to see the world about which his father had dared dream, just as he himself had never stopped believing that one lifetime was not enough. The man drove him down dirt roads for the better part of two hours, after which he said the fifty-dollar bill was pretty much used up. The old man had the taxi drop him off back at the station, where he sat reading and smoking until the next train West came along.

He went to Toronto by train and by bus, and he stayed at a cheap hotel and visited with Ann, who had only a bachelor apartment and certainly not enough space in the single room to hold all the smoke the two of them would create when talking together. He went to bars with her, and while she played Trivial Pursuit, he chased beer with double rum and Coke, one ice cube. He went to Blue Jays games with Jim. He came over to Ottawa and fished the Rideau River and visited the Military Museum and sometimes just had us drive him around Eastern Ontario looking for reminders of where his people had originally come from—Burnstown and White Lake along the Madawaska River chain. We even checked graveyards for familiar names. At White Lake we found a McGregor who had been buried in the early 1920s, and he remembered standing there, a half-century earlier, when this man—"I think he was my uncle, but he might have been my father's cousin"—was laid to rest. But like so many who lived and worked in the bush, he had no idea beyond this graveyard where his lineage began or how, exactly, it ended up here.

He took the Polar Bear Express up to Moosonee just because he wanted to see James Bay. I had written a book about the Cree chief Billy Diamond and his long battle against the massive hydroelectric developments of the Far North—the so-called Project of the Century—and he wanted to see where the Cree lived. He loved my stories from Northern Quebec as much as I had always loved his from Algonquin Park, and next to the ridiculous tale of the Rapalla and the duck decoy he had been fascinated by another trip North I had made with an Ottawa friend, Doug Sprott, who went on to work on several building projects with the Crees. We had flown up to the Cree village of Waskaganish, on the banks of the Broadbank River where it empties into James Bay, for the launch of the Cree-Yamaha boat, which the Cree and Yamaha of Japan had designed together to replace the famous, but dangerous, Hudson Bay freighter canoe. We had, in fact, gone out on the last trial run before the Japanese investors were due into Waskaganish, where the boats were to be manufactured, along with Cree trappers Lawrence Katapatuk and Charlie Diamond, Billy's older brother. We had been "lost at sea" for three days, marooned on little Obejiwan Island while a freak summer snowstorm ravaged the coast. Had we been in an old freighter canoe, we would never have made the island, as we had been far out in the shallow bay when the storm struck. As it was, we very nearly did capsize as we raced for shelter, but the new boat held against the rolling, pounding waves and we made it, finally, onto a stony beach somewhat sheltered from the wind. Once we'd landed, the two trappers then saved us from freezing to death by constructing a make-shift tent and even turning an old, abandoned forty-five-gallon drum into a stove. They set nets for whitefish and monkfish, made bannock and tea, and we passed, in retrospect, as pleasant a stay as possible when others were imagining the worst about our fates. The Japanese had flown in and flown out without ever seeing their boat. They did, however, find out from us when we returned to Waskaganish that it did float, and that it stayed floating.

The Old Man had called first from Cochrane, where the regular trains stopped and the Polar Bear Express continued on north. It had become, in the summer, a popular tourist attraction, and he was lucky to be able to get a seat.

"I've met some good lads," he barked into the phone. "Hitch-hikers from Europe. Speak good English, too. I told them I'd get a room in Moosonee. They're welcome to stay."

I said all the right things, thought all the wrong ones. An eighty-year-old man and a couple of young hitchhikers? He didn't have a credit card. His wallet would be stuffed with bills for his trip.

Why would they want to be with an old man? Just to get at his money when he was sleeping? The child might have gotten over his fear of the woods, but the adult he had become still shivered sometimes from the unknown.

He called again from Moosonee. He said that they had gone out to Moose Factory by freighter canoe—"Just like the boat you were in"—and he had seen the residence where Billy Diamond had been sent off to school and where he had won his first great battle against white authority by refusing to eat his vegetables, even if it meant, as it did, sitting up all night with his little arms folded in front of a cold plate. The Old Man could relate to that.

Duncan had seen James Bay, the endless water, and he had seen, when the wind turned, how quickly it can shift from pleasant view to frightful sight. "You were damn lucky to be with those trappers," he said. I said I knew I was.

One of his new friends wanted to speak to me, he said. They had taken a hotel room and they'd been out for a good dinner and a few beer and now they were back in the room. They'd be headed back on the morning train south.

"Hello," a young voice said. Dutch? German? Danish? I couldn't tell. "Your father's been taking care of us," he said. "He's a fantastic guy, you know?"

"Yeah," I said, waves of guilt as high as James Bay whipping over me. "I know."

He took delight in knowing that he sometimes appeared in my writing. I used him as a partial model for the old man, Russell Pemberton, in a novel on the life of Tom Thomson, and again as Poppa in a novel set in the Polish community of Wilno. He loved it when Tom wrote about him in *Legion* magazine. He was astonished that Ann could work for *Maclean's,* a magazine he had read virtually since its founding and one where his favourite writers —Gregory Clark, Pierre Berton, later Allan Fotheringham—all appeared. It pleased him that he could have three children who would all end up working with the printed word, something he had worshipped for a lifetime, but the three of us knew that he was little short of amazed that the fourth—Jim, the banker—would end up a successful and competent manager of money. Helen's genes, he would have argued.

Two or three times a year after he moved to Huntsville, he would ask her to drive him up to Barry's Bay, on the other side of the park, and there he would book into the Balmoral Hotel and pass a couple of weeks sitting in the taproom with his old mill friends. He became such a regular that they reserved room No. 4 for him and gave him a key to keep. He was, for the Billings family that ran the hotel, family himself, a charming old fellow who liked a beer and liked, as well, to sit in the leather seats at the front of the office and talk about everything from the state of Blue Jays pitching to the disintegration of the Soviet Union. He had his own seat in the Balmoral beer parlour, and no one dared occupy it when he, like the royal family, was in residence. They fought for the chairs around his when he came in, sharp at noon, for his first of the day.

Eric was the first to suggest that the Old Man might be being taken advantage of by the odd fair-weather friend when he went for his daily libation at the Empire Hotel in Huntsville. Most who sat with him either had known him for years or were genuinely entranced by this witty old bugger from Algonquin Park. But Eric, who had himself quit drinking, noticed that there were times when moochers were hitting up Duncan for rounds and never reciprocating. The Old Man refused to discuss his finances, as always, but the wastebasket in the upstairs bedroom told its own story of losing lottery tickets. So what? we thought. He had earned the right to do whatever he wished with what little he had. If he wished to be overly generous, if he wanted to gamble endlessly on lottery tickets that never came true, then that was his business—just as he himself would tell you if you asked.

He switched from the Empire Hotel to the local Legion at one point, heading there for his afternoon beer with his cane and plastic bag of library books swinging at his side. He took out an affiliate membership. The beer was cheaper, the company a little more his own age. And the Legion always had Nevada tickets, those little fifty-cents-a-try lotteries where the purchaser is either instantly gratified or instantly disappointed. A deft player can break one open every few seconds, seeing if the cherries or bells or lemons match up and, if they do, cashing them right back in for whatever value the match is. Winning tickets pay anything from two to fifty dollars.

Every day he spent five dollars or more on Nevadas. His dream was to break open three straight cherries and claim the fifty-dollar payoff. And he finally won it one slow afternoon at the Legion, when he was well into his eighties. He handed the big winner and a smaller winning ticket to the man selling them and waited, as always, at his table for his reward to be brought to him. When the man returned, he put down only two dollars for the minor ticket.

He asked where his fifty dollars was. The man told him there was no fifty-dollar winner. The Old Man insisted there was. The man told him he must be mistaken; the two dollars represented his total winnings.

It was an unfortunate incident. There were no witnesses, but no one who knew the Old Man had to have been there to know he was right. The money meant nothing to him; victory over stingy providence meant everything. He might have been more than eighty years old, he might have been barely able to walk, and he might have had a pint too many, but this was also a man who knew Caesar's campaigns, Plutarch's biographies, the capital of every country in the world, circa 1920, and could take one glance into a hardwood stand and tell the number of board feet that could be cut from it.

He knew what was happening. The man was playing him for an old fool. He had hoped the old fool wouldn't remember when he brought back the two dollars and had pocketed the big winner to be cashed in himself later. And if that strategy failed, he knew it would come down to his word against the Old Man's. The ticket seller, surrounded by people who knew him, versus the tipsy old man just in off the street.

"You owe me fifty dollars!" he told the man.

"I'm sorry, sir, you're mistaken."

"No goddamned way I'm mistaken. Give me my fifty."

"You're wrong, sir. There was no winning ticket in the ones you handed me. You've made a mistake."

"*The hell I have!*" the Old Man shouted, lifting his cane and pounding it down, hard, on the little table.

Eighty-three years old, and they had to hold him back. Stiff and with one good leg and a cane, he attacked, but failed when others in the room dashed to the aid of the man who had stolen his ticket.

They threw him out of the Legion and banned him for life for what they termed "disorderly conduct." He thought it one of his finest moments, and now, so too do we.

We moved back to Toronto briefly when I went to work for the *Star*, and when he came down by bus to visit, I took him first to see where I worked. Usually I moved around the newsroom un-noticed, but the moment he walked in it seemed the place had come to a halt. Whatever it was—the cane, the cocky fedora, the twinkle in the eyes—it had an effect on everyone, even supposedly-jaded journalists. He doffed his hat to a young woman reporter. "Oh," he said as he bowed. "Roy never told me they have models working here." It was a time when to speak that way in a newsroom was to head for court, and yet because he seemed so sincere, because he seemed so quaintly out of this time, or any time she could ever have known, the young woman responded as if it were the sweetest thing that had ever been said to her. I took him over to visit one of his long-time sportswriting heros, the legendary Milt Dunnell, who was approximately the same age. They flipped coins together and talked about Dempsey. By the time he left, they were lining up at the elevator to shake his hand and wish him well.

That same visit, he and Ann took in a hockey game between several NHL old-timers, a few media fantasizers and the Flying Fathers. It had been arranged by Ken Dryden and me with the full support of the *Toronto Star*, and the money would go to a special fund that had been established for Jocelyn Lovell, the world-class cyclist who had been severely injured when a truck sideswiped him on a training run. We were hoping to raise enough money to allow Lovell to have his home rebuilt to accommodate a wheelchair. Thanks to the *Star's* promotions department, the tickets had gone fast. We had sold out St. Michael's College arena and would be turning $30,000 over to the Jocelyn Lovell Fund.

At a luncheon, and at the reception that followed the game, Duncan met many of the greatest players who had ever played the game—Dryden, Frank Mahovlich, Andy Bathgate, even Eddie Shack—but the one that overwhelmed him the most was Gordie Howe, the very one he had pointed out to Jim and me nearly thirty years earlier, telling us never to forget that we had once seen the Great Howe play. But it wasn't Howe's play that astonished Dunc this time, even though Howe, at fifty-five, had been retired only three years. None of the former stars took the game very seriously and it was far more a celebration of the past heroics of the NHLers and the current slapstick of the Flying Fathers than it was a true hockey game. No, what amazed Duncan MacGregor was the time the Great Gordie Howe gave an old lumberman from

Algonquin Park. They sat together at the luncheon and talked together after the game. They talked about names that rang so far in the past some of us could barely recognize the sound—Metro Prystai, Earl Reibel, Jack Stewart—and they talked about growing up poor in the Depression and how no one today appreciated how hard people had to work back then just to make ends meet.

"People have no idea how tough it was," Dunc told Gordie Howe. "I tell you, there were a good many nights I went to bed hungry."

"My brother and I were so poor," Gordie Howe told Dunc, "that Christmas Eve we'd go to bed praying we'd wake up with an erection—just so we'd have something to play with Christmas Day."

Dunc MacGregor stared at Gordie Howe, unsure for a moment, and then both men burst with a knowing cackle. Gordie Howe could have scored a half-dozen goals that night (he didn't), it could have been the last game of the Stanley Cup final (it most certainly wasn't), but all would have paled beside the fact that Gordie Howe and Dunc MacGregor had shared a joke. He would count it among the highlights of his life, his own Stanley Cup.

He made his last long trip on August 11, 1994. It is marked down in the cottage log: "Up and away on cloudy day. Dunc decided to come along on our trip to Toronto to see the new Hockey Hall of Fame." My son, Gordie, and two of his hockey-playing friends had come over to the cottage for a few days of swimming and fishing, but cool weather had dampened the visit. The water was warmer than the air. The fish weren't biting. I had suggested we make a run to Toronto to see the Hockey Hall of Fame, and the three peewee hockey players had enthusiastically agreed. There was room in the van for a fourth, so I had called into town and tried to talk the Old

Man into coming along, but he hadn't shown much interest. The Blue Jays were on television. He had library books to take back. The boys at the Empire would be expecting him. He was three weeks away from his eighty-seventh birthday and hardly needed a long day of walking around and standing in lines.

We stopped by in the morning, however, just to double-check, and he was ready, almost as if he had planned it that way to see if we would come by and try to twist his arm a little. He liked to be fussed over, even if he liked to shake his head and argue the other way. The boys fussed. They wanted him along. And soon it seemed I was driving four kids south along Highway 11, headed for Toronto, stopping twice so they could eat and he could smoke.

The rest of the time, he talked. He talked sports, about seeing Sprague Cleghorn—a player so mean he was once arrested for hitting his wife with his crutch while he was out with a broken leg—and King Clancy and Frank Nighbor, the Pembroke Peach, and about reading of Enos Slaughter and Three Finger Brown and Tinker, Evers and Chance. He talked almost constantly, Highway 11 fading behind us as the rock and bush of Muskoka gave way to rolling, sloping farmlands, Highway 400 spreading as the traffic picked up and we began the frenetic final screaming run through the outlying industrial areas and onto the main junction feeding into Highway 401 and from there to the army-ant-like Don Valley Parkway.

"Tch-tch-tch-tch-tch-tch-tch."

"Just imagine," he said after a short while, "if people from a hundred and fifty years ago could wake up and see all this." And from there he launched into a talk about Lord Simcoe and the first roads in Upper Canada, and then from Simcoe into a dissertation on the sparkling rhetoric but abysmal organizational skills of an early revolutionary, William Lyon Mackenzie. "He was right, you know. The Family Compact did control everything—and it still does, as far as I'm concerned."

No wonder he loved Runyon and Lardner. Turn a game on, and he was automatically for the team behind. Catch a boxing match, and he was against the favourite. Take him to the races, and he had eyes only for the long shot. Long shots, underdogs, little guys—he cheered them all and considered himself always standing with them, everywhere from Wrigley Field to the jungles of North Vietnam. If you stood against the establishment, if you fought when the odds were stacked against you, then you were his. From William Lyon Mackenzie and Louis-Joseph Papineau and the rebellions of 1837, he leapt, seamlessly, to the sports establishment of 1994. He railed against the high cost of tickets; he grouched about tax dollars having to pay for SkyDome, where the Blue Jays played, when the average taxpayer couldn't even afford to go to the games; he cursed greed wherever it was found: player, owner, agent. But what he was really upset about was his own inconvenience. The 1994 baseball strike was on and he was put off, to say the least. The greatest joy of his forced retirement had been the opportunity to follow his sports on television, as well as in the papers, and now his enjoyment had been taken away by greed.

With the Toronto skyline rising in our windshield, he began talking about the first NHL game he ever saw—the Ottawa Senators versus the Hamilton Tigers—and how the Hamilton team went on strike in 1925 for more money.

"They didn't get it, either." The team folded not long after.

"Tch-tch-tch-tch-tch-tch-tch."

The parkway rolled and folded into the downtown, his memory moving faster than the traffic. He talked about the Ford Hotel, where he stayed when he came down to see his first Leafs game and where he and his cousin Donald stayed before Donald headed off to war and Dunc, knowing what was expected of him, took the train back north and headed back into the Algonquin Park bush. The Ford had been torn down a generation ago. He talked about the time he and his good friend Eddie and some of the other mill workers were summoned to a hearing in Toronto over a failed attempt to form a union at the mill, and he described how none of them had ever before seen a streetcar. We passed by a pay phone where a woman was hanging half-in, half-out, talking easily.

"Eddie had never seen one of those things before."

"A pay phone?"

"Yeah, a pay phone. He had no idea how it worked or what you did."

He was off and running. Even the boys in the back seat were now listening to him, not sure if he was making things up or not. From the pay phone he moved to radio reception, telling how, as a young man, he was invited to try the first radio to arrive in Eganville one memorable Saturday night. "You had to put earphones over your head, eh? We had to take turns. The crackle'd almost knock your head off, you know, but just to hear a voice, that was something. None of us ever even had a telephone, you know. We'd never heard a voice that way before. We couldn't believe how it was happening.

"They discovered radio by accident, you know. They heard voices coming over the telegraph wires. The first commercial broadcast we heard was the Dempsey-Tunney fight in 1926. It's been all downhill since then, far as I'm concerned."

The boys obviously disagreed. We had no sooner reached the foot of Yonge Street, parked and slowly made our way to the Hockey Hall of Fame but the three young visitors were racing off in their own direction. "This way!" Stan shouted to the others. "All the electronic stuff is over here." The three boys bolted left. The Old Man was already headed to the right: all the memory stuff was over there.

I caught up to him, pulling his cane arm slightly. He stopped and turned, wondering what I wanted. What I needed was a way to bring up what I had to say. I had called ahead to see if wheelchairs were available—they were—but I had never mentioned it to him. A wheelchair seemed sensible, meaning it didn't have much of a chance with him.

"Well?" I said, pointing ever so subtly towards one of the hall's wheelchairs. "Should I get us one? They're free."

He stared at it a while, then back at me, a look of incredulity growing.

"What will people think?" he finally asked.

What, I wondered, could he possibly be imagining? That someone would see him in it and report back, and the next time he hobbled down to the library there would be people hanging halfway out of their car windows to point and laugh at him?

"No one here even *knows* you!" I said, the whispered exasperation of the grown child coming through. But still he wasn't sure. We struck a compromise. I would get the chair—they were free, after all—we would start off and, well, if he needed to sit at some point, he could sit. We started out, an old man hobbling ahead, a younger man pushing an empty wheelchair right behind him. No one would ever make the connection.

Soon, however, the wheelchair was all but forgotten. We turned right and entered a world in which the imagination does all the necessary travelling. He came to a display of original skates—Starr Skates, made in Dartmouth, Nova Scotia, a brand-new pair still in their original box—and he stopped to tap the glass with the end of his cane.

"That's what I wore. You had to put them right onto your boot."

We passed the showcase on the career of the great little Montreal Canadiens player Aurel Joliat, and the mementos sent the Old Man's memory spinning. "His father used to be the chief of police for Ottawa, did you know that?" I, of course, did not; I never knew when he specifically asked, which was likely why he asked. "You know what he did after he stopped playing?" No, I did not. "He worked as a clerk on the work trains. Used to bring men up into the park to build roads and airstrips. He came into Whitney one day, and everyone in town came down to see the great star. I went down, too. Everybody was there."

I could, in fact, see it. Poor Aurel, a green visor on his head, clips on his shirt, sleeve protectors for the lead-pencil work; Aurel blinking as the train's car door slides open and an entire bush village is standing there, waving and cheering for something he had done so many winters before. Aurel's memory; my father's memory; now mine.

He hobbled from showcase to showcase. The display in honour of Rocket Richard started him talking about the Montreal Riot of 1955. Dunc would have been at the Hay Lake mill then. He would have read about it in the *Journal* and the *Citizen,* and he would remember every detail for forty years: who Richard hit to cause the suspension, what they threw at Clarence Campbell, what happened in the streets. He stopped at the Bobby Orr exhibit—Orr's old Victoriaville stick, with the single strip of tape around the blade—and he smiled to think that he had been so fortunate as to see Orr as a child, and to have seen in that child the man that would emerge.

At the Household Finance "Family Room," he marvelled at what had been done with 1950s furniture and dummies dressed in 1950s styles. There was an old black-and-white television with a Leafs–Canadiens game on, the screen going periodically snowy with poor reception, the players sometimes overlapping images, ghosts of themselves. It reminded us both of Saturday nights at Sandy's, when he and Sandy would drink beer throughout the game and wait for "Juliette." Too many memories. The wolves. Sandy and Annie now long since dead. We all have colour television and cable. But the games have never been as rich since.

He stopped for a long while in front of the Gordie Howe exhibit. Howe's Northland Pro sticks, his skates with their blackened toes, his gloves with the number 9 painted in white at the base of the thumb. There was a photograph of Howe in a Hartford Whalers' uniform—Gordie standing at centre with Marty on his left wing and Mark on his right. The three Howes are facing off against the Detroit Red Wings. We began talking about what it must have meant to Gordie Howe to play this game with his sons, but just as we were stating the obvious, my own son and his friends caught up to us, the electronic attractions having held them for only so long. Our own Gordie insisted on reminding everyone of the old hockey cards—surely a thousand Gordie Howe rookie cards included—that I once had and either destroyed or threw out. The grandfather then took his turn reminding me, once again, of that moment in Maple Leaf Gardens when he had first pointed out the great Howe to us. Grandfather and grandson moved together to the other side of the showcase, pointing things out to each other in a manner that presumed each would already know. And it seemed they did.

We travelled together as a group for a while, the names on the exhibits familiar to all, the meaning different to each of us—Bobby Hull is a youngster to the old man, the most exciting player of all to the younger man, a lost rookie card to the youngest—but the game is still hockey. We saw the Stanley Cup, the Hart Trophy, the Art Ross, the Lady Byng. The boys bored easily in the trophy room and hinted about returning to the electronics displays, particularly the broadcast booth where they were able to take turns calling a game.

They left and we were again alone. I could see that he was sagging. He was leaning heavily on the cane, moving even slower.

He turned to face me and the waiting wheelchair, defeat in his eyes. "I guess maybe I will sit in that thing."

I said nothing. I put the wheelchair in position and helped him settle down. He seemed embarrassed by it, but too tired to protest, and I felt for him. He didn't like the idea that anyone might stare at him. He hated to think that the boys who had laughed at his jokes and marvelled at his stories would see him like this.

I suggested we take in one of the old films on hockey. It would be quieter there, and he could sit and relax in the dark. He thought it a fair idea and agreed. The daily film took place in what the hall calls the Hartland Molson Theatre—beer money, so the Old Man had every right to claim his seat. I pushed him in through the doors and right to the front, where he could sit between the rows and see well enough and yet not be in anyone's way.

It was a large room, and when there were enough people gathered in it, they closed the doors and turned down the lights and began the film. It was, as would be expected, a film heavily dependent on nostalgia: old footage of kids playing shinny on farm sloughs, shots of kids putting old catalogues in for shin pads, a scene of kids divvying up sticks as a way of choosing sides before playing. Just the way he had played down on the river. Just the way I once played down on the bay. Just the way Gordie and his pals play at the schoolyard rink. An eighty-year link, and growing.

The soundtrack was syrupy and smooth, but soon began to grate, almost as if there was dust on the needle or a broken speaker. I sat watching the film, but could sense that people were looking around, trying to locate the source of the grating noise. I turned to check and saw that a man and a woman had located the trouble. The man was pointing, smiling, and the woman laughing one of those silent, open-mouth laughs.

The man was pointing at my father, whose head seemed to have fallen off and onto his chest. He was snoring loudly. To everyone else in the room—now all aware of the sound, many of them smiling and laughing—he was an old man in a wheelchair, sound asleep in front of a movie screen, with young players flickering in grainy black-and-white behind him.

But to me he was something quite apart from what they believed they were seeing. When I looked up, I could see my father on exhibit in the Hockey Hall of Fame. And I could see, on the flickering screen in front of his lolling head, exactly what he was dreaming: Duncan Fisher MacGregor, forever young, skating faster and faster through his long, long life.

When Sigurd Olson, the distinguished American wilderness writer who was so taken with the Ontario bush that he was once issued a guide's licence, died just short of his eighty-third birthday in 1982, his family found his final assignment still rolled into the old Royal typewriter that sat in front of the window of his simple office. "A new adventure is coming up," he had written, "and I'm sure it will be a good one."

Olson had lived a wonderful life. He had paddled the voyageur routes that led up the Ottawa River and across the mighty Nipissing and on into the northwestern Ontario bush that the Chicago native seemed to love more than anywhere else on earth. It was here, deep in the Ontario tangle, that he had formulated the notions that would be his legacy: the idea of a *singing* wilderness, where peace must not be mistaken for silence; the notion that almost anyone, from the bottom-line stockbroker to the young camp girl, can, if only given the opportunity, develop an easy *oneness* with the wilderness that is energizing, sustaining and, he might add, spiritual. Olson even said, at one point early in his life, that there were only two known states that could make a person feel so wildly alive: wilderness and war. Wilderness, he wrote, "is a spiritual necessity, an antidote to the high pressure of modern life, a means of regaining serenity and equilibrium." He sought to put into words something many Canadians feel, even if they feel less need to articulate it, and that is that there is a deep need for periodic contact, a natural, human response to the "potency of their primitive inheritance." Perhaps he so loved the deep Ontario bush because here there are still those in constant contact, those whose inheritance is neither primitive nor lost, but as real, if as invisible, as the chill in the morning air as they head out for another day that is vocation rather than vacation.

I like to think Sig Olson and Dunc MacGregor would have got on fine together, just as I'm convinced Dunc would have loved Calvin Rutstrum and Rutstrum Dunc. Olson, the city dweller who fell in love with the bush, spent most of his life fighting to see a wilderness preserve established along the U.S.-Canadian border area around the western nose of Lake Superior. He fought passionately for Superior National Park in Minnesota and Quetico Provincial Park in Ontario. He had hoped, at the outset, that they would be fashioned as true wilderness preserves, safe from foolish tourism as well as rampant logging. It was a long and at times nasty battle, pitting those who wished for pristine wilderness against those who wished to use the bush largely as they had always used it. The visitor, leaving a vehicle at an access point and heading out by canoe to the interior, returning days later with the evidence of their having been there locked in memory and tied carefully in a garbage bag, versus those who wished to penetrate by snowmobile, by motorboat, by four-wheel all-terrain vehicle, those who wished to hunt and fish and log, the evidence of their having been there slashed and dumped and tied, in spring and fall, to the hood of their four-by-four.

It was, and remains, the wilderness movement's most gnawing question. Is the bush for those who are privileged enough to visit, who have the economy and the time and the equipment to come, usually in the best weather, and then can have the bush shelved for the off-season? Or is the bush a resource for those who live and work in it, a farm for trees and a playground for hunters and fishers? Or is it something in between, not fully satisfying to either, but sensible under the circumstances? What Sigurd Olson and his fellow preservationists won in Quetico and Superior was preservation through management, a compromise whereby the wilderness values would be preserved even if they could never really be returned to those pristine imaginings. Natives used the bush and, despite the fancies of those who believe otherwise, left a mark, even if one admirably small by comparison to those swaths later cut. The voyageurs Olson so revered used the bush and left their marks. And those settlers who eventually followed, who set up along the Ottawa River and the Madawaska, who headed down the Muskoka and into the Great Lakes system and ever farther west, who took the trains and the corduroy roads deeper and deeper into what might once have been pristine—they had no choice but to leave their marks, for these, in fact, were their lives, not their holidays. Bush to be cleared, bush to be cut, bush to burn, bush to hunt in, bush to fish in, bush to trap in. In seeking to live, how could they possibly have committed the crimes of which the more privileged sometimes believed them guilty? And it was not that they could not learn. Having destroyed the white pine for the sake of money a century earlier, they understood only too well that you cannot endlessly take without putting back. The bush, despite first impressions, is not infinite.

Sigurd Olson accepted compromise. Preservation made sense when pristine made, in the end, not enough. Both sides could have a little, just as Algonquin Park loggers have always known that those vacationers who come there from all over the world to see the "wilderness" could not reach it if it were not for their being there first, could not drive on the roads or walk on the renowned nature trails or even find the perfectly groomed canoe portage if, at one time, men with axes had not passed this way. Those who were so busy working in the year-round bush, who rarely, if ever, travelled for comparisons, were never able to articulate their desires as fine and powerfully as those they so often seemed pitted against, but their lack of writing and speeches and political contacts never meant they did not care as much about preserving the same way of life. When Duncan MacGregor drove on the Camp Lake road that day and said he deeply regretted being party to so much tree-cutting and hauling and sawing up and shipping out, he did not mean that he regretted that he had spent his life working in the bush. Just that he wished they had been more careful, as perhaps now, thanks to the likes of Olson, they will be.

Like Olson, Dunc knew a "new adventure" was coming up. He felt forty-nine less and less in the mornings. He was finding his walking laborious. In the fall of 1994, now eighty-seven, he found it difficult to go down to the library and then to the beer hall, and would go, instead, whenever Eric, who was now driving a taxi in Huntsville, dropped by and picked him up and drove him downtown. If he dared walk in those final years, it took a long, long time. He would sit along a stone wall on Main Street, catch his breath and watch the passing parade: tourists headed for their cottages and into the park; the odd logging truck heading through town and south towards the markets; snowmobilers in winter, water skiers in summer, hunters in fall and young men at all hours of the day, revving their engines and double-clutching down the Main Street hill, not a second glance for an old man sitting on a stone wall smoking a cigarette at the same time as he tries to catch his breath.

Tch-tch-tch-tch-tch-tch-tch.

*　　*　　*

In December he came down with a heavy cold that wouldn't lift. Jim's wife, Stephanie, a nurse, worried about him. He stopped going downtown, even if Eric came by to offer a free lift. He counted on visitors to bring him tobacco, lottery tickets and new books—the staples of his life. Helen worried that he would burn himself, and her, to death. She worried that he'd fall from his bed and she wouldn't be able to get him back up. She worried that he'd cough until his last breath had leapt out of reach and she would be able to do nothing for him. She worried that he wasn't eating enough, and so began carrying his meals upstairs for him, an unexpected development that surprised both of them. We found it touching, four children, all now grown, but clinging to the hope of when they were still young.

Stephanie spoke to his doctor and arrangements were made for them to get some home care on the provincial health plan. It wouldn't cost them anything, but Helen resented the idea that another woman might think she should clean or do the shopping, and she refused, after the first few visits, to have anything to do with such charity. The nursing care was another matter, however, and once a week an area health nurse began coming in to check on the Old Man. She was as stubborn and sure in her ways as he was, and they fought from the first meeting.

"One of you should speak to your father," she told me one day when we were visiting and she dropped by. The concerns, it turned out, were less physical than financial. He was no longer passing on any of his savings to help with the house. There was necessary work to be done and he wanted nothing to do with it.

I tried to reason with him. "That woman came right out and told me I was going to die!" he shouted. "I told her she was god-damned well going to die herself! We all die."

I doubted this was a time for existential conversation. I tried to explain her point. He said he had no money. It was the first hint, though it would be a few months before we had it confirmed by the bank manager who thought there really should be more than one small account, that he was running dry. He wouldn't ask any of us for money. He wouldn't take it if offered. He seemed to think that if his bank account was about to be closed out, he may as well shut down as well. But he didn't need any pushy nurse telling him the obvious.

He was so angry at being told he was dying, he rallied magnificently just to prove them wrong. By March he was looking, and feeling, better, and was even up to taking the odd lift downtown with Eric. Eric was willing to do anything for his old friend. He would practically carry Dunc out the back door to his cab, take him first to the library and drop him off, then pick him up and drive him the short block to the beer hall, where he'd pick him up yet again two hours later for the trip home, which included a quick stop at the drugstore for lottery tickets. Perhaps it wasn't too late for the ship to come in. If his existence was directly connected to his dwindling bank account—at least in his own mind—then it must have also seemed that if the bank account suddenly filled up with lottery money, he might live forever—or at least outlive the public health nurse who had unwittingly rallied him back.

It was March when the family stopped worrying about him and began worrying about something far more unexpected and alarming. Ann, who had been feeling poorly and keeping it a secret for far too long, finally took herself to a doctor in Toronto and was, almost instantly, under the surgeon's knife at Wellesley Hospital, where fifteen years earlier they had repaired her father. This time the operation was a failure. The tumour they found when they opened her up was so twisted around intestine, vital organs and major arteries that they didn't even attempt to cut any of it out. It was three weeks before her fiftieth birthday. She was forty-nine, Duncan's golden age.

Ann returned to Huntsville to recuperate from the operation. Dunc was now so weak that he rarely left his room, except to go to the bathroom, and she was virtually an invalid upstairs as well, with Helen now caring for both of them, struggling up the difficult staircase with three meals a day for each and a dozen more trips just to check on them. Ann could barely walk, but often grew bored sitting and reading and would go to sit and talk with her father. They got along, as always, wonderfully—two heavy smokers, one now having quit, but both with the same droll wit—and he soon gave her one of her final, favourite stories.

"We were sitting there and he asked me, 'How are you feeling today, dearie?' I said, 'Fine.' I still had the stitches in, you know. I could barely walk, I was so sore and weak. He smiles at me and says, 'Do you think, then, you might go downtown for the Old Man?'"

Everyone knew what he wanted. A bottle. A mickey of rye. And the papers for the sports scores. And, of course, a few lottery tickets. No one knew then quite how badly he wanted them.

Ann recovered well enough to return to her apartment in Toronto and, for a while, to her job at *Maclean's*. She began a long series of radiation treatments, and naturally everyone thought of her and hardly any attention was paid to the Old Man. But Helen noticed he was getting so thin and so weak he could barely make it to the bathroom any more. She was feeling the strain. She wanted to go to Toronto and help Ann through her treatments, but she didn't dare leave Dunc at home alone. She called us all. We knew it was time to get him into a home, at least for the time being.

I went over to talk to him about it. I see by the cottage record it was May 22: "Rained all night, but nice in morning. . . . Ellen and Roy went to town to see Dunc, who hasn't been feeling too well. . . ." He had been taken, at one point, to the emergency department at the little Huntsville hospital, but was discharged with cold medication after a check. The cold that he had shaken over the winter returned in full force.

I sat for a good part of the afternoon with him. He was reading *The Last Tsar: The Life and Death of Nicholas II* and he had taken a pen and checked off the sections he liked about the myth and murder of Rasputin. Inside the cover, I later discovered, he had thanked us for the book and scribbled, "I love history." Like Plutarch, who took up Latin heading for his eighties, Dunc could never stop learning. On the other side of the table he had set out George Seldes's *Witness to a Century*, the elderly American journalist's memoirs of Trotsky, Isodora Duncan, Freud, Lenin, Teddy Roosevelt, and Mussolini. "A real book!" Duncan had scribbled inside that cover. "Like I say, 'I knew them all.'" Seldes's acquaintances were face to face. Dunc's were through reading and imagination. But he knew them all the same, and well.

He wanted his hair cut. He insisted on a haircut. I got him downstairs and out the back door to the car, and we drove down and parked on Main Street, right outside Rudy Baker's barbershop. Rudy was still cutting hair here, just as he had when I was so small he had to put a board across the seat for me to sit on. Rudy had worked then with his father, now he cut with his son. He was glad to see the Old Man but noticed, as everyone did, that he could barely walk to the chair. Dunc announced that this was going to be "My last haircut," and everyone laughed or shook their heads, no matter what they might have been thinking. Once Rudy had the cloth wrapped about him and tucked into his collar, the shrunken body was out of sight and all that was left was the Old Man's head, talking and joking about politics and, on Rudy's prodding, telling some of his wilder fishing stories. It could have been 1954 again, me waiting on the chair for the board to be slapped down and my turn to come.

We went back to the house and talked at length about the situation. It was not the first time a nursing home had been discussed. He had often suggested that this was where Helen wanted to "put" him, when, in fact, it had been only recently that she had stopped believing she was capable of caring for everyone forever. But when the words passed his mouth this time, they contained no anger, only resignation. He knew himself his health was deteriorating.

I said I would like to get him into a new home that was being built in Renfrew, not far from Eganville, where he had been born. There would be other old Ottawa Valley types there, perhaps even a few he might know. Certainly there would be others there who had spent lifetimes in the bush, and who would still be there if only they could.

"All right," he said. "Let's get it done."

It was not, however, quite that simple. Calls to the new facility were promising, but it was going to be slowly moving to full capacity. In the meanwhile, he might like to be elsewhere. He was willing, he said, to move temporarily into a home that would take him: the Lady Isabella Nursing Home in Trout Creek, on the way to North Bay. His great old friend Wam Stringer had gone there when even the bootblack could no longer convince people he wasn't an old, old man, and Wam had recently passed away there. Dunc wasn't interested in following suit: he wanted me to get him over to Renfrew as soon as possible.

He seemed, for the first time in all the years that I had known him, suddenly smaller. He sat on the edge of the bed, book open, tobacco marking his place, ashtray filled, poor roll-your-own smouldering, and he just nodded, staring straight ahead. I sat down beside him on the edge of the bed and put my arm around him, surprised at how much lower his shoulder was than mine. We said nothing.

"You're sure it'll be all right?" he asked finally.

"I'm sure."

"I can't afford it."

"It won't cost you a cent."

"You're sure about that?"

"I'm sure."

I took a piece of paper off a small yellow pad, took the pen with which he'd been marking off the Rasputin parts of the book, scribbled, in large letters, "DON'T WORRY!" and handed it back to him. It seemed to take him a long time to read it. The next time I saw his reading table it had been taped to the spot where, normally, he would lay down whatever book he was reading.

On Monday, after the Victoria Day long weekend, we headed home from the cottage. The medical network went to work, and by the end of the week he had been accepted for temporary residence at Lady Isabella. Eric came to see him on Wednesday night, sitting up in the room overlooking the town, and Dunc, for no apparent reason, launched into, first, a complete recital of D'Arcy's "The Face on the Barroom Floor" and then Service's "The Shooting of Dan McGrew."

Perhaps it was just to prove that his mind, at least, was still fortynine. By the weekend he was headed north for Lady Isabella, Don McCormick volunteering to drive him up and settle him in. I went to work back in Ottawa arranging for a permanent room for him at the new nursing home in Renfrew. It seemed all to be working out fine.

He stayed less than a day at Lady Isabella. The staff there listened to his breathing and took his temperature and decided his presence would only be putting the other residents at risk. They sent him, by ambulance, to the North Bay Hospital, where he was instantly admitted.

We all kept in contact by telephone. Helen called from Huntsville and was told he was on antibiotics and resting. Tom called from Ottawa and was assured that he was doing fine, that it was pneumonia but they were treating it aggressively. Jim's wife, Stephanie, who over the past several years had taken over more and more of Dunc's care, called several times and was told he was responding fairly well. We were told not to worry.

"Would you like to speak to him?" the voice at the nursing station asked when I called to check on him.

I was surprised. I had thought we were able to call for information only. I was delighted to find out that he was well enough to speak.

The telephone rang a few times and I presumed he was just ignoring it. Telephones in his life were always for other people, never him, and it was rare for him to answer until ten or more rings, if he bothered even then.

Finally, the telephone clicked and a quiet voice came on. It was a nursing assistant. I identified myself and spoke to her. She seemed more worried than anyone else I had spoken with over the previous two days.

"How is he?" I asked.

"Not too good."

"Is he awake?"

"Yes."

"Ask him if he wants me to come."

There was a long pause, some mumbles I couldn't make out, then her breath back on the receiver. "Yes."

I left immediately, a sunny Sunday afternoon, and drove the five hours to North Bay in less than four. He was on the fourth floor, and when I reached the nursing station it seemed the cheeriness had gone.

They had him alone in a four-person ward. I did not know enough about hospitals to realize that this is a bad sign in a crowded facility. It wasn't to keep his germs away from the other patients. It was to keep death away.

He was sleeping when I got there. They were feeding him intravenously and he looked peaceful.

I went over and sat beside him, holding his hand. He awoke and stared up, blue eyes clear and holding not the slightest surprise. He seemed calm and, yes, happy that I had come. But the calmness was what struck. No panic. No calls for priests who held nothing for him anyway. No pain. No worry. Like that Tolstoy story in which the old coachman lies helpless in the kitchen of the country inn and the woman asks him how he feels. "Death is here," he says. "That's how it is."

The nurse leaned down into him, checking through his gaze for other signs of life. "Do you know who's here?" she asked him as if he were a child.

"Yes," he said.

"Who?" she asked.

"Roy!" he shouted, insulted that she would dare check.

We were together twelve hours in that room. He slept, I sometimes dozed; I made a few calls to let the others know it was not looking good. I held his hand and talked to him. About fishing. About the grandchildren. About the family. About all those years in Algonquin Park and about how those times, as Ann was now best positioned to say, meant more to us than anything else in the small, unnoticed lives that make up a family. It seemed he was dreaming, perhaps of the places I was talking to him about. Perhaps he had finally found his walnut tree.

In the late evening they decided his breathing was much too rough and came in to set him up with oxygen. The nurse putting the plastic mask over his face had trouble fitting it correctly over his stubble.

She laughed uneasily. "We're going to have to give you a shave in the morning, Duncan."

"Why?" he asked in a voice so clear it made her start. "I won't be needing one."

It was the last thing he would ever say. Certainly not as enigmatic as Thoreau's "Moose. Indians," but more in keeping with the Old Man's sense of mischief. For the next five hours I sat there listening to his "death breathing," as the poet A.E. Housman once described the terrible rattle and gasp and eerily long silences that link Cheyne-Stokes breathing. How little I had known then of the way we really go. I thought of myself standing with that small broken mirror at Cooperstown, checking his breath to see if he was still alive. I thought of the four of us kids listening in the cabin at Lake of Two Rivers to the smoker's hacks and coughs that had convinced us he would never get out of the fifties alive. This breathing was so very, very, very different, so alarming and every pause so convincing that the end had come, that the only certainty between rattle and gasp and the next long, unnerving pause was that it was now certain he would never, ever get out of the nineties alive.

At 4:20 in the morning, May 29, 1995, the pause seemed to go on forever. I thought for sure he had died. I stood up, crying, thinking I should call for someone, then I stared down at him just as, I suppose, his heart gave out.

He clenched twice, top lip folding into bottom lip, cheeks puffing, nose wrinkling, jaw setting.

The exact motion of him, forever forty-nine, at the precise moment of a trout strike.

I sat down again after that, realizing that he wasn't going to get away this time, and oddly calmed myself by it all.

The Old Man was dead. It was late spring in Algonquin Park, and the ironwood had finally, stubbornly, shed its leaves.

We buried him four days later in Huntsville. There was no one there to take a leak in the junipers, but that doesn't mean there was no laughter at the funeral. There was very little else. What else could you do? Eighty-eight good years, sharp to the very end, and the only regret he could have had was the pile of unfinished books on the larger table in his upstairs room. The books were every-where, spilling out of every cupboard, covering every possible space. His Plutarch was one of the few long-time favourites that had survived. It still held the advice Themistocles gave to Antiphales: "Time, young man, has taught us both a lesson."

The cleaning up of such a long life was almost effortless. The shirts and pants and single drawer of clothes were off to the Salvation Army. The books would go to the library. There was a working jackknife and several non-working watches. A few old photographs of Eganville days and Algonquin Park fishes. A visit to the bank, where the manager let us know, with an expression that betrayed her bewilderment, that there was only one account and, it turned out, only enough money in it to pay the funeral bills. He had indeed been on the verge of closing out.

He left us nothing, someone else might say.

In the desk drawer of his room, Tom came across a few lottery tickets and scratched them with the side of a penny.

"He won!"

Everyone rushed to check and then double-check. He had died with a winning ticket in his possession.

Only ten dollars, but, damn it, he had beat the system.

*   *   *

After the burial, our family drove back to Ottawa through the park, past Cache Lake and the Lake of Two Rivers point, past the turnoff to the Whitefish and Rock Lake mill, past the turn to Opeongo and on into Whitney. I am glad the four kids and Ellen were there; otherwise, no one would have ever believed the tally of animals that stood at the side of Highway 60 as we passed through: twelve deer, nine moose, four fox, one bear, one wolf. A fine turnout, he would have thought.

It took a while for us to get a proper marker out to the cemetery at Huntsville. The delay was partly caused by the sad fact that we required two—Ann having died of cancer less than six months after him—but eventually a small stone was chosen and Ellen designed a pair of loons to grace the simple inscription.

After the markers had been installed, I drove out to check on them. It was a bright, early December day, with the sun shining on a recent snowfall. The snow was just beginning to melt, dripping from the pine branches and wet along the paths.

It took a while to locate the exact position of the grave, the wet snow covering making it impossible to read the upturned stones. But eventually I found it. There were footsteps in the packy snow leading to it, and they came from the direction of town. Someone had walked up through the snow and brushed away enough that his name—Duncan Fisher MacGregor, August 28, 1907–May 29, 1995—was visible.

A single red rose had been laid on the stone.

And behind the stone there were other tracks, also fresh.

A deer.

I can explain none of it.